Race and Gender Discrimination at Work

Race and Gender Discrimination at Work

Samuel Cohn

Texas A&M University

Westview
PRESS

A Member of the Perseus Books Group

Copyright © 2000 by Westview Press, A Member of the Perseus Books Group

Published in 2000 in the United States of America by Westview Press, 5500 Central Avenue, Boulder, Colorado 80301-2877, and in the United Kingdom by Westview Press, 12 Hid's Copse Road, Cumnor Hill, Oxford OX2 9JJ

Find us on the World Wide Web at www.westviewpress.com

A CIP catalog record for this book is available from the Library of Congress.
ISBN 0-8133-3201-X (hc)—0-8133-3202-8 (pb)

The paper used in this publication meets the requirements of the American National Standard for Permanence of Paper for Printed Library Materials Z39.48-1984.

10   9   8   7   6   5   4   3   2   1

To Mark Fossett,
who convinced me to study race in the first place,

and to Chris Williams,
who reminded me that integrated theories
of discrimination matter

Contents

1 *Has the Problem of Discrimination Gone Away?*

This book is about race and gender discrimination at work. It is a grim subject. It is not grim because discrimination is awful (although discrimination, when it exists, *is* awful). The subject is grim because most discussions of discrimination, both conservative and liberal, are pretty tedious. This is a debate with a large amount of posturing and hot air. Most people have already made up their minds about this topic *before* they study it. Either people think discrimination is an important force in U.S. society or they don't. Once they have decided this matter, they have their speeches written and ready to give, and they don't want to hear much about material from the other side.

If you are a committed leftist or feminist, you see the world in terms of the victimization of the weak by the strong. The world is filled with gross inequalities that are the results of predation by the powerful. The poor are poor because of exploitation by the rich; blacks are poor because of discrimination by whites; women are poor because of the sexism of men.

If you are a committed conservative, you see the world in terms of bureaucratic obstacles to meritocracy. The world is full of nonperformers who use special pleadings to keep the talented and energetic from getting their just rewards. The government taxes the successful so that it can write checks to the less enterprising. Minorities seek set-asides so that they don't have to compete with majority members with better test scores and greater abilities. Women seek reverse discrimination lawsuits to counterweight their own lack of commitment to the labor force and to cloud the legitimate accomplishments of men.

Because people have made up their minds about these issues already, they prefer to ignore facts that are inconsistent with their own

1

preconceived views. There are plenty of these facts to deal with. Race and gender in the United States are subjects that have been studied exhaustively. With these studies have come statistics that may be dry but that have a story to tell. They fit some aspects of the liberal's story, some aspects of the conservative's story, and some aspects of nobody's story. The statistics that fit nobody's story are the most interesting, because they suggest that what is going on in the workplace is not what most people expect.

If there is going to be a good-faith discussion of race and sex in the workplace, it has to be done with the facts; it has to be done with the numbers. Statistics are the ultimate honesty test. You can't just take one isolated example of blatant discrimination or blatant abuse of affirmative action and wave it around in the air as if this is what happens every day all the time. What happens every day all the time is what is measured in census statistics. Census statistics are numbers that count what happens to the population as a whole. Interesting stories occur, but it is important to know what is a "typical" horrible situation, what is "exceptional," and therefore not worth making a big fuss over.

Occasionally, national statistics do not speak to a critical issue. Then we are forced to go to the anecdotes, to the stories of what happens to particular people in particular firms. Even here, however, a little scientific discipline can depoliticize a discussion and allow for more careful consideration of the facts. There are a lot of good quantitative studies that allow one to carefully test liberal, conservative and neutral accounts of what is happening to men and women in specific companies. These studies suffer from not being economy-wide, but they gain by being able to rule out particular scenarios at particular times and places. To know that no discrimination occurred at Company X, or that at Company Y discrimination was severe against blacks but only when certain conditions occurred, helps frame a larger discussion. We can try to do as many studies of this sort as we can, collect the results from various companies, and see if the pieces of the mosaic we can find suggest what the larger picture may look like.

The studies presented here suggest that discrimination exists. It does not always take the form that many orthodox feminists and liberals claim. It does not occur for the reasons most people think it does. Discrimination is often absent from many places where it is supposed to be pervasive. Everyone knows that stereotypes about women and blacks are often false. Stereotypes about stereotyping are also false, however, and these need correction as well.

The story presented here is not the standard account of discrimination. The book provides statistics in lavish and copious detail because statistics are the only cure available for preconceptions. Most readers will probably finish the book with the same political persuasions they began with. However, if liberals can now argue a liberal position in a manner consistent with the facts, and conservatives can argue a conservative position in a manner consistent with the facts, then the book will have served its purpose.

Some Introductory Definitions

Few things in the world are more boring than definitions. However, on controversial topics in which inflammatory language is common, developing a common agreed-upon language can take the sting and insult out of "buzzwords" and allow for calmer, more consensual discussion.

Ascriptive Status is a feature that one is born with. Gender, race, and ethnicity—and in some cases, religion and sexual preference—are attributes one can be born with.

Inequality is the unequal allocation of benefits. We normally study inequality among groups with different ascriptive statuses, although any subgroups can be studied in this way. Any benefit can be distributed unequally; people differ in their access to social status, leisure, relationships, and power. However, the most obvious unequally distributed resources are economic: income, jobs, and wages. Income is the total revenue that people receive. This includes salaries, bank interest, dividends, capital gains, lottery winnings, gifts, and other more obscure sources of funds. We care about income because how much money people have determines the general quality of their lives. The largest component of most people's income is wages. This book will spend a lot of time discussing the determinants of inequality in wages—and employment matters as well, because anyone without a job has earnings of zero. Therefore this book gives a lot of attention to differences in who does or does not have a job and why.

Establishing racial or gender inequality in income or employment says nothing about the causes of this inequality. It also says nothing about the social desirability of this inequality. In a hypothetical society where French people earn all the money and Germans earn none, it could be that none of the Germans wants to work and everybody's happy. The mere presence of inequality says nothing about sexism, racism, or any other underlying social property. What causes inequality in each case has to be assessed individually.

Discrimination is the provision of unequal benefits to people of different ascriptive statuses despite identical qualifications and merit. Race and gender inequality may or may not be caused by discrimination. Whether or not discrimination is occurring in a given setting is an enormously political question for which social scientists are expected to have defensible answers. Many of the debates about discrimination are arguments over whether hidden qualification and merit considerations explain away differences that superficially look discriminatory. These debates can become impassioned. Other arguments explore *why* discrimination exists, if it does exist. There is legitimate disagreement about these issues as well.

Prejudice is an attitude of hostility held by members of one ascriptive group towards members of another. Prejudice and discrimination are not the same. Prejudice involves what people think; discrimination involves what they do. One is attitude; the other is behavior. Prejudice is measured with social surveys. There are a number of fairly reliable indices that can be used to measure people's feelings about other social groups. Discrimination is measured with economic behavior. Who is hired? How much are they paid? Are there "neutral" qualification factors to account for these differences?

It is possible, even common, for people with very prejudiced attitudes to engage in very little discrimination. It is also possible for people who always think and speak in egalitarian terms to discriminate substantially in their economic actions.

Note as well that it is not at all obvious that discrimination is caused by prejudice, or that changing levels of prejudice will affect levels of discrimination. *Discrimination is affected by differences in levels of prejudice and by differences in people's ability to act on prejudiced beliefs.*

Imagine a Ku Klux Klansman as an employer in an isolated all-black town. He may despise African Americans, but if he wants to hire someone, he may have no choice but to hire a black. This is an extreme example but illustrates an important theme of this book. Economic and social realities often prevent prejudiced people from acting in a prejudiced way, or encourage nonprejudiced people to engage in active discrimination.

One can only understand the racial and gendered dynamics of workplaces by understanding not only the attitudes of individual workers and employers, but also the realistic constraints they are operating under that limit their freedom of action. Sometimes these constraints are political; sometimes they are legal. Sometimes they are narrowly sociological.

However, often as not, in a profit-maximizing organization, the factors that provide the most crippling constraints are economic. Market realities are an overriding fact of life in corporations. Rising international competition and corporate reorganizations have made profitability and rational response to financial pressure a key component of modern organizational life.

One cannot study discrimination just as a psychological process, or as a cultural process, or as ethnic identity, or as childhood socialization. These things are important, but one has to come to terms with the hard, cold economic realities that managers and workers face when they make decisions about staffing and remuneration. Supervisors are making calculations about their bottom lines at the same time they are implementing policies that may have profound impacts on men and women, blacks and whites. The policies are not implemented in a race-blind or gender-blind vacuum. However, understanding the interactions between market pressures, organizational realities, and race and gender roles becomes the key to explaining whether or not discrimination will occur and who will benefit from changing patterns of inequality within the corporation.

Recent Trends in Inequality

The first question one should ask in any study of racial or gender inequality is, "Is there any?" There is no sense in reading a⋆ whole ⋆book on a phenomenon that doesn't exist. Most readers would be willing to grant that some sort of racial and gender inequality exists without poring over tables of social statistics.

However, an intelligent conservative could argue, "Sure, race and gender discrimination exist, but they are steadily diminishing. There may have been massive inequalities in the 1950s and 1960s. However, these were based on attitudes that have long since disappeared. It is no longer socially acceptable to manifest the crude forms of prejudice that used to exist at an earlier time, and nowadays people behave themselves. Elaborate discussions of racism and sexism only increase the divisions between groups when these differences are quietly being resolved on their own. Why study the problems of the sixties with the rhetoric of the sixties when today these things no longer apply?"

Such an argument becomes even more cogent in the light of policy debates. In a world where racial and sexual inequality are declining rapidly, the case can be made for the weakening or even the elimination of antidiscrimination programs (such as affirmative action) because the problems these policies were designed to solve are largely disappearing from view. However, if levels of race and gender inequality today were the same as those found in the 1940s, one could hardly claim these problems are evaporating, and the case for continuing antidiscrimination programs would be more convincing.[1]

Racial Inequality

One of the reasons why for so much debate over how much racial inequality exists in the United States is that different statistics show different things. The issue is not that quantitative data are all screwed up and that anybody can make anything look like anything by cooking numbers. Actually, the statistics are relatively consistent and hard to manipulate. The issue is that some aspects of American life show persistent discrimination and some show extraordinary reductions in discrimination. There has been progress on some fronts but not on others.

If you want to make the strongest possible case for the existence of discrimination, consider employment and unemployment statistics. No numbers look quite as bad as employment and unemployment figures.

Table 1.1 shows the employment rates for the U.S. male civilian population over the age of 16 by race. The employment rate is the ratio of people with jobs to the general population. The left column shows the white male employment rate, the middle column shows the black male rate, and the right column shows the difference. Note that the racial employment gap for 1997 is virtually identical to the gap that existed in 1950. Racial inequality in job holding has not changed one bit. From an employment standpoint, it is almost as if the Civil Rights Movement had not happened. Note that from 1950 to 1980, the gap actually got worse rather than better. This surprises many liberals, because the 1950s, 1960s, and 1970s include the years of the Civil Rights Movement, the years of the inner city riots of the late 1960s, and the years in which the federal government was strongly committed to racial progress and the elimination of inequality. Reynolds Farley (1996) presents detailed historical data on the black-white employment gap showing that not really

TABLE 1.1 Employment Rates for the U.S. Male Civilian Population over the Age of 16 by Race

	White	Black	Gap (W–B)
1950	77.6	73.0	4.6
1960	79.4	73.5	5.9
1970	76.8	69.7	7.1
1980	73.4	60.4	13.0
1990	73.2	61.8	11.4
1997	76.7	72.2	4.5

SOURCES: 1950: Census of Population. 1955–90 White and Black: Economic Report to the President 1996. 1997: Bureau of Labor Statistics Website. Black figures for 1955–70 are adjustments to published statistics for nonwhites. See Technical Appendix for details.

until 1988 was there any significant reduction in racial inequality in job holding. Even the improvements of the Bush-Clinton years only brought the gap back to that of the 1950s, hardly a period associated with glorious equal opportunity for all.

Note as well that white employment ratios changed only slightly during this period. All the fluctuation comes from black employment rates, which vary significantly. Farley's statistics strongly suggest that the driving force here is the national economy. When the economy was bad, as it was in the 1970s and early 1980s, blacks are particularly likely to be unemployed. Although whites suffer from recessions too, they experience far less job loss than do blacks. African Americans tend to bear the full brunt of downturns in the national economy, while whites are relatively cushioned. It appears that whites were preferred employees and blacks were less preferred. When the economy is strong enough to absorb everybody, both blacks and whites find jobs. When the economy is weak, the preferred workers are kept, and the less preferred workers are discarded, exacerbating racial differences in overall employment.

Table 1.2 shows estimates of unemployment rates rather than employment rates. Unemployment rates are the ratio of people looking for work but not finding any to all people participating in the labor force. This is not the same as the opposite of employment, because there is a third category, not in the labor force: people not looking for work, and therefore not working at all.

TABLE 1.2   Unemployment Rates for the U.S. Male Civilian Population over the Age of 16 by Race

	White	*Black*	*Gap* (W–B)
1950	4.7	8.5	3.8
1960	4.8	10.3	5.5
1970	4.0	6.5	2.5
1980	6.1	14.5	8.5
1990	4.8	11.8	7.0
1997	2.5	5.0	2.5

SOURCES: 1950: Census of Population. 1955–90 White and Black: Economic Report to the President 1996. 1997: Bureau of Labor Statistics Website. Black figures for 1955–70 are adjustments to published statistics for nonwhites. See Technical Appendix for details.

Unemployment rates still show significant racial disparities, but the differences are not as bad as those observed for employment rates. Like the employment situation, unemployment rates show no consistent trend towards improvement. Some decades show a reduction in gaps; others show gaps becoming intensified. Nevertheless, about one third of the 1950 gap in unemployment between blacks and whites has been eliminated, a reduction that is nontrivial. However, note that in 1990, not so long ago, the gap was almost twice that of 1950, and that this rate jumps around a lot. There is thus no guarantee that we are on any steady path towards progress, even though current indicators are not bad.

Why do such similar indicators as employment and unemployment show such different results? Cotton (1989) argues that one of the reasons the black unemployment indicator has declined is that obstacles to black employment are so high in some places that blacks become discouraged workers and drop out of the labor force. They stop looking for work, not because they are lazy but because there are no jobs for them. This removes them from the denominator of the fraction unemployed/looking for work, and therefore the unemployment rate improves. As a result, he argues, the unemployment statistics are practically worthless, and that instead employment statistics should be used. These numbers have a straightforward meaning: what percent of the population is holding jobs.

Cotton's complaints would seem to be like whining about a lobster dinner. After all, what can be bad about unemployment statistics going down? Unfortunately, his arguments have some merit. Later on, we present data from a study in Chicago (Tienda and Stier 1991) that shows a large percentage of the population really does fall into this category of discouraged worker, making the interpretation of unemployment rates quite ambiguous. The employment rates therefore come closer to the truth of what is actually happening to the job market for blacks and whites.[2]

That said, for the reader who adores unemployment statistics and does not want to give them up, the best that can be said from these is that race gaps are going up and down in a wild and somewhat random way, with no consistent trends towards improvement. If one accepts the tale of the employment statistics, there has been racial progress in the 1990s. However, these merely counteracted losses that occurred in the previous forty years. Overall since midcentury, no significant improvement in total black job holding or in black job holding relative to white job holding has occurred.

The story is less gloomy when income statistics are considered. Here real racial progress has occurred.

Table 1.3 shows the ratio of black male mean annual earnings to white male mean annual earnings from 1950 to 1997. In 1950, blacks earned slightly more than half the amount whites earned. In 1997, they earned slightly less than three-quarters the amount whites earned. This improvement from 53 percent of parity to 73 percent of parity is significant. Note as well there is a more or less consistent trend for the income gap to shrink over time. Progress has been stalled since 1980, but nevertheless, there is no period in which there has been a significant deterioration in black income relative to white. This is in contrast to employment statistics where such deterioration is relatively common.

Of course, the presence of racial inequality in income does not guarantee that discrimination is occurring. It could be that these differences stem from "legitimate" factors. For example, if blacks worked fewer hours than whites, they would earn less money. Working less could reflect discrimination in the job market. However, some conservatives might say it reflects lack of job skills or welfare dependency. Regardless of what caused the working less, working less by itself is a reasonable cause for lower earnings. Furthermore, blacks may have less education, and thus be less qualified for high-paying jobs. One could certainly not blame an employer for paying skilled workers a higher wage and unskilled workers a lower wage. On top of that, blacks may live in parts of the country that have a lower cost of living than that of predominately white areas. Because prices in the South are generally lower than those in the North, and blacks are more likely to live in the South than are whites, this could cause part of the income differential.

Farley (1985) investigated these factors, and all of them contribute in some way to the racial income gap. Using these factors, he was able to

TABLE 1.3   Black Median Annual Earnings as a Percentage of White Median Annual Earnings: U.S. Males

1950	53%
1960	58%
1970	64%
1980	73%
1990	72%
1997	73%

SOURCES: 1950–1990 Farley (1996). 1997: United States Statistical Abstract (1998).

make two-thirds of the racial gap in earnings disappear. After adjusting for hours worked, education and region, the 1979 black-white earnings ratio was 91 percent rather than 73 percent. 91 percent is a much less serious gap than 73 percent. However, a 9 percent shortfall is still noticeable. If you were in a job where someone else with the same qualifications as you working the same hours as you was earning 9 or 10 percent more than you, you would complain and rightfully so. If there is any income discrimination at all, it appears in this remaining gap. These gaps are small and shrinking but they are real.

There is one other piece of bad news to report. Farley (1996) repeated his analysis with 1989 rather than 1979 data. He found that when one adjusted for education, region, and other statistical controls, the "residual" black-white earning gap (the gap that could not be explained by nondiscriminatory factors) increased between 1989 and 1979. The component of earnings inequality that could not be explained by neutral factors such as education or hours worked increased over the course of the 1980s by about 20 percent. Overall, income differentials are declining, a trend that may be the result of improving black education and increased entry by blacks into high-status professional occupations. The statistics suggest, however, that it is not obvious that blacks and whites receive comparable treatment once they enter these high-status occupations.

The area where the most racial progress has been made is education. Educational gaps between blacks and whites have practically disappeared. Table 1.4 shows the median years of education completed by black and white males over the age of 25 between 1950 and 1997. In 1950, there was a sizable difference between the races. The average white male had a three-year educational advantage over the average black male. The average black man had less than a seventh-grade education. Such lack of education would truly have disqualified many African Americans from high-status occupations. Whites had just less than a tenth-grade education, but the difference between grade nine and grade six is substantial.

By 1997, these differences had vanished. Both blacks and whites had more than twelve years of education. They were separated by only 0.4 years. Over 85 percent of the racial gap in education had been eliminated! This is a remarkable turnaround. Note as well that the progress here has been relatively steady. Every decade except the 1980s produced improvement, and even the 1980s produced no harm.

The story gets a little more complicated when one considers high school and college graduation rates separately. The greatest progress has been made in high school graduation, where the two races in 1997 are practically equal. College graduation rates still show some racial differentials, due in part to blacks being less likely to attend college in the

TABLE 1.4   Median Years of Education Completed by U.S. Males Age 25 and over by Race

	White	*Black*	*Gap* (W–B)
1950	9.8	6.8	3.0
1960	10.9	8.2	2.7
1970	12.1	9.8	2.3
1980	12.5	12.0	0.5
1990	13.0	12.5	0.5
1995	13.1	12.7	0.4

SOURCES: 1950: Census of Population. 1955–90 White and Black: Economic Report to the President 1996. 1997: Current Population Survey, January 1997, from Ferret Website. Black figures for 1955–70 are adjustments to published statistics for nonwhites. See Technical Appendix for details.

first place. However, despite some adverse trends in the 1980s, college graduation differences between the races are declining as well (Hacker 1995). The few significant racial differences in the percentage of adults without a high school diploma or GED are especially notable. Because the lack of a high school diploma is an extremely serious barrier to employment, the creation of equal high school graduation rates means that there is no longer an educational deficit among African Americans that forces membership in the underclass; African Americansare no longer incapable of qualifying for a respectable blue collar job.

Some individuals, both liberals and conservatives, are still convinced that differences in skills between the races continue to exist. Liberals might argue that school funding is unequally distributed. If whites go to lavish well-financed schools and blacks attend underfunded schools with inadequate resources and teachers, then blacks will still have a skills deficit even after graduation because their schools taught them less. Conservatives might make a related case, arguing that blacks have been the beneficiaries of social promotions and school systems that are reluctant to impose standards on lower-class children who pose disciplinary problems. It is also sometimes argued that blacks are more likely to come from households headed by single females and where financial pressures, social psychological stress, and reduced parental capacity to monitor children lead to lower motivation and performance in school (Garfinkel and McClanahan 1986).

Some of these arguments may have merit. However, even if there was once a skills deficit between blacks and whites, it is shrinking quickly. This shows up most conspicuously in test scores.

Table 1.5 shows trends in test scores for 17-year-olds from 1975–1990. The figures in Table 1.5 are National Assessment of Educational Progress scores for reading, math, and science. For all years, there was a gap in test scores between blacks and whites in every subject that was examined. However, what is dramatic is how fast that gap is closing. Between 1975 and 1990, 44 percent of the racial gap in both reading and math disappeared. That nearly half the differences between blacks and whites in test scores could be made to go away in fifteen years is remarkable. Improvements in science scores have not been as pronounced, but differences in scientific aptitude are decreasing as well.

Thus, the argument that blacks suffer from a human capital deficit relative to whites is becoming increasingly invalid. Such an argument may have had some credibility in the 1940s and 1950s when Jim Crow laws and segregated schools produced high rates of black illiteracy. However, contemporary conditions are different. Some of this improvement can probably be linked to increased social mobility among African Americans. Educational attainment is strongly related to the social class of one's parents. Upper-class parents, both black and white, pressure their children to do well in school. Lower-class parents, both black and white, tend to have lower educational aspirations for their children. A garage mechanic who always got Cs in school will not think it is the worst thing in the world if their son also gets Cs and becomes an auto mechanic just

TABLE 1.5   Trends in Racial Differences in National Assessment of Educational Progress Test Scores for 17-Year-Olds 1975–90

	Reading	*Math*	*Science*
Gap 1975 (In Points)	52.4	37.5	57.5
Gap 1990 (In Points)	29.3	21.0	47.9
Percent of Gap Eliminated	44%	44%	17%

SOURCE: Bernstein (1995).

like Dad. For this family, a son who is a tool and die maker or the owner of a liquor store would represent real upward mobility. None of these jobs require a college education.

During the 1960s and 1970s, there was a substantial increase in the black middle class as a result of an increase in African American employment in the public sector. Much of this was due to affirmative action programs in federal, state, and municipal government. Another cause was an outmigration of white workers in response to declining salaries and working conditions in government jobs. These new vacancies created opportunities for African Americans. Black children of farm workers and factory operatives became urban planners, college professors, school superintendents, and civil servants. For this new black bourgeoisie, education was the road out of poverty. They internalized norms of educational attainment and passed these on to their children. This factor alone would have caused significant improvements over time in black test scores.

It is possible that changing priorities within school systems accounts for some of the improvement as well. In 1950, it would have been completely acceptable to run a school system catering entirely to white children and providing minimal educational services to the black population. Today, this double standard is no longer viable. Educational professionals are evaluated by how their districts perform on objective tests with the results broken out separately by race. School superintendents and principals are expected to raise both black and white test scores alike. Both education professionals themselves and political actors such as community activists and elected officials place great emphasis on eliminating disparities in test scores. It is noteworthy in this regard that most of the racial progress in the National Assessment of Education progress results have been in reading and math rather than science. Typical reading and math scores receive much more publicity in the mass media and in public discussions of the adequacy of school systems than do science scores, which receive less attention.

The improvement in black educational attainment and qualifications has implications that are not obvious at first glance. Remember that between 1950 and 1998, black-white employment disparities have stagnated and shown no improvement. Nevertheless, black white educational differences have been nearly eliminated. If blacks are becoming more qualified to obtain employment, why have the job-holding statistics remained unchanged? Remember that the definition of discrimination is providing unequal rewards to people of equal merit. If between 1950 and 1999 blacks became more qualified to hold jobs (relative to whites), but during this period the racial employment gap did not decrease, then in 1999 there was more discrimination against blacks in the job market, from a technical, legal standpoint, than there was in 1950. This is a sobering conclusion. Employers seem to be treating blacks as if they were uneducated and have no skills. This is less defensible today than it has been in any other period of American history. That racial employment gaps are continuing is bad enough. However, that these are stagnating while the most popular legitimation for this gap becomes invalid gives more and more credence to the explanation that discrimination is currently behind this gap, and may have been behind the gap all along. Thus, although there may have been progress in some aspects of black-white inequality in American society, it would seem that there is still quite a long way to go, particularly in the area of eliminating unequal treatment in the hiring process.

Gender Inequality

There has generally been a greater reduction of gender inequality than there has been for race. This is particularly noticeable when one considers male-female differentials in earnings.

Table 1.6 shows female annual earnings as a percentage of male annual earnings for the United States from 1955 to 1997.[3] In general, there has been increasing pay equity between men and women during this period. After 1955, women's wages declined relative to those of men until 1970 when they reached a low point; women earned the famous "59¢ to the dollar." Thereafter, conditions began to improve, with 1980–90 being a decade of particularly dramatic amelioration. Currently, women are earning 73¢ to the male dollar. This is not perfect parity, but it is a significant improvement over conditions in either 1955 or 1970.

TABLE 1.6   Female Annual Earnings as a Percentage of Male Annual Earnings: U.S. all Races

1955	.64
1960	.60
1970	.59
1980	.60
1990	.72
1995	.72
1997	.73

SOURCE: 1955–70 Reskin and Padavic (1994). 1980–1997: Women's Bureau Website. 1997 Annual figures estimated from 1996 annual data and 1996–1997 changes in hourly and weekly earning gaps.

As we shall see, much of this improvement came from increased access by women to jobs that had been traditionally male. Table 1.7 shows the index of occupational dissimilarity for males and females in the United States from 1950 to 1995. The index of occupational dissimilarity is a measure of the extent to which men and women hold different occupations. If males and females had exactly the same occupations, this index would be 0. If men exclusively worked in all-male occupations, and women exclusively worked in all-female occupations, the index of dissimilarity would be 1.

In general, significant occupational segregation exists in the United States. Scores for every year in Table 1.7 range between 0.5 and 0.65, both of which are substantial figures. Still, the index shows a steady decline beginning in 1960. By 1995, occupational segregation in the United States had declined 22 percent from what it had been in its worst year, 1960. This is noticeable progress.

Men and women, however, continue to work in jobs that are fundamentally male or female. This tendency for men to work in some jobs and women to work in others is called *occupational sex-typing*. This process has enormous consequences for men's and women's economic well being.

The extent to which occupational sex-typing is still alive and well in the United States is illustrated in Table 1.8. Table 1.8 shows the twenty least female and most female jobs in the United States in 1997 as measured by the Current Population Survey. In this case, least female means having the smallest proportion of women workers; most female means having the highest proportion of women workers.

Table 1.8 lists twenty jobs that are less than 1.8 percent female (or put otherwise are more than 98 percent male). Most of these are classic blue-collar jobs; mechanics of all kinds, oil well drillers, and such construction

TABLE 1.7   Index of Occupational Dissimilarity between Males and Females: U.S. all Races

1950	.64
1960	.69
1970	.67
1980	.60
1990	.55
1995	.54

SOURCES: Gross (1968); Jacobs (1989; Wooten (1997).

workers as masons, HVAC (heating and air conditioning) installers, plumbers, and carpenters figure prominently in the list. Many jobs are 90 percent female; these include clerical jobs, such as secretaries and bookkeepers, child care workers, bank tellers, hairdressers, nurses, dressmakers, and female helping professionals such as speech therapists and dieticians.

TABLE 1.8   The Twenty Least and Most Female Jobs in the United States: Current Population Survey 1997

Least Female	Percent Female	Most Female	Percent Female
Mason Supervisors	0.7%	Secretaries	98.7%
Bus, Truck, Farm & Heavy Equipment Mechanics	1.0%	Family Child Care Providers/Child Care Private Household	98.3%
Carpenter Supervisors	1.1%	Teachers, PreK and K	97.8%
Marine Engineers	1.2%	Dental Assistants/ Hygienists	97.3%
Mason/Concrete Workers	1.2%	Early Child Teach Assistant	95.9%
HVAC Mechanics	1.3%	Receptionists	95.7%
Electric Power Installer	1.4%	Typists	94.4%
Duct Installers	1.4%	Registered Nurses	94.3%
Oil Well Drillers	1.4%	Private Household Cleaners/Housekeepers	94.0%
Plumbers	1.5%	Licenced Practioner Nurses	93.6%
Roofers	1.6%	Dressmakers	93.4%
Longshore Equip. Operators	1.6%	Health Record Technician	91.6%
Excavating Mach. Operators	1.6%	Speech Therapists	91.1%
Elevator Repair	1.7%	Billing Clerks/ Stenographers	90.6%
Carpenters	1.7%	Bank Tellers	89.8%
Rail Brake & Switch	1.7%	Hairdressers	89.6%
Grader-Dozer Operators	1.7%	Welfare Eligibility Clerk	89.6%
Small Engine Repair	1.8%	Occupational Therapists	89.6%
Automobile Mechanics	1.8%	Bookkeepers	89.6%
Structural Metal Workers	1.9%	Dieticians	89.3%

Table 1.8 does not mean that progress has not been made in breaking down gender barriers in jobs. Wooten (1997) shows that between 1985 and 1995 significant progress was made in integrating many occupations. The percent female of medical managers rose from 60 percent to 80 percent, The percent female of technical writers rose from 36 percent to 54 percent. The percent female of purchasing managers rose from 24 percent to 42 percent. The percent female of postal carriers went from 17 percent to 32 percent. Overall, Wooten identifies 53 occupations in which the percentage female increased more than 5 percent, a noticeable change over one decade.

However, increased access to male jobs is not the same as increased access to good jobs. Women continue to be in relatively less desirable occupations than those held by men, although this differential is decreasing. The phenomenon of being confined to low-status jobs is referred to as *status segregation*. Status segregation continues to exist in the U.S. economy. Some of this should be evident from the pay differential statistics that have already been discussed. As a general rule, high pay is associated with jobs with high status and organizational power.

Table 1.9 illustrates gendered status segregation directly by contrasting the percentage female for superior and subordinate jobs in parallel work settings: medicine, law, and office work. In health care, physician continues to be a male occupation; fully three quarters of all doctors are male; they supervise a largely female labor force. 87 percent of all nurses are female; 63 percent of all physician assistants are female. Most lawyers as well are men; only 27 percent of all attorneys are women. They, too, supervise a largely female labor force: 84 percent of all legal

TABLE 1.9   Percent Female Jobs in Particular Status Hierarchies: Current Populations Survey 1997

Physician	25%
Nurse	87%
Physician Assistant	63%
Lawyer	27%
Legal Assistant	84%
Executive/Administrator/Manager	44%
Clerical Worker	79%

assistants are women. The job of executive is becoming relatively balanced. In offices, fully 44 percent of executives, administrators, and managers are female. Males continue to hold the majority of these positions, but their lead is becoming increasingly slim. That said, regardless of whether one considers executive to be a male or mixed-sex occupation, the fact remains that clerical worker continues to be a female occupation. Practically 80 percent of all clerical workers are women. In all three organizational settings that we consider here, a male or mixed-sex occupation supervises and controls a larger and more poorly paid set of female workers.

Table 1.9 is suggestive, but it does not represent the entire economy. It contains little information on blue-collar jobs or on other occupations within the service sector. Furthermore, the national census does not provide data on power, authority, or promotion prospects. All these are components of what we mean when refer to "good" jobs. Information on power and promotion prospects is available for the state of North Carolina. In 1989, the North Carolina Employment and Health Survey obtained detailed information on the working conditions of a large scientific sample of North Carolina men and women, including their powers, responsibilities, and promotion prospects. The study was able to differentiate between true managers (people who had the authority to make substantive decisions), nominal managers (people whose job titles suggested decision-making powers, but who in actuality had little real power), true supervisors (people who had the authority to give orders to workers), nominal supervisors (people whose job title suggested the oversight of personnel, but who in actuality had little control over their people), and people with no power of any kind whatsoever. It was also able to obtain information on promotion prospects. None of this type of subtle information is available in traditional census materials.

Table 1.10 shows the results of this analysis. Most of the true managers in North Carolina were men. Men filled over 80 percent of these positions; fewer than 20 percent were filled by women. Women were far more likely to be nominal managers, workers with titles but with little real decision-making ability. True supervisors were even balanced 50–50 between males and females. Note that the true supervisor category included foremen, shift supervisors, senior secretaries, and other low-level personnel. That said, there were fewer women in these positions than in nominal supervisor positions, jobs that tended to be almost two-thirds female. Jobs with absolutely no power were divided roughly 50–50 with a slight tilt towards women. There are many menial powerless male positions in the economy; women scarcely have a monopoly on subordinate status.

Promotion prospects showed a similar pattern, although the gender differentials were not quite so pronounced. Jobs with excellent prospects

TABLE 1.10 Percent Female in Jobs by Power and Promotion Prospects: North
Carolina 1989

Power	
True Manager	19.2%
Nominal Manager	45.5%
True Supervisor	50.2%
Nominal Supervisor	65.0%
No Power	56.9%
Promotion Prospects	
High	40.6%
Middle	49.6%
Low	52.3%
None	65.9%

SOURCE: Tomaskovic-Devey (1993).

for promotion were divided 60–40 between men and women, the advantage being towards men. The percent female steadily increased as the
hopes of promotion decline. Dead-end jobs were divided nearly one
third-two thirds between men and women, with women getting the
brunt of these positions. Still, 40 percent of jobs with high upward advancement were held by women and 34 percent of dead-end jobs were
held by men. Even though women were more likely to be under a glass
ceiling, there was male company on the bottom, and opportunity for
some women to escape.

The most important mechanism for creating gender inequality in
power and status is occupational sex-typing. Occupations with formal
authority are more likely to be male; occupations with little formal authority are more likely to be female. However, this is not the only way in
which power differentials are created. Often within occupations that in
principle should allow for significant status and autonomy, men are
given high-level positions and real power, while women are languishing
at entry-level or low-visibility positions with little substantive clout. This
varies enormously, with plenty of exceptions, in terms of industries or
occupations that provide equal promotion probabilities to workers of
both sexes, and in terms of women in atypical industries who somehow
manage to struggle to the top. These exceptions are extremely important, and in some settings the exceptions are becoming the rule.

A good example of the issues involved can be found in management. Openings in executive jobs for women have increased dramatically in recent years. According to the census, in 1970 only 18.5 percent of all executive, administrative, and managerial jobs were held by women; in 1990, this number was 44.0 percent (Cohen, Broschak, and Haveman 1998). This is an awesome change, a transformation of the most powerful occupation in the U.S. economy from a male preserve in 1970 to a nearly balanced occupation in 1990.

It is possible to try to dismiss these changes by showing that women executives are generally concentrated in the lowest rungs of management. As far as it goes, this statement is true. In 1996, only four women were CEOs in the Fortune 1000—the remaining nine-hundred and ninety-six CEOs were men (Zweigenhaft and Domhoff 1998). By 1994, the majority of Fortune 1000 corporations had a woman on their boards, but she was generally a token. Only 5.6 percent of all directors were women (Zweigenhaft and Domhoff 1998).[4] More important, the duties of female directors were marginalized. Women directors were less likely to be placed on the subcommittees of the board where real, substantive decisions are made, namely, the executive committee, the compensation committee, and the finance committee. They were more likely to serve as goodwill ambassadors or public relations figures, serving on the less important subcommittee of public affairs (Bilmoria and Piderit 1994).

The interpretation of this phenomenon, however, is ambiguous. Consider the case of the California savings and loan industry, an industry that has been conspicuously supportive of the recruitment and advancement of female managers. Rates of promotion for male and female managers are roughly similar. However, although there are significant percentages of female vice presidents, treasurers, and secretaries—a secretary of a bank, like the Secretary of the Treasury is an executive, not a clerical worker—fewer than 5 percent of the chief executive officers, presidents or chairmen of the board are female (Cohen, Broschak, and Haveman 1998). Superficially, this looks remarkably like a glass ceiling.

There is, however, another explanation for this. The California savings and loan industry, like much of the rest of the United States economy, has only recently begun to hire female executives. In the 1960s and 1970s, these banks would have hired primarily male labor. In the 1980s and 1990s, the savings and loans industry increased its hiring of women. Let us pick an arbitrary date, say 1985, at which all discrimination in California banking would have come to an end. (This is an assumption made just for the sake of argument; further analysis would be needed to determine whether or not the late 1980s and 1990s were discrimination-free at all.) By this logic, from 1985 on, entering cohorts of women were hypothetically experiencing no gender-related barriers to their promotions.

This does not mean there would be a 50–50 male-female split of all top executive positions by 1986. An entry-level bank manager trainee cannot expect to rise all the way up to president of Golden State Savings and Loan in one year. Advancement up the corporate ladder takes time. Outside of some unusual industries that offer rapid advancement for the very young (computer hardware and software being two such examples), most managers have to grow through the ranks and obtain seniority and experience before being considered for upper-level positions. It can easily take thirty years to obtain a top position in an auto company; most Fortune 500 executives have similar career paths. Therefore, in the case of a 1985 elimination of discrimination in promotion, one would expect women to start reaching the top between the years 2000 and 2015. (One might not have to wait the full thirty years to see results, because there may be senior women predating the 1985 change who would be raw material for late 1980s and 1990s promotions). The presence of women at middle executive positions combined with their absence from top positions may be an indication of discrimination, or it may be a mere indicator of the newness of a regime of gender fairness.

This ambiguity, however, does not apply when one considers populations of managers who enter their occupations at the same time. If all of the workers have roughly the same organizational age and the men are obtaining higher positions than the women, one cannot argue that this is due purely to accidents of seniority. One can do the same thing by considering a population of managers of many different ages but statistically controlling for their levels of experience. Both types of study tend to find that women face difficulties in obtaining promotion that are not due to seniority alone.

Reskin and Ross (1992) studied a random sample of managers in Illinois; their findings are illustrated in Table 1.11. They found that women systematically had less decision-making authority than did men. They were more likely than men to have no final decision-making authority whatsoever and less likely to have final responsibility for large numbers of different areas. This lack of power may reflect their marginalization within a prestigious job title; in most cases, however, it also represents not being promoted to a sufficiently high position to be "in the loop" for the setting of major policies.

Reskin and Ross explicitly considered whether seniority was the cause of these gender differentials. This turned out to be not the case. They statistically controlled for firm tenure, firm size, and formal qualifications. Even when the researchers allowed for this, they found that women managers were substantially less likely to have decision-making authority than were men.

TABLE 1.11   Number of Arenas in Which Managers Had Final Decision-
Making Authority: Reskin-Ross Illinois Sample

Arenas of Final Decision Power	Men	Women
0	16.8%	27.2%
1	28.4%	14.7%
2–5	33.6%	27.1%
6–10	23.2%	9.8%
11–15	11.2%	7.4%
16 +	0.7%	0.0%
Total	100.0%	100.0%

SOURCE: Reskin and Ross (1992).

Reskin and Ross's data has another peculiar twist. In their equations, they also controlled for managerial level and formal supervisory authority. This study represents how high women had climbed in the organizational pyramid both in title and in number of workers supervised. Even allowing for these statistics, women had less decision-making power than men; this strongly suggests that women are marginalized even when they hold high-status titles. Confining women to staff roles rather than assigning them line roles may account for part of this. In many corporations, engineering, finance, and marketing are the centers of organizational power. By contrast, women may be disproportionately assigned to human resources or to support staff, away from the key issues facing the firm. In other cases, this may represent management's avoidance of incorporating particular women into the decision-making process as a result of the vagaries and flows of office politics. Whatever the reasons for women's marginalization, the Reskin and Ross study showed that women's rise to power in business was being hampered by more than lack of experience.

What is occurring in business is occurring in other professions, too. In 1996, only 8 percent of the directors of Wall Street's largest investment and brokerage houses were women (Truell 1996). In that year, only 14 percent of the partners in the 250 largest law firms in the United States were women. Female partners are significantly less likely than are male partners to be entitled to a percentage of the firms profits (Deutsch 1996; Zweigenhaft and Domhoff 1998). Kay and Hagan (1998) studied lawyers practicing in Ontario; although the attorneys in their study entered the profession at roughly comparable times, the researchers found that the male lawyers were almost twice as likely as the females to make partner.

Paula Nesbitt (1997) examined the careers of clergy in the Episcopal and Unitarian churches in the United States. Fully aware of the dangers of conflating discrimination with seniority, she carefully divided her pastors into cohorts who took the cloth at roughly the same period. As such, her findings are strictly a result of the internal dynamics of these organizations and not a function of age per se. In general, women clergy had less prestigious postings than did men. They were more likely to be assistants and associates than seniors, more likely to be employed part-time than full-time, and more likely to have to leave a congregation and take employment elsewhere. Similar findings exist for other Christian denominations (Carroll, Hardgrove and Lummis 1983; Prichard 1996) and for Reform Judaism (Marder 1996). Suffice it to say, female clergy are paid significantly less than are male clergy. Zikmund, Lummis, and Chang (1998) show this salary differential exists even when one takes into account the years of experience of the clergyperson. This is further evidence that the gender gap is not caused by some neutral effect of seniority and that women still suffer significant obstacles to attaining promotion to positions with higher pay and responsibility.[5]

Occupational Typing
Versus Status Segregation

Occupational typing and status segregation are two different sociological processes. Occupational typing sorts people into occupations. These occupations held by people of group A may be better, worse than, or equal to the occupations held by people of group B. Status segregation is the confinement of people to low-status jobs by virtue of their ascriptive status. This can be done by occupational typing. It can also be done by confining people to low status positions within a given occupation.

Occupational typing and status segregation exist both for women and for blacks. There is, however, an important difference between these two groups. The male female split in the United States is characterized by intensive occupational typing, with a lesser degree of status segregation. The black-white split in the United States is characterized by intensive status segregation with a lesser degree of occupational typing.

What does this mean in plain English? In the United States, there are male jobs and female jobs. However, many women rise to superior positions and supervise men. By contrast, relatively few jobs are uniquely white or black. Blacks and whites are more likely to share occupations rather than work in occupations labeled as being one color or the other.

Blacks, however, suffer from limits on their access to high-status occupations and are forced to work in mixed occupations on the low end of the prestige scale.

This finding is shown statistically in Table 1.12. Table 1.12 shows indicators of occupational typing and status segregation for gender and race respectively. The indicators used are relatively complex and require some explanation.

The measure of occupational typing is the index of occupational dissimilarity. This is a general measure of the extent to which two groups hold the same jobs or different jobs, with 0 implying they have very similar occupations and 1 implying they have very different occupations. This is the same measure that was used in Table 1.7.[6]

TABLE 1.12   Indicators of Occupational Typing and Status Segregation by Gender and Race in the United States

Indicators of Occupational Typing *(1=High Occupational Typing, 0= Low Occupational Typing)*	
Index of Occupational Dissimilarity: White Males & White Females	.604
Index of Occupational Dissimilarity: White Males & Black Males	.293

Indicators of Status Segregation *(1=High Status Segregation, 0=Low Status Segregation)*	
Correlation of Male Job Advantage & SES: White Males & White Females	.152
Correlation of White Job Advantage & SES: White Males & Black Males	.657

SOURCE: Indices of Occupational Dissimilarity. King 1992. Figures are for 1988. Correlation of Male Job Advantage and SES: Author's calculations from data organized by Mark Fossett from Current Population Survey 1997. See text for details of construction of index.

The level of occupational dissimilarity by gender was 0.604; the level of occupational dissimilarity by race was only 0.293. Blacks and whites are not in the same occupations as each other, but racial differences in occupational distribution are less than half the gender differences in occupational distributions. Blacks and whites, then, are more likely to work in the same occupations than are men and women.

The measure of status segregation used here is the correlation of white male job advantage with socioeconomic status. White male job advantage is the extent to which the occupation in question is filled with white males as opposed to women or blacks. Socioeconomic status is a standard sociological index of occupational prestige. Supreme Court Justices do the best. Janitors do poorly. Doctors score high. Waitresses score low. If white male job advantage is highly correlated with socioeconomic status, it means that white males are more likely to get high-status jobs than are members of the competing groups. If the correlation of white male job advantage and socioeconomic status is not very high, this means the disadvantaged groups have strong possibilities of obtaining high-status jobs, and that the white male advantage in obtaining good jobs is not very great.

The correlation of male job advantage and status is 0.152. The correlation of white job advantage and status is 0.657. The indicator of status segregation for race is over four times as great as the indicator of status segregation for gender. Earlier in the chapter, we saw noticeable differences between men and women. Table 1.12 shows the status gap between blacks and whites is more than four times as great as the status gap between men and women.

To summarize the complicated message of Table 1.12: Men and women work in jobs that are distinctively male or female; status differences exist between them, but they are not large. Blacks and whites are likely to work in racially mixed occupations. Hhigh-status jobs, however, have a lot of whites and relatively few blacks; low-status jobs have fewer whites and more blacks.

The consequences of these differences will become more apparent in later chapters. A simple first lesson from this analysis is that gender and race are not the same. Loose discussion of white male privilege often conflates women and blacks as being subordinate groups sharing a victim status relative to white males. Both of these groups do have real problems, but the issues facing women and blacks are different. As a result, the experiences of these groups are different. Women have made real strides in eliminating the wage and employment disadvantages between them and men. Black progress has been much more limited. Many of the barriers to racial equality in education have been substantially eliminated. Discrimination in the labor market and in employment, however, remains as great as ever.

Conclusion

This discrimination is why this book is about race and gender differences at work. The workplace is the primary stratifying institution in our society. Employers make organizational decisions that determine workers' pay. Workers' paychecks determine workers' incomes. Workers' incomes determine workers' access to economic resources and power, and, in turn, their ability to obtain all the good things in life. Employers also make organizational decisions about whom to hire and whom not to hire. Hiring decisions determine who gets work and who doesn't get work, which determines who has money and who does not. Thus, in an extremely fundamental way, much of the race and gender inequality that we observe in modern life has its start in the managerial policies of firms and corporations.

If we want to understand inequality, then, we need to understand managerial logic. Why do employers make the decisions they do? Why do they pay people this amount and not that amount? Why do they hire this person but not that person? If one wants to understand social stratification in our society, we need to get inside the heads of managers. We need to know what they think and why they think it. We need to know the economic constraints under which they operate. We need to know the organizational realities that limit their freedom of choice. If the decisions of top executives affect the way we live, the only way we can understand our own lives is to understand the managerial logic of these top executives.

Understanding the logic of a top executive means learning how to think in economic terms. Firms exist to make money. Although top management has discretion to act in independent ways, they are under constraint to pay attention to the bottom line and to consider firm profitability when they make organizational decisions. This means that if we want to understand the logic behind the creation of opportunities for women and blacks, we need to understand firm profitability and financial constraints. The student thus has to know how to think like a businessperson and deal sensibly with economic realities.

The next chapter begins to consider the economic factors that go into determining whether or not employers will discriminate. Chapter 3 uses this economic analysis to understand what kinds of jobs are male and female. Chapter 4 considers the problem of status segregation for women. Chapter 5 considers why women are still paid less relative to men. Chapter 6 is a lengthy consideration of the distinctive problems experienced by blacks, analyzing why the black employment rate continues to be low relative to the employment rate for whites. Chapter 7 integrates these statements into a general statement of the causes of racial and gender discrimination in the United States.

We now move to a discussion of the economic models that underpin the analysis of the remaining five chapters of the book.

Technical Appendix

Before 1972, the Bureau of Labor Statistics did not publish statistics for blacks per se, but combined them with all other nonwhites. Before 1960, most nonwhites in government statistics were African Americans, so that the distinction between nonwhite and black during this period is academic.After 1960, however, the number of non–African American nonwhites in government statistics began to increase. This increase was caused by a number of factors. American Indians who had previously declared themselves whites began to declare themselves Indian. A similar process occurred among Hispanics. There was furthermore a bona fide increase in Asian in-migration. Thus, from 1960 on, substantial differences emerge between the black and the nonwhite populations.

In this book, black data is used for African Americans whenever possible. When only nonwhite data is available, it is used with the following technical corrections: The difference between nonwhite and black scores is calculated for 1975. This is applied as a correction factor to nonwhite data for 1955 to 1970 and is phased in over time in linear increments. For example, in 1975, the nonwhite male employment rate was 1.5 points higher than the black male employment rate. Black male employment rates for 1955 were calculated by subtracting 0.3 from the nonwhite rate. In 1960, 0.6 was subtracted; in 1965, 0.9 was subtracted; in 1970, 1.2 was subtracted.

Comparable corrections were applied to other series.

I offer my sincere gratitude to Mark Fossett for providing the information necessary to produce these adjustments.

Notes

1. Technically, diehard liberals could claim that declining social inequality justifies affirmative action because government programs are reducing racial gaps; diehard conservatives could argue that unchanging inequality means that affirmative action should be dropped because it doesn't work. In politics, people will say just about anything. However, liberals rarely exult about the absence of social problems, and conservatives rarely boast about the persistence of fundamental inequality.

2. Bruce Western and Katherine Beckett (1999) have suggested an even more sinister interpretation: Unemployment fell because of the drug war. Police incarcerated large numbers of blacks, often guilty of only trivial offenses, and by removing them from the population searching for work, coincidentally removed

them from the unemployment statistics. This sounds paranoid, but unfortunately there is nontrivial statistical support for this position.

3. Most gender time series on earnings begin in 1955 rather than 1950 due to the lack of consistent data before 1955.

4. Three percent of all corporate directorship seats were held by blacks (Zweigenhaft and Domhoff 1998).

5. This review of the literature on female career prospects in the clergy is largely drawn from Chaves 1997.

6. Technically, the occupational dissimilarity measures in Tables 1.7 and 1.12 are not strictly comparable because they are calculated on slightly different populations (King 1992).

2 *Discrimination and Market Competition*

One of the great paradoxes of discrimination is that if firms were entirely economically rational, gender and race discrimination in the workplace would not exist. This isn't because discrimination isn't "nice" or because the world would be a wonderful paradise if everybody treated everyone else kindly. Many forms of economic cruelty are entirely rational; these include paying your workers the smallest amount of money possible consistent with maintaining their work effort, laying off workers you don't need if you won't need them later, and avoiding paying for ecological cleanups. Firms are more likely to survive and prosper if they focus on making money rather than concentrating on solving all the problems of the world. That said, discrimination is rarely a viable strategy for making money, and its existence poses problems for economic theory.

This argument was made most cogently by the University of Chicago economist, Gary Becker (1957). Gary Becker is viewed within economics as having done the pathbreaking work on discrimination. His theory, developed in the 1950s, has stood the test of time far better than most of the rest of social science of that decade (which is not to say it has not been the subject of intense controversy, both then and now). The model requires the operation of a strong and fully competitive free market. Assuming this precondition, he argues that economic forces will ultimately eliminate discrimination from both hiring and wages. This strong claim sometimes works surprisingly well, because Becker's assumptions capture the experience of a nontrivial proportion of the U.S. labor market. However, there are other settings when the assumptions do not apply. Where Becker's assumptions do not apply, discrimination persists.

In this chapter, I explain the Becker model in some detail, along with a feminist rendition of this argument from Heidi Hartmann. I then discuss how discrimination may continue to exist even in the face of the type of free market processes Becker documents. I consider not only situations in which Gary Becker's assumptions are violated, but also those where his assumptions apply with full force.

The Becker Model: Core Assumptions

Gary Becker, in his *Economics of Discrimination* (1957), argued that the free market has the capacity to eliminate discrimination. To understand how economic forces can do this, we need to know exactly what Gary Becker meant by the concept of a fully competitive market.

A competitive free market (or its namesake, perfect competition) is a setting in which individual firms are capable of trading for goods under the conditions of the highest rationality without anyone's having a unique or permanent advantages. It is a setting where no one makes any enduring mistakes, and no one can obtain a permanent edge that would relax their need to continue behaving rationally in the future. This can occur under the following conditions:

1. *Profit Maximization.* Every firm's primary goal is to make the largest possible profit. The only goal that any businessman has is to make the largest amount of money possible, and they pursue this goal relentlessly and single-mindedly. Workers also share this motivation. All they want is the highest possible wages, making their work as profitable as possible.

2. *Perfect Knowledge.* To behave rationally, everyone needs complete access to all the information required to make intelligent decisions. In this model, all the knowledge anyone requires to make an intelligent investment or job choice is readily available.

3. *Perfect Liquidity of Capital and Labor.* The highly rational businesspeople posited by this model will want to invest their time and money in the most lucrative enterprises possible. Should there be a trap s that once one put money or labor into an enterprise one could not get it out, one could be stuck in unprofitable endeavors. In a perfect market, no such obstacles exist. One can get any factor of production out of a bad company instantly and instantaneously put that factor into a new company with the highest rate of return available. Economists call this *liquidity of capital and labor.* Liquidity refers to the ability to move something almost immediately to where it would be most

desirable. *Capital* refers to the nonhuman factors needed for production. These refer to any of the following: money, technology, raw materials, or machinery. *Labor* refers to the human factors needed for production; this generally means workers.

If people are maximizing profit, if they are fully informed, and if their capital and labor are perfectly liquid, they will never tolerate being in a less profitable situation and always immediately transfer their resources to more profitable situations. This has the important implication that investors will instantly pull the plug on underperforming firms. If a firm is anything less than perfectly rational, and the mistake shows up in the form of lower profits, the funds that were originally put into the firm will be dispersed and other more lucrative investments will receive the resources that were placed in the original company.

The core implication of the neoclassical model, then, is that one mistake means sudden death. Sudden death can come in a number of ways. It could be that all the investors pull their funds out of a firm and invest elsewhere. It could also be that some astute raider notes that the underperforming businessman is making a hash out of his firm. He could then offer to buy out the underperformer, paying the underperformer the low rate of return that businessman is getting on his investment. The raider would then apply rational policy, making the firm worth more than he paid for it, thus making a profit for himself.

There are other methods for eliminating irrationality in firms besides buyouts. A board of directors could be aware of stupid decisions being made by their executives and simply fire those managers, replacing them with smarter people. Furthermore, a top manager could make an error and start seeing the warning signs of trouble: investors pulling out, raiders making hostile offers, and boards of directors becoming restive. This would give the manager a chance to reconsider his or her ways, and as long as it was done quickly, institute a new and more rational policy. One can thus see the argument that irrational policies are often eliminated from firms in competitive markets is not entirely without justification. In real life, we see bankruptcies, buyouts, firings, and managerial U-turns all the time.

The Becker Model: Operation

Assuming therefore that perfect competition exists, why would market forces eliminate discrimination? Assume that for some reason a set of employers chose not to hire members of a particular group, say blacks. Whites could find themselves hired just about anywhere. Blacks, however, could find employment only with a limited set of tolerant firms.

Under these conditions, neoclassical economics predicts that black wage rates would go down. This is because all the firms that blacks work in have a large supply of labor competing for those positions, while the firms that whites work in will have a small supply of labor competing for these positions. The firms that hire blacks will have black workers and white workers trying to get jobs in these establishments. The firms that hire whites will have only white workers trying to obtain jobs. The discriminatory firms will have fewer applicants bidding against each other to obtain work. The lower competition for jobs in these firms means higher wages for the workers involved; employers will have fewer alternative workers to turn to as replacements should workers' wage requests increase. By contrast, the nondiscriminatory firm is flooded with job applicants and can easily play one applicant against the other to obtain the lowest possible wages. Because blacks can get jobs only in the firms with these low-paying employers, overall black wage rates will tend to be low.

Because the discriminatory firms are paying higher wages than their more egalitarian counterparts, they are going to be less profitable overall. In a perfectly competitive free market, companies with lower-than-normal profits are driven out of business by the competition for funds. This will put an economic squeeze on discriminators; they are faced with one of two choices:

1. They can hire blacks, who will be working more cheaply than whites. This will lower the firms wage rates, restoring their profitability and allowing them to survive.
2. They can be driven out of business.

In an economically rational world, most employers will take the first alternative. The result is that discriminatory firms will start hiring minorities overall. They will continue to do so until the wage difference between blacks and whites disappears. This wage difference will only disappear when the difference in the hiring rates of blacks and whites disappears. When the process comes to an end (or in economic jargon, comes to an *equilibrium*), blacks and whites will have identical employment and wage rates, and there will be no discriminatory employers whatsoever in the labor market.

The logic of Becker's position is reasonable. There is just one problem, however. Obviously in the modern world, economic discrimination is robust and pervasive. If discrimination is supposed to go away, why is it so persistent? Becker had two answers to this question.

The first is that he himself decided to relax the assumption of profit maximization. He argued that employers have a "taste for discrimination." In noneconomic jargon, this means that employers love discriminating so much that they are willing to take a loss to exclude minorities

(Becker 1957). This is a somewhat less than wonderful answer. It is undoubtedly true that many employers prefer to be surrounded with workers of their own kind. However, in a neoclassical free market, one cannot just decide one would rather not make a profit and have the market tolerate it. In general, unprofitable firms will be driven to near extermination by other competitors who are willing to be less discriminatory.

Becker's free market/taste for discrimination formulation is relatively fragile. The only case where a free market could tolerate discrimination is when *everybody* discriminates without exception. In this case, there would be no profitable nondiscriminators who could compete with the high-wage discriminators and there would be no reason for profit maximizers to move their funds out of all-white firms. However, the claim that "everybody discriminates" is as implausible as the claim that "nobody discriminates." We can all think of many employers who are especially likely to hire blacks, women, Hispanics, or the physically challenged. Many employers find discrimination of all kinds offensive, and some are even prejudiced the other way with a positive preference for groups other than white male Anglos. Differences exist within employers in the extent to which they provide equal or unequal opportunity for minorities. By the free market logic, this should provide an incentive for profits to flow from the discriminating firms to the egalitarian firms. "Taste for discrimination" alone does not explain how inequality can survive in a free market.

Becker provided a second explanation that was equally problematic. He argued for the existence of "employee discrimination." Employees have a strong preference for working with members of their own group. If forced to work with members of some other gender or ethnicity, workers would be likely to go on strike, unionize, or all quit to take other jobs. If the cost of hiring minority workers would be to lose one's majority workers, employers would supposedly have no choice but to hire majority workers (Becker 1957).

Let us bracket the troubling and not obvious question of why firms, given workers who will not work with other groups, would prefer majority over minority workers. Instead let us consider the more basic questions. How obvious is it that white male workers will never under any circumstance work with members of other groups? White men play football with black men all the time; they serve together in the army; they even run together on political tickets. Furthermore, even if it were viewed as being distasteful for whites to work with blacks, employers routinely get workers to do distasteful things. Getting to work by 8 A.M. is distasteful, especially if it means fighting the interstate from 6:30 to 8 every morning. Taking a pay cut is distasteful. Working with toxic chemicals, or with dangerous, poorly repaired machinery is distasteful. People do these things all the time. Working with someone from another ethnic group would seem to be mild in comparison.

Furthermore, since when in U.S. capitalism do employees tell employers whom or whom not to hire? The control of the labor process in the United States is firmly under the control of management. The voice of worker sentiment in the United States is the union. The majority of firms in the United States are not unionized. In those firms whose workers belong to unions, the union generally concentrates on issues of wages and conditions. Very few unions have ever been able to force an employer not to hire minority workers.[1] As for the argument that white workers would all quit if a minority worker were hired in their firm, just ask yourself if you personally are familiar with any work settings in which such a phenomenon has occurred.

The Feminist Gary Becker: Heidi Hartmann

What's useful in Gary Becker is the postulation of a fundamental tension between profit maximization and discrimination. Not all readers are going to intellectually accept the neoclassical economic assumptions behind his reasoning. His argument, however, has also been made by Marxist feminists who approach these problems from an entirely different angle. The school of feminist scholarship that emphasizes the contradictions between economic and gender considerations is "dual sector" theory. The leading exponent of this theory is one of the pioneers of Marxist women's studies, Heidi Hartmann.

Heidi Hartmann (1976) was writing in reaction to earlier Marxists who argued that all of women's oppression was the product of capitalism. Engels (1964) had maintained that women's subordination was a product of the institution of private property and the need of men to control the inheritance of capital. Seccombe (1974) had argued that women's housework was a form of extraction of surplus value (a form of Marxist exploitation) that directly allowed capitalists to accumulate wealth. An alternative formulation is that capitalists exclude women from the labor force to make a "reserve army of labor," a docile set of workers who work for very low wages and who can be used as a threat to replace male workers should the males ask for higher wages or become militant.

Heidi Hartmann argued that it is difficult to say that capitalists benefit from women's oppression in any monetary fashion whatsoever, a position that makes a great deal of sense. The old Marxist gender-profit links were always dubious. Capitalists can survive as a class regardless of who inherits any particular piece of property. Whoever gets the property becomes a capitalist, and the class reproduces itself nicely. The link between housework and capitalist profits is tenuous. Has any corporation ever tried to improve its balance sheet by making the spouses of its employees do more housework? The reserve army of labor argument is also weak. It is true that the existence of a large body of workers exists outside the labor force who could replace the current set of workers will reduce militancy among currently employed workers who have reason to fear immediate replacement. If these unemployed and desperate workers are willing to work for less, however, why do capitalists put up with their expensive current employees in the first place? Why not fire everybody, hire equally from both sexes, and let suicidal competition from workers of both sexes drive wages to a rock-bottom level? Instead of just threatening to let in cheap women workers, employers could actually act on this intention and get immediate and sizable reductions in their overall wage bill.

Hartmann argued that two separate social forces are at work in the work world. The first is *capitalism*, which represents the process of economic profit maximization. From Hartmann's standpoint, this is the logic by which capitalists oppress workers. The second is *patriarchy*, which represents the defense of male privilege. From her standpoint, this is the logic by which men oppress women.

Hartmann argued that men of all social classes prefer to keep women home and not working for the preservation of male status and the continuation of female dependency. By insuring that men are the sole breadwinners of their families, women become dependent upon a man for their economic survival. Unmarried daughters cannot afford to leave their father, insuring that his authority in the household will be unchallenged and absolute. Women who leave their fathers have to do so through marriage, insuring a contract of sexual and domestic service to a different male. Because in the absence of employment married women cannot provide for themselves without a husband, they are forced to accept whatever terms the husband imposes on the relationship. At worst, their lack of economic power may put them at risk of being subject to domestic abuse, or might require them to tolerate antisocial behavior. More frequently their lack of an exit option forces them into submission to a beneficent but autocratic authority. This dependency supplies men with permanent access to domestic and sexual services as well as reinforces their psychological status as the dominant members of their households.

To show the gendered rather than class base for the exclusion of women from the workplace, Hartmann traces the history of nineteenth-century laws, which made it illegal for women to work long hours or to work in dangerous workplaces. Although employers were often supporters of such legislation, what is marked is male unionists' vociferous advocacy of the limitation of female factory work. Hartmann's history shows that working-class men explicitly argued that the exclusion of women would maintain the status of men as the sole breadwinners of their families; the manly nature of paid employment was a good thing and should be reinforced and perpetuated. Thus the exclusion of women from paid employment was not imposed on working-class women by a capitalist class eager to seek profits but by a coalition of working-class and upper-class men, both of whom sought to keep women out of work and in the home.

Let us set aside the participation of unions in these campaigns (this topic gets proper attention in Chapter 5). Consider for a moment the actions of the patriarchal factory owner. In Hartmann's argument, it would not be rational for a male employer to refrain from hiring women even if he as a man benefited from the perpetuation of male domination. The subordinate status of women in the labor market depends on the global or national exclusion of women from employment. The actions of any one firm will not change the balance of power between the sexes at a global level. A company that hires two hundred women will not change the fundamental balance of power between the genders in the nation because those two hundred jobs represent an infinitesimal percentage of all activity in the labor market. However, hiring two hundred women will produce significant wage savings for the company that does so. Any company that refuses to hire women is thus having a negligible impact on the overall gendered division of labor. If employers insist on keeping women out, it is because they enjoy doing so, pretty much a restatement of Gary Becker's "employers' taste for discrimination".

Decision Theory: Why Organizations Don't Behave So Rationally After All

The entire dilemma posed by Becker and Hartmann's work is that left to its own dynamics, the free market has the potential to eliminate any form of discrimination. That said, both Becker and Hartmann would rightfully claim that no such elimination has occurred. The question then arises why this elimination has not occurred. Instead of following Becker and Hartmann's lead in considering other forces such as tastes and patriarchy, let us look critically at the institutions of markets themselves. Maybe they were limited in their capacity to remove discrimination in the first place.

The most convincing arguments in this vein were developed in the 1950s and 1960s by the Decision Theorists. These were a set of organizational analysts and institutional economists who empirically analyzed the process of decision making in large firms. They found massive deviations between how decisions are really made in business and how economic theory claims these decisions are made. The predictions of neoclassical economic theory were not entirely disconfirmed; they were however, embarrassed on a number of critical points. Their work suggests a modified economic theory in which market forces and rational decision making obtain only under a specific and limited set of conditions.

Although there are a number of writers in the Decision Theory tradition, many of whom—Herbert Simon (1957) and Richard Lester (1951) among them—made powerful arguments, the present discussion is going to focus on the work of Cyert and March (1963), whose formulation of these issues is particularly compelling. Cyert and March identify three problems with traditional neoclassical economic thinking.

1. *Businesspeople have other goals besides profit maximization.* Cyert and March's argument begins in a similar fashion to the arguments of Becker and Hartmann. Becker said that businessmen pursue profits and their taste for discrimination. Hartmann argued for the simultaneous existence of capitalism and patriarchy. Cyert and March would agree with these authors that sometimes male managers pursue their gendered aspirations instead of maximizing profits. They might therefore not hire women, or hire women only for positions in a personal service relationship to powerful men (secretary, nurse etc.).

However, Cyert and March's critique runs deeper than just acknowledging the presence of sexism. Managers have many goals *besides* profit maximizing and acting on their ethnic or gender concerns. Some of them are seeking personal glory and ego gratification; they pursue personal projects that will advance their names even if these projects aren't especially lucrative. Some of them are seeking higher salaries. Although sometimes higher salaries come as a reward for being productive, managers who give themselves extraordinary stock options or nominate board members who will give the managers raises even in the face of indifferent performance are not acting to maximize the profits of the firm. Some managers just love certain lines of business regardless of their profitability. The ownership of professional sports teams is a conspicuous example of this phenomenon. And last, some managers are flat out lazy. They want to go home at five or seven o'clock and not have to rationalize their product line, research what the competition is up to, or change the comfortable ways of doing business that served them well in their youth.

If managers are pursuing pet projects, padding their salaries, or carving out some leisure in their daily schedule, they are not going to be vigorously pursuing every legitimate profit opportunity that comes along. Their private agendas and the limits on their time mean that they are going to miss potential investment opportunities; they will fail to implement new technologies that are being adopted by their competitors; they will let stale investments sit too long because they are too distracted and busy to notice that parts of their portfolios are stagnating. Put simply, the presence of other goals gives firms a certain level of inertia. Such inertia makes capital and labor illiquid rather than liquid; it allows unprofitable economic arrangements to persist because other competitors are simply too slow and sluggish to notice the vulnerability implicit in the inactivity of their partners. To use a sports analogy, when a competitor fumbles the football, if the remaining players don't pay attention, the sloppy runner will maintain possession.

2. *When making choices, businesspeople miscalculate.* The previous section argued that businessmen don't always pay attention. Not only do they not pay attention, but when they do pay attention, they use the wrong information in their calculations. As Kenneth Arrow (1973) would argue later, one cannot make correct decisions without information, and information is not free. There is no universal data bank that executives just tap into to get all the data they need to make intelligent decisions. Information shows up in idiosyncratic ways. An outside agent, such as a lunch partner or a vendor, brings an investment opportunity to a manager's attention. A subordinate writes a report for his supervisor filled with information that would coincidentally imply a bigger role for the subordinate in the running of the firm. A company is considering three suppliers for a product, but the saleswoman working for one of them is especially vigorous and articulate.

Cyert and March's key concept is that information is considered on a *sequential* basis. Because the company knows that it will never have all the information it could possibly have, it at some point stops seeking data and makes a decision. Because all the information is not (and can never be) put into consideration, all economic thinking in some way is biased. Biased decision making is irrational decision making. If corporate actions generically are irrational, then imperfect policies can survive in the market for a long time.

3. *Businesspeople can be rational when they have to be.* Just because managers can be irrational doesn't mean they *have* to be irrational. In some settings managers will exert themselves to approximate the level of focused, intelligent decision making implied by traditional economic theory. Rational choice is particularly likely in crisis situations when the survival of the firm is in immediate jeopardy. Although managers may have a variety of personal goals, they are all united by one goal: the survival of the firm. If everyone's job is likely to be eliminated unless dramatic actions are taken, even the most rugged individualist is likely to make common cause with other managers, temporarily abandon side projects unrelated to firm survival, and concentrate in a narrow, focused way on eliminating the immediate threat at hand. Cyert and March refer to the survival of the firm as a *primary* goal. They refer to private projects

as *secondary* goals. Generally managers pursue primary goals until it seems likely that these goals will be met. Once this occurs, they concentrate on secondary goals, often losing sight of the primary goal altogether. Once it appears, however, that minimal standards will not be met on the primary goal, attention returns to this primary focus. Cyert and March refer to this process of partially meeting the needs of primary goals as *satisficing*. When one satisfices goals, one does not maximize one's efforts to act on these goals. One does just enough to avoid performance in this area from reaching crisis levels. One then moves on to other things. Students who do just enough to insure they pass the physics midterm and then just enough to see they get an OK grade on the anthropology presentation before they hit the bars are classic examples of satisficing. Sure, one could really kill oneself on either of these projects, and if one was on probation one might put some extra sweat into the physics and the anthro. However, once one's grade is at an acceptable level, one can concentrate one's efforts in other areas.

The concept of satisficing also applies to the process of information search. People stop searching for information when they feel secure about their decision process. If the firm is undergoing a challenge to its very survival, the centrality of the issues at hand will be clearly impressed in everybody's mind; few managers will feel comfortable with a cursory or superficial examination of the available data. The search for information will be relatively exhaustive and the probability will be greater that the firm will develop a response to the situation that more or less approximates a rational solution.

4. *What Determines the Level of Rationality of a Firm is the Level of "Organizational Slack."* Organizational slack is the level of surplus resources available to an organization. In a loose market, where not everyone is competing rationally, firms will be able to make money easily, even if their decision making is less than perfect. As such, firms will accumulate surplus resources; these can be used to advance a wide variety of projects. Managers may invest in Research and Development, expand their facilities, support the local opera, or, more notably, hire a more expensive grade of worker than they otherwise could afford. Weak market competition permits the accumulation of such slack; were rival firms making more rational decisions on their part, the firm might not have the profitability that allows the accumulation of organizational slack. When an organizational crisis emerges, slack resources evaporate. The firm finds itself operating on the margin where every penny lost can be catastrophic. When there is no slack, managers cannot satisfice on primary goals. Information search becomes intense in those areas, which are critical to firm survival. Cost-cutting and efficiency become the order of the day and the firm overall becomes more rational.

The Link Between Decision Theory and Discrimination: Buffering from Competition

Discrimination is a secondary utility; it is not the primary reason people go to work. People do not go to college, get an MBA and then work fifty-hour weeks so that they can intentionally deprive women and blacks of good jobs. Employers go to work to make money, just as the rest of us do. Their salaries and careers depend on the survival and health of the firm. Therefore, this survival is their primary utility.

That said, if they were to be able to work with a mix of coworkers whom they find congenial, this would be a desirable fringe. A prejudiced white male hiring an all-white male staff is like a company executive redecorating the offices or hiring a fancier caterer for the company cafeteria. He is using company resources to improve the personal quality of his life while costing the corporation money.

Such luxuries are fundable when the corporation is well off. They become less viable when corporate resources are strained. If market competition can eliminate the organizational slack that exists within the firm, then the firm's capacity to discriminate will be severely reduced. A world with no organizational slack looks like the world of Gary Becker, a world where savage market competition makes discrimination an economically nonviable policy. A world with organizational slack looks like the world of decision theory, where weak competition permits management to pursue secondary utilities using sloppy data. In such a world, arbitrariness in hiring policies can flourish.

The critical element here is *buffering from competition*. Buffering from competition refers to the presence of some force that protects the firm from the unimpeded pressures of the free market. In the previous discussions, the primary buffer we examined was human stupidity. Lazy, misinformed managers were doing a lousy job running competing firms, giving the home firm a break from the economic wars. Other factors, however, can produce buffering from competition; each of these increases the potential for discrimination.

Competition can be buffered by other factors as well, he most common being monopoly or oligopoly. A company may have a dominant position in a given industry because of superior technology, product design, or marketing. The reputation of the company is sufficiently strong that it can charge a premium price for its product and still command a huge percentage of the market. As of 1999, most people would rather drink Coca-Cola than Harry's Cola, use Microsoft Windows rather than the MeToo operating system, or charge their purchases with Mastercard rather than a First Elgin Bank Defer-Your-Payments Card. The dominant position of Coca-Cola, Microsoft, and Mastercard suggests that none of these firms is likely to see a crisis in organizational survival anytime soon. If necessary, they could afford to let their costs rise somewhat. In contrast, Harry's Cola, Metoo Software, and the First Elgin Bank Name Brand Credit Department (all fictional examples made up for this book) are likely to be economically marginal enterprises. The continuous threat to their survival from the major players means that their costs have to be kept to an absolute minimum. Such firms can afford to discriminate only at their peril.

This logic leads to the following hypothesis: Large, wealthy firms with relatively monopolistic market positions should be relatively more likely to discriminate and thus less likely to hire women and minorities. Large monopolistic firms are more buffered from competition than are small marginal firms and can afford a more expensive labor force. Such a prediction flows smoothly from the arguments we have just been developing. Such a prediction is also dead, flat wrong!

There is no evidence whatsoever that women and minorities are more likely to work in small impoverished firms than in rich wealthy firms. Evidence shows that just the opposite occurs. The definitive test of this hypothesis for gender was done by William Bridges (1980) on 1970 census data. Bridges studied the extent to which industries characterized by small, economically marginal firms were more likely to employ women. Analyzing industries is not quite as strong a test as that of analyzing individual firms; this is, however, a standard shortcut used in the literature which in most cases produces reasonable results. Bridges considered several different measures of industry marginality, including average size of firm, average wealth of firm, absence of concentration of sales, and average earnings of male workers. With one exception, which will be discussed in a later chapter, no indicator of industry marginality was significantly associated with female employment. This finding was replicated by Wallace and Kalleberg (1981). Wallace and Kalleberg repeated this analysis as well for race; the relationship between race and employment in marginal industries was practically zero. Further evidence on race comes from Harry Holzer. Holzer (1996) measured the effect of enterprise size on the employment of blacks in four separate cities in the United States (Atlanta, Detroit, Boston, and Los Angeles). Holzer had the advantage of knowing the actual size of the plants and race composition that he was studying rather than having to infer these from crude industry averages. In all four cities, blacks were far more likely to work in large plants than in small ones. The effect of size was not linear. There was a rough dichotomy between enterprises of less than 50 workers and enterprises with more than 50 workers; the latter were particularly likely to hire blacks.

Buffering from competition has important effects on discrimination, as we shall see, but not because such buffering steers minorities into small firms. Such steering is effectively counterbalanced by affirmative action and antidiscrimination legislation. Laws against discrimination have been a major force in steering minorities into large companies rather than small. This is because large corporations are more subject to enforcement of affirmative action policies than are small firms. There are three reasons for this:

1. *Many affirmative action laws do not apply to small firms.* Many antidiscrimination laws exempt the smallest firms from coverage. For example, Title VII of the Civil Rights Act, the major federal legislation governing discrimination by race, gender, and ethnic origin in the workplace, only applies to firms with fifteen or more employees. In earlier years, the ceiling was higher (Burstein (1985).

2. *The most stringent antidiscrimination policies apply to government contractors and the public sector.* Above and beyond federal and state laws that prohibit exclusionary treatment by gender are affirmative policies that mandate aggressive proactive attempts to increase the hiring of women and minorities. These are most commonly found in government employment because the state imposes high standards of equality on itself; alternatively, the state imposes these on contractors who wish to do business with government agencies. Because government contracts are often quite lucrative, vendors are generally willing to comply with affirmative action as a condition for being allowed to bid. Neither of these considerations is germane to small private sector firms. They are not subject to civil service regulations, and they are generally too small to compete for federal or state business. Note that most Fortune 500 companies do some government business; even if the primary component of the business is private sector, the effect of imposing affirmative action on public contractors is to increase minority hiring throughout the larger corporations of the United States, even in their nongovernmental activities (Burstein 1985).[2]

3. *It is more efficient to enforce antidiscrimination laws among large rather than small firms.* Even if it were wholly illegal for firms with even one employee to discriminate, as a practical matter it is highly likely that such firms could continue to do so with impunity. Prosecution costs the government money. Limits on public budgets constrain the amount of funds available to law enforcement in general and the amount of funds available to antidiscrimination prosecutors in particular. The EEOC has far more cases to investigate than they can possibly handle, a constraint that applies to every other police force and

regulatory agency as well. From the standpoint of cost efficiency, taking a case involving the employer of seven workers
to court is not that much cheaper than litigating a case involving an employer of 45,000 workers. If, however, the EEOC wins
the second case, 45,000 workers get immediate relief; if they
win the first case, only seven workers get relief. As a result,
smaller firms are going to be a lower enforcement priority, giving them greater de facto latitude to discriminate.

Note that the empirical studies we reported showed weak relationships between size and percent female or minority. Legal considerations
alone ought to suggest a strong positive relationship between size and
percent female or black. In real life the absence of relation between size
and percent female or black suggests that legal considerations and
buffering from competition effects are occurring and that the two forces
are canceling each other out.

The effect of buffering from market competition is manifest not so
much in cross-sectional differences, but in longitudinal trends in hiring
over time. The decrease in buffering from competition is one of the key
reasons that the improvement in employment prospects of women and,
to a lesser extent, minorities has occurred. The all-white-male labor
forces of the 1950s and 1960s were fostered by a buffered economic environment that prevented many large firms from having to economize
on labor costs. Such policies became less and less viable in the harsher
economic markets of the 1980s and 1990s.

Before the Arab oil crisis, many Fortune 500 firms were in relatively
comfortable and secure niches with significant monopolistic advantages. Nearly all U.S. cars were purchased from General Motors, Ford, or
Chrysler; agricultural machinery was made by John Deere or Caterpillar;
clothing and shoes were made on U.S. soil, and the labor making these
items was paid full U.S. wages. The U.S. dominance of the home market
was the product of many circumstances: the technological weakness of
many non–U.S. firms, weak educational systems in much of Asia and
the third world inhibiting the training of engineers and skilled workers,
sophisticated marketing on the part of U.S. corporations, political and
agrarian systems in the third world that stifled the development of an in-
digenous entrepreneurial class, and strong social democratic systems in
Europe that raised wage costs in many developed competitors of the
United States, thus reducing their capacity to increase market share
through price wars.

The result was that between 1940 and 1970, U.S. firms were heavily
buffered from international competition. High union density and personnel costs were tolerated; these, in fact, were more than tolerated. High
personnel costs were judged to be an indicator of having "progressive,

constructive" union relations where the profits of capitalism were divided equally among management and labor in the interest of social and industrial peace (Slichter 1947). In such an environment there was little pressure for management to think about employing women or blacks. The sheltering from market competition facilitated the continued maintenance of discrimination and the employment of primarily white male labor forces.

The 1970s brought significant competition to U.S. manufacturers from Japanese and Korean competitors. The 1980s and 1990s brought about offshore production in which it became increasingly viable to transfer production to the third world, dramatically reducing labor costs for the plants that were transferred and intensifying the pressure to lower wages for the plants on U.S. soil that remained.

The globalization of production was accompanied by a wave of mergers and acquisitions among large U.S. firms. The rise of the junk bond market and the development of shareholder advocacy on the part of institutional investors facilitated hostile takeovers by corporate raiders and challenges to the boardroom control of chief executives whose stocks were underperforming on the market. The reduction in the job security of the managerial elite intensified pressures to generate immediate short-term profits to bolster share prices. This, combined with the forces of globalization, constrained managers, even those running the wealthiest corporations, to reduce costs in any way they could.

As a result, many large firms in the 1980s and 1990s began to cut labor costs relatively aggressively. Plants were closed or transferred overseas. Workers were laid off. Unions were decertified. Union contracts were renegotiated, gutting wages. Even white-collar workers and managers were not immune because downsizing eliminated job and wage security for workers of all income brackets, social classes, and occupations.

Because firms were under pressure to lower personnel costs through whatever means they could, it became important to substitute cheap labor for expensive labor whenever possible. In the downsizing environment of the 1980s, discrimination became more economically unviable than it had been in earlier eras. This discouraged the employment of white adult males and created opportunities for groups who were willing to work for less.

Note that the more stringent environment of the 1980s and 1990s had different effects for women and blacks. Women's employment improved and their pay differentials decreased. In contrast, black employment deteriorated, along with whatever progress blacks were making towards income equality with whites. Why did the cost-saving priorities of the current period benefit women and not minorities?

The key issue, laid out in Chapter 1, is the differential use of women and blacks in the labor force. As tables in Chapter 1 show, women are placed into distinctive sex-typed jobs. These, however, are dispersed all over the status hierarchy. There are male and female professional jobs, male and female managerial jobs, male and female sales jobs, and male and female blue-collar jobs. Within any given cluster of related jobs it is often possible to find male and female versions of similar work. In contrast, blacks and whites are separated by a status hierarchy. Whites work in high-status jobs; blacks work in low-status jobs. Over and above considerations of simple occupational prestige, there are no "black" and "white" jobs, the way there are male and female jobs. To put it another way, there are no distinctively black high-status jobs, or even distinctively black low-status jobs. Blacks simply are more likely to get low-status jobs, although uneducated or working-class whites might obtain these positions as well.

This means that a manager seeking labor savings is more likely to substitute women for men than to substitute blacks for whites. If a firm is trying to reduce its labor costs, it will want to replace expensive workers with inexpensive workers who do similar jobs. Normally, this does not imply firing old costly workers and hiring new cheaper workers with the same job title. One does not usually want to fire all one's veteran workers at one time, because this means losing everyone with experience and the know-how to do the job. If one fires some workers and puts in new workers with the same job title but a lower pay scale, however, this undercuts the incentive for workers to perform.

Often it is more tactful to assign the new workers different job titles and slightly different job assignments than the old workers had. It is then easier to justify paying more to the old veterans for doing the "difficult" or "challenging" or "supervisory" jobs and paying less to the new workers for doing the "easy" or "elementary" jobs. Over time, the range of activity of the cheaper workers may increase, and the range of activity for the more expensive workers may decrease. Bringing in newer workers with new distinctive job titles as well as lower pay provides a virtually no-cost device for maintaining morale of older workers in the face of cost cutting. One can claim that the pay and conditions for the older workers is not being changed; one can provide the older workers with status advantages over the new entrants; one can ascribe the lower pay to the work or the ethnicity or the gender of the new workers, thus providing some implicit promise of protection for one's preexisting white male veterans. None of this diplomacy is absolutely necessary. However, it allows one to cut wage costs while maintaining the morale of one's scarce superior workers, preventing them from quitting, joining the competition, or degenerating into passive-aggressive deadwood; the fiction of titles, furthermore, costs very little to implement or maintain.

There is a long history of employers' cutting wages by introducing a new job title in a male domain and giving these new positions to women.

During the Industrial Revolution, the first mechanized spinning machines were called mule spinners. They were operated by men—generally skilled men—because the machines were crude and difficult to operate. The next wave of technical progress produced ring spinning, a far simpler technique that could use a less skilled operator. Employers generally gave ring-spinning jobs to women, although technically either sex could have done either job perfectly well. The introduction of the new machines gave employers the excuse to discover a "naturally female" occupation that would allow them to substitute women for men to obtain cheap labor (Abbott 1910).

U.S. cigar making in the late nineteenth century had a similar transformation. In Tampa, cigars used to be hand-rolled and made by men. When it became possible to manufacture cheap cigars mechanically, women were put in charge of the new machinery and paid less than men. Traditional gender stereotyping would see men performing the machine work and women the handwork because men are often linked to heavy equipment and high technology. Since, however, there was no "technical" reason to favor one sex over the other, but women did work for less than men, the technical reorganization provided a good excuse to "invent" a new job title and fill it with cheaper women (Kessler-Harris 1982).

In the modern economy, it is not hard to find examples of poorly paid women with low-status job titles replacing men with more advanced job titles and higher nominal salaries. Consider the recent revolution in health care, in which HMOs (Health Maintenance Organizations) and insurers are attempting to reduce medical expenses in every way possible. One method for doing this is to expand the number of services provided by nurses and medical assistants and to restrict the number of services provided by doctors. Physician is a male occupation (although it is becoming more balanced). Nurses and medical assistants are generally (although not always) female and work for far less than doctors. Within the helping professions, the moving of counseling jobs from psychiatrists (a medical specialty divided between men and women with a mild emphasis on men) to social workers (a heavily female and less well-paid occupation) would be another example of this process. A similar process can occur in offices that offload managerial functions to secretarial or administrative staff. The old managerial jobs were typically performed by males. The clerical and administrative workers underneath them are female. In banking, for example, loans often were made by bank presidents or branch managers who were important figures in their communities and these presidents and managers had intimate knowledge of their most important commercial and residential customers and were thus in a position to apply their personal understanding of individual circumstances to the approval or denial of credit. Some high-level officers were typically male. Currently, loan approvals are centralized in large national credit offices, where most of the discretionary work is handled by an administrative staff. Typically a small male programming staff is in charge of designing the algorithms for the computer and a larger mixed but heavily female administrative staff is in charge of daily operations and implementing the machine-made decisions (Smith 1990). Again, a substitution of cheap females for expensive males has been accomplished by changes in technology and job title.

Of course, feminization does not necessarily require a change in job title. Sometimes, in the face of reorganizations of production, employers just add female workers and enjoy the job savings. Reskin and Roos (1985) have documented many examples of this phenomenon. Pharmacy work has been steadily losing status in the last twenty years. Pharmacists who once ran their own businesses, compounded their own prescriptions, and gave personal medical advice to regular customers are being replaced. The new workers are also called "pharmacists" and have the requisite academic degrees. They typically work as employees of a large retail chain, such as a supermarket or a discount store. They merely dispense premade medications, fabricating relatively little on their own. Even the advisory function has been taken away; the druggist's warnings and recommendations are now stored in computer databases and are automatically dispensed with each new prescription. As the pharmacist's job has been deskilled, a change of gender has occurred as well; relatively inexpensive women have been replacing more expensive men. The pay differential is legitimated by the location of the new work locations in retail chains that just "naturally" offer inferior pay and conditions.

The job of branch bank manager has not gone away; it has simply become deskilled; most of the decision-making functions have been removed to administrative and data processing centers, leaving the branch managers with limited sales and supervisory functions. As the status and pay of bank manager has declined, the job has become progressively female.

The job of bartender has become feminized as well. Some of this is due to the elimination of laws that kept women out of working in establishments that primarily serve alcohol. Just at the time that women have entered the occupation, however, the job has deskilled because of the rise in beer and wine consumption over the consumption of hard spirits. The decline of whisky, gin, and vodka, relative to softer beverages, has meant that the bartender in 1995 has to hand mix far fewer cocktails than did the martini and manhattan artists of 1955. It is harder to make a good brandy alexander than to fill a glass with someone else's microbrewed beer. Add to this the widespread prevalence of premade mixes for such popular beverages as margaritas, and it is evident that the job of bartender has undergone significant simplification if not technological change. Adding women doubles the labor supply for this occupation and allows wages to remain comfortably low.

There have thus been ample opportunities in the economy of the 1980s and 1990s to reduce labor costs by feminizing work. Could employers have accomplished the same thing by hiring blacks over whites to produce a more minority-based labor force? In a superficial sense the answer to this question is yes, because in the largest sense any employer can hire anybody to do any job. But in other senses, the opportunities were not as strong as they were with women.

If one wanted to introduce a two-job-title system, with the one group having inferior occupational status and pay, it would be harder to do with blacks than with women. The absence of traditional race-typed jobs would make the presence of a blacks-only occupation suspicious and worthy of note, particularly to affirmative action authorities. The bifurcation of one job into two is easier to do with two groups who are used to sharing work worlds of similar status. Men and women share far more work settings than do blacks and whites. Consider the medical case. Because doctors and nurses have habitually worked in the same setting, the expansion of the nurses' domain at the expense of the doctors' can be done noncontroversially and almost invisibly without any disruption of traditional staffing norms. Substituting a new all-black suboccupation into doctors' offices would have been extremely conspicuous and transparent. The concentration of whites in high-status positions and blacks in low-status positions lowers the number of settings where a white occupation could be cheapened by the expansion of a black occupation just one status rank below it.

But what about just bringing in blacks and using the same job title just to increase the labor supply and thus lower wages overall? Here again, creating gender inequality is a far more potent tool for labor cost reduction than is creating race equality. There are approximately the same number of males and females in the population. In contrast, if blacks represent only 12 percent of the U.S. population, then there are more than eight times as many whites than blacks in the population. Adding blacks to the labor mix simply does not increase the overall size of one's recruitment pool that much. Adding women doubles one's potential number of job candidates. Adding blacks increases the pool by a mere three twenty-seconds.

Consider, furthermore, the regional differences that exist in the supply of black labor. In some southern labor markets, such as the Atlanta area, blacks can represent practically a quarter of the total workforce. In heavily white areas such as the Pacific Northwest, however, blacks may represent less than 5 percent of the labor pool. The ratio of men to women, by contrast, is virtually constant in all forty-eight states. To be sure, many large firms allow their managers to adjust their hiring patterns to local labor market conditions. A national policy of reducing personnel costs by promoting gender inequality, however, will produce far more systematic effects than will a comparable policy of promoting racial inequality. A corporate racial progressive might almost be condemned to making his argument on the narrow basis of justice and fairness rather than on labor force expansion per se.

Conclusion

So what can be said about Gary Becker's theory of discrimination? In principle, free market competition ought to eliminate racial and gender inequality in employment. If workers are excluded from jobs, their wage rates will go down; rational employers will hire these new cheaper workers and restore wage parity; the hiring rates for majority and minority workers will become equal. All of this assumes, however, that employers are under intense pressure from a free market to minimize costs. In contrast, we saw that buffering from competition is relatively common. When firms are protected from having to cut costs to the rock bottom to survive, they will pursue other noneconomic goals; maintaining a white male labor force could be such a secondary utility that it becomes feasible in the face of attenuated competition.

The decline of white male economic advantages in recent years can be seen as a response to the greater economic competitiveness that has characterized our economy since the augmentation of global competition with an increased emphasis on short-term profits. Naturally, this simplistic picture requires some adjustments to capture the nuances of what has occurred. Increasing hiring of women and minorities has also been a response to equal opportunity laws and the banning of the most overt forms of explicit discrimination. Furthermore, increased competitiveness has affected women and blacks differently due to the different capacities of each group to serve as cheap labor.

This chapter has only dealt, however, with the simpler and more superficial aspects of labor cost buffering. Other implications of Becker's model are more complex; they affect the racial and gender composition of jobs in deep and profound ways. The most important application of labor cost buffering theory is its predictions about corporate cost structures. The next chapter considers these cost structures in some detail.

Notes

1. There are some exceptions to this principle. Construction unions were effective for many years at excluding blacks and women from their apprenticeship

programs, effectively barring them from employment. There were also some famous ethnic strikes in the pre–Civil Rights South. See Hill (1984) for the history of these incidents. For a balanced view showing the limits of such union exclusion see Marshall (1965).

2. These laws have recently been challenged and partially eliminated in states such as Texas and California.

3 What Determines If a Job Is Male or Female?

In the previous chapter, labor cost buffering was introduced as an important principle of occupational sex-typing. That discussion, however, was incomplete. The theory was not used in any satisfactory fashion to explain the broad, general patterns of which jobs are male and which jobs are female. Furthermore, no other theories were considered that could provide plausible alternative accounts of how sex-typing is determined.

This chapter is a general discussion of the overall determinants of occupational sex-typing. Labor cost buffering will play a major part in this argument, although in a somewhat more sophisticated form than that presented in the last chapter. The primary appeal of this theory is that it works. Support for the model is provided with a statistical examination of occupational sex-typing in the United States, a historical analysis of the introduction of women in clerical work in Britain, and a contemporary look at the use of female managers in India. Having a theory of occupational sex-typing theory that works is slightly unusual because most theories of occupational sex-typing don't.

To appreciate the significance of these dynamics, the chapter commences with a lengthy discussion of the traditional arguments that are usually provided to explain why some jobs are male and some jobs are female. These traditional positions are usually held both by students and academics alike. Most of them sound good. Their intuitive appeal makes undergraduates and professors relatively reluctant to give them up. Unfortunately, the logic of these traditional positions is dicey and they run into flagrant contradictions with the historical evidence. Comfortable theories of occupational sex-typing tend to be wrong theories of occupational sex-typing. The student who seeks a compelling explanation of why certain jobs are open or closed to women often needs to turn to more exotic sources such as the material at the end of the chapter.

The Myth That Women Exclude Themselves from Employment: Supply-Side Theories of Occupational Sex-Typing

Overview. When, in my classes, I ask students why certain jobs are male and certain jobs are female, the most common answer I get is that "women would like to work in job X but don't want to work in job Y." Examples might be

"Women don't work as night clerks in convenience stores because they might get held up. Who wants to hang out with the rowdy crowd who buys beer at 4:30 in the morning?"

"Women work as day care workers because they really like being with children."

"Women don't work as coal miners because it is hot, physical labor. Who wants to get black lung and die?"

"Women work as light assemblers in factories because being more patient they don't object to boring work nearly as much as men do."

I even heard one male student argue

"Women don't work as corporate managers because who wants to have to take all that responsibility?" (He was shouted down by the rest of the class.)

Sometimes these arguments take a historical form. They argue that changes in the types of jobs available to women are due to changes in women's historical aspirations. In the early twentieth century, women were very traditional and only wanted standard women's jobs such as teacher, nurse, and secretary. In the 1960s, 1970s, and 1980s, women's consciousness changed. Women became a lot more ambitious and career oriented. Because of women's greater occupational aspirations, they are applying for more demanding professional jobs that involve more responsibility and higher pay. Because women are more liberated in the 1990s than they were previously, they are appearing in all sorts of occupations that were previously reserved exclusively for men.

All these arguments are fairly similar in that they maintain that the sex composition of jobs is determined by the occupational choices of women workers themselves. Women take jobs that are consistent with their needs, and they don't take jobs that are inconsistent with their needs. Women take only the kinds of jobs they want.

In the language of labor economics, these theories are called *supply side* theories. They argue that occupational gender composition is determined by the relative *supply* of men and women that apply for these positions. Women wish to work in some jobs; men wish to work in others. They mostly apply for jobs suitable for their gender; therefore any employer who wishes to fill a certain position will note that the *supply* of candidates applying for his "female" jobs is mostly women, and the *supply* of candidates applying for his "male" jobs is mostly men. The employer, then, is somewhat constrained by the composition of the applicant pool to hire people into gender-appropriate positions that reflect the needs and desires of his labor force.

The opposite of a supply side theory is a *demand side* theory. Demand side theories argue that occupational sex types are determined by the choices of employers themselves. An employer can hire men or women, blacks or whites, Anglos or Hispanics. They can even be very particular and insist on Greek-speaking grandmothers who bird-watch in their spare time. Whatever the employer asks for is what the company will get. Workers who know the employer is interested in their kind will apply for jobs in the hope of being selected. Workers who know that they don't have a reasonable chance of being hired will save their energy and not apply.

From a logical standpoint, supply side explanations of sex- typing don't make much sense. Employers have the last word in determining who is accepted and rejected for any given job. People do not walk into personnel offices and say to the interviewer, "You must hire me." (Well, maybe a small number do and get the one one-hundreth of 1 percent of all jobs reserved for very, very pushy people). In most cases, job applicants submit their applications and are placed in a competition with a large group of candidates. A few applicants are successful. Most receive thin letters. No matter who wants to work for a given company, the final decision as to what worker with what gender will fill a given vacancy is made unilaterally by management.

At the same time, the argument that "women wouldn't want to do job X because it is so Y" does not make a lot of sense either. There are all sorts of jobs the average person would not want to do that nevertheless get filled because the employer can find a nonaverage person who is willing to do them. Consider the argument

Women would not want to work as prostitutes. The work ruins your romantic life. It is dangerous and uncomfortable. Furthermore, the social stigma associated with prostitution is enormous. Working in the sex industry ruins your possibilities for getting a good job later in your career. On top of that many respectable people will want to avoid getting close to you.

These claims about prostitution are all reasonable and realistic. Most men and women would not accept any form of sexual employment and would be extremely offended if it were even suggested they might be interested in sexual employment. By the logic of majority opinion, one would think that no one would ever work in the sex industry and that paid sexual service would die out from a shortage of employees.

That said, there is no shortage of sex workers in the United States even though the work repulses most Americans. In most cities, you will find a generous number of prostitutes, streetwalkers, strippers, escorts, lingerie models, phone sex operators, massage parlor workers, and in some cities, stars in pornographic movies. The average person would not want to accept such employment. Plenty of people in the labor market, however, are not average. People become sex workers for a number of reasons. Some sex workers are just daring, shock-the-bourgeoisie risk takers. Some are mentally ill or have a history of being sexually abused. Some are pressured into it by boyfriends with connections to the industry. Some are forced into it by economic desperation. Others just take it for the nonstandard hours or because it offers higher pay than the other jobs available to people without educational qualifications. Whether they enter the occupation for positive or negative reasons, sex workers are fairly atypical people. However, there is an ample supply of atypical people in the labor market. Even if a job were rejected by over 99 percent of the people in an economy, there will always be that 1 percent who will buck the trend and take jobs that defy orthodox convention.

The same argument that applies to sex workers also applies to other occupations. Most women may not want to work the graveyard shift in a convenience store, but there will always be some who will. Most women may not want to work as coal miners, but there always will be some who will. To know that the average woman in a population would not be interested in a certain form of work tells you nothing about whether employers could staff that position with women if they wanted to. Consider a city of 3 million people (Chicago would be a good example). Such a city would have 1.5 million females, and if half of these were prime working age, maybe 750,000 potential working women. Now imagine an employer with some incredibly unpopular job that only 1 percent of all women would even consider. If only 1 percent of the working women of Chicago would consider working in this extremely unsavory occupation, it would still mean that the employer would have 7,500 women to choose from to fill his vacancy. One should be able to fill ten or even one hundred positions with 7,500 women, and this is without using any of the women in the suburbs!

Evidence from the nineteenth century. The historical evidence suggests that relatively few jobs have been unable to feminize because they were unable to attract female job candidates. The experience of the nineteenth century is particularly informative here. The experience of Victorian England and America is an important test of the role of supply-side considerations and women's choice because the Victorian era was one in which gender ideologies were especially traditional and strict. In the nineteenth century a woman's place was in the home. Religious revivals during the first half of the century brought on a popular recommitment to abstinence, self-control, and dedication to family and church. The relation of Victorian ideology to sexual restraint and temperance is well known. With this, however, came a glorification of domestic life, a flourishing of popular literature emphasizing women's role as homemaker and mother, widely supported political reform movements advocating the limitation of women's employment, and encouragement for active women to devote their time to noncommercial endeavors such as participation in missionary societies and providing comfort to the poor. It was a difficult time for women to choose careers over family, and female labor force participation rates fell to relatively low levels (Kessler-Harris 1975; Davidoff and Hall 1987).

That said, there seems to have been no shortage of willing women workers. Virtually every employer who entertained the prospect of opening their jobs to women found themselves deluged with female applications. In the early Industrial Revolution, the owners of textile mills had frequent problems obtaining enough male laborers. In Britain, owners had to turn to prison labor because so few men were willing to accept the relatively strict discipline associated with factory labor. For this reason, both in England and the United States, employers turned to women as an alternative labor force. Most of the early factories were staffed with heavy contingents of female labor. Women applied for these jobs in copious numbers, delighted with the wages and independence associated with millwork (Pollard 1965; Dublin 1979). Women continued working in the factories throughout the nineteenth century in some settings on the continent, regardless of traditional sex role ideology. In other settings in Britain and the United States, these labor forces became more male over time. The diminished use of female labor, however, was not the result of women's failure to apply for textile jobs. They were the result either of factory legislation that legally restricted the use of women or of employers substituting male ethnic minorities for women as a strategy for reducing labor costs.[1] Invariably, male exclusion rather than female occupational choice was responsible for the creation of male job settings (Kessler-Harris 1982).

Over the course of the nineteenth century, employers began to return to the use of female labor because of the enormous potential cost savings involved. Whenever they did so, they found plenty of women

job candidates. When the British General Post Office opened up telegraph jobs to women, they found female job applications outnumbered
male job applications by a factor of twelve to one (Cohn 1985). There
were dramatic feminizations in ring spinning (an important form of
mechanized textile work), carpet making, cigar making, schoolteaching,
and clerical work. Furthermore, many women worked as governesses—
a miserably paid form of private tutoring, and as domestic servants—
work that was even less lucrative (Abbott 1915; Rose 1992; Holcombe
1973; Strober and Tyack 1981; Davies 1982).

One would think that if women particularly valued traditional sex
roles and staying home with their husbands and children, they would
have been reluctant to take on paid employment. If this were the case,
one could predict that women would have accepted only very attractive jobs, because only well-paid high-status employment could remunerate women for the psychic costs of giving up their roles as wives
and mothers.

Just the opposite seems to have occurred. Women in the nineteenth
century were on the bottom of the status hierarchy. In textile factories,
they had the lowest-paid and least skilled jobs. In other industries, including in some cases cigars, they were only brought in when work was
mechanized, lowering the wages that were prevalent in the industry.
Employment as a governess or domestic servant was especially unattractive because, over and above the paltry economic rewards, servants
were expected to reside on the premises and completely subordinate
their social lives to those of their employers. One could neither raise a
family nor do much to start a family when living in one's employer's
home and only having Wednesday afternoons off.

Assuming that women had to take jobs inconsistent with family
roles, if they were choosing jobs voluntarily, they would have chosen
the most respected jobs in Victorian society: minister, physician, attorney, banker, mill owner. Instead, the jobs they took that conflicted with
family roles were among the most miserable: factory slave, sweatshop
worker, overworked maid. This suggests that their choice of occupations was not voluntary because they selected jobs that were neither
consistent with traditional domestic roles nor with choosing work for
economic advantage. This strongly suggests that women's entry into
occupations in the nineteenth century was based on some factor other
than their own volition. This would be consistent with demand-side
theory rather than supply-side theory.

Evidence from the Twentieth Century. The definitive work on the supply-side considerations in the twentieth century has been done by Valerie Kincaide Oppenheimer. Her *Female Labor Force in the United
States* (1970) is the classic analysis of the relative contribution of
women's occupational choice and employer behavior in determining

female labor force participation and the willingness of women to apply for work.

Oppenheimer's analytical strategy was ingenious. She looked at census data to determine in what decades women were more likely to enter the labor force. If you asked this question of the typical undergraduate, he or she would guess that women's work started with women's liberation and that women started to give up their traditional roles in the 1960s, and continued to do so in the 1970s, 1980s, and 1990s. I sometimes refer to this as the "Beatles theory" of women's work. Women's work came with the Beatles, marijuana, antiwar protest, and Woodstock. Oppenheimer's data showed that this was not at all the case. Female labor force participation had been increasing throughout the twentieth century, with only one minor interruption during the 1910s. Furthermore, although the sixties did produce the major expansion of female labor force participation, one would have expected, there was a rise that was almost as large in the 1950s. Oppenheimer argued that any compelling theory of women's work could not just base itself in the sixties, but had to be able to explain the entire century including the second big burst in the 1950s.

Superficially, women's liberation, consciousness-raising, and general all-purpose radicalism would not seem to be a good explanation for increasing labor force participation in the 1950s. These were the Eisenhower years. This was a period of Republicanism and conservatism. The major domestic political trend was McCarthyism, the systematic legal pursuit of communists. Gender ideologies during this period were fairly traditional. This was not the decade of Janis Joplin or Grace Slick. It was the decade of Alice Cramden, the stay-at-home wife on the *Honeymooners*, or Lucille Ball, who only took jobs because she was wacky.

Oppenheimer examines this paradox of rising women's labor force participation during a conservative era. Her argument is that if women's personal choices were driving the change in labor force participation, then it should be possible to identify some objective factor in women's private or domestic lives that would make more women want to go to work rather than stay home. If employers' behavior is changing, a demand-side model would be a more appropriate explanation. If a supply-side model is to hold, then some independent factor relevant to women's lives outside the workplace must be identified that can explain why suddenly women decided to increase their participation in paid employment.

But what could such an independent factor be? One possibility is fertility. In the 1990s, fertility rates are low. Women can choose to pursue careers because they are deferring childbearing and having small families. This reduced commitment to large families facilitates a greater commitment to market work. If women were also reducing their fertility in the 1950s, this would explain why more women were choosing to go to work.

The 1950s, however, were the years of the baby boom. Between 1850 and 1945, fertility had been on a steady decline; between 1945 and 1960, childbearing reversed trend and rose dramatically. The typical couple from 1945 to 1960 had one extra child above the typical family size of the 1930s and 1940s; these large families reflect the return to traditional values that was associated with the 1950s. It would be hard to argue that women could go to work because they were facing lighter child-care loads. If anything, the burden of child care was greater in the 1950s than in most other decades of the twentieth century. Thus Oppenheimer argues that if the rise in female labor force participation is to be explained, it must be explained by using something else.

One possibility is that housework became easier. During the twentieth century, there were a wide variety of technological innovations that reduced the amount of work associated with taking care of a family. The invention of dishwashers, washing machines, dryers, electric irons, freezers, canned food, and vacuum cleaners all dramatically cut into the time it took the average housewife to cook, clean, and take care of her house. This allowed women to finish their domestic duties early; they could then apply for work to fill out the rest of their time.

Unfortunately, Oppenheimer shows this approach doesn't work either. Most of the major innovations in home appliances and prepared food occurred earlier than the 1950s. Sales figures on the use of electric appliances and canned goods shows these products entered most homes from 1920 to 1940, not the 1950s. Had female labor force participation increased dramatically from 1920 to 1940 and increased slowly during the 1950s, it would be credible to explain such an increase by invoking technological changes in homemaking. However, because the appliance revolution was already largely over by the 1950s, the increase in women's work must have come from something else.

A third commonsense explanation for women deciding to come to work in the 1950s is that they had rejected traditional attitudes disapproving of working homemakers; they had become relatively more liberated. One does not need an objective stimulus to change one's mind; new ideas can sweep the country even in the absence of structural change, and these new ideas can produce new behavior. Oppenheimer takes this consciousness explanation quite seriously and tests it with survey data drawn from many different opinion polls taken from 1936 to 1960. If women really changed their minds about the desirability of working, such a change should show up in attitude data because women in the later periods answer survey questions about women's work more positively than did women in the earlier periods.

Such a test is technically hard to do because nobody did comparable surveys in 1935 and 1960. Lots of surveys about women's attitudes towards working were conducted throughout the 1930s, 1940s, 1950s, and 1960s; each was performed in a different way, using a different type of woman in each sample, and few of them asked the same question as the others. As a result, comparing these polls across several dates is a lot like comparing apples and elephants, and the conclusions that one can draw are limited.

There was a mild tendency for attitudes towards women's work to improve between the 1930s and the 1960s. Oppenheimer downplays this tendency and argues that it would have been insufficient to produce the dramatic changes in female labor force participation she observed. In the 1930s, the population was extremely hostile towards female employment; only 15 percent of all respondents approved of women working. Oppenheimer rightfully argues that much of this came from the Great Depression, a time when widespread sensibility dictated that women should stay out of the labor force to save jobs for men who could not find work. This was a distinctive reaction to a national crisis and did not reflect general attitudes about how women should behave in normal times. In the 1940s, attitudes towards women's work became more variable with between 10 percent to 50 percent of the population that supported women working (depending upon the exact question that was asked). By 1960, only 34 percent of the population approved of women working, a figure not dissimilar to that observed in the 1940s.

Interpreting these materials is ambiguous, and Oppenheimer is rightfully careful about drawing strong conclusions. Some doubt remains about what interpretation should be made of the 1930s data. That said, a cautious middle-of-the-road reading of these materials indicates a small increase in popular tolerance for women working. The population in all periods was divided on this issue, and people's feelings about female participation in the labor force fluctuated wildly depending on the precise circumstances involved. Attitudes were fluid and highly changeable, and people were capable of seeing positive and negative aspects of women's work. To say that attitudes were exactly the same throughout the twentieth century would be inaccurate. To say that the population as a whole disapproved of women's work in 1930 and approved of it in 1960 would also be inaccurate. Some people became more tolerant of women's work, although they limited this toleration to some situations. Would this attitude change have been enough to produce a massive increase in female labor force participation? Oppenheimer is skeptical and thinks the change was much too small. My own opinion (for what it's worth) is that nobody knows how much attitude change can be expected to produce how much change in female labor force participation and that it is hard to gauge how big a survey change would have to be to produce a gender revolution. Certainly the changes were not enormous. If attitude change had any effect at all, it was to support other transformations that were occurring, not to be the prime mover of women returning to work.

There was a prime mover that did account for the reason female labor force participation exploding in the 1950s, and the role of this factor is clear and unambiguous. Oppenheimer shows compellingly that in the 1950s there was an enormous expansion of traditional female sex-typed jobs. Before the 1950s, women had always worked in a relatively predictable set of well-known women's jobs. Women were employed as clerical workers, as nurses, as schoolteachers, as social workers, as librarians, and as waitresses. They also worked in white-collar jobs in banking, insurance, and finance. Before the 1950s, the number of these jobs rose slowly. Not surprisingly, female labor force participation rates also rose at the same slow rate.

In the 1950s, a set of happy coincidences produced explosive growth in virtually every traditional female job sector. The rise of big government required a huge expansion in the numbers of clerical workers and social workers (and, to a smaller extent, public librarians). Rising middle-class demand for financial services produced double-digit growth in banking and insurance, sectors that had always hired large percentages of women. The baby boom produced a need for schools and schoolteachers, jobs that have traditionally gone to women. The 1950s also saw a dramatic expansion in health care as the nation went on a long overdue campaign of hospital construction. Furthermore, growing prosperity put health insurance and medical care within reach of a large percentage of the previously poor. Prosperity and the automobile sparked an explosion in the restaurant industry. More and more people could afford to drive five or ten miles to take the family to dinner. Drive-ins and full-service restaurants (such as Howard Johnson's) became a staple of American living. As a result, demand for clerical workers, nurses, schoolteachers, social workers, librarians, and waitresses went through the roof, and employers sought every female employee they could find.

It is not surprising that many women decided to enter paid employment during the 1950s. This was not due to any particular change in women's ideologies but to an economy that generated simultaneous growth in all the preexisting female occupations. If anyone could take the credit for the expansion of women's opportunities, it would be this nation's employers. They were, to some extent, responsible for the general expansion of employment. More important, it was their preexisting policies of hiring women for teaching positions, secretarial work, and other traditional female occupations that insured this employment growth would disproportionately benefit women. Change in popular attitudes concerning women's work may have played a small role in encouraging homemakers to enter the workforce; however, the demand-side factors promoted by employers hiring policies were the dominant factor in producing the 1950s transformation.

Do Supply-Side Factors Ever Make a Difference? In general, the larger point of this section is that supply-side factors rarely determine occupational sex types. One exception where limits on the availability of female job candidates can produce a male sex-typed occupation occurs in settings where occupational training times are very long. Where extensive preparatory schooling is required before a worker can enter an occupation, an immediate change of gender policy by employers may not be capable of generating an adequate supply of female job candidates, a situation that would force employers, even involuntarily, to continue using men.

The most obvious example of this process is engineering. Engineering has traditionally been a male occupation for reasons that will be discussed at length in the sections below. Engineering requires extensive and specialized formal education. When the populations of working engineers and engineering students are entirely male, inertia sets in against the rapid transformation of the occupation's sex type. An employer who wants to hire female engineers can find few qualified candidates coming from engineering schools. Very few women enter engineering schools, however, due to the perception that opportunities for them would be limited because most working engineers are male. One creates a Catch–22-type paradox that can persist for some time.

Long training times need not be an absolute barrier to feminization; they certainly were not in law. After the passage of affirmative action policies, law schools rapidly committed to admitting equal-sex cohorts of law students. Because law schools are administered by lawyers, who are generally on the cutting edge of the discipline, they were among the first population to realize the potential legal liabilities they risked by excluding women, and therefore they moved quickly to amend their practices. This change in admissions policies produced an explosion in female applicants to law school. Because legal training is generally short (allowing B.A.'s with any major to train in from two to three years), qualified female lawyers entered the labor market and were rapidly available to most law firms (Epstein 1981).

In general, long training times will delay but not eliminate feminization. The absence of women in a job involving extensive preparatory formal training can stem from three sources: discrimination on the part of employers, discrimination on the part of the schools themselves, and reluctance of the part of students to enter the relevant training programs. Disentangling these three is a tricky business. In general, students will attend training for any lucrative occupation for which attractive opportunities exist both in education and in employment. A paucity of job candidates usually indicates students' perceptions of adverse prospects in prep school or adverse prospects on the job. These problems could exist in the professional schools. In the past, some professional schools have explicitly discriminated against women. In the current environment, however, most U.S. universities are staffed by liberals and professionals who are committed to affirmative action in more or less aggressive form.[2]

Thus, in the post–1990 world, it would seem that managers' complaints that their plans for feminization are impeded by an absence of qualified female (or black) job candidates may reflect employer prejudice rather than any objective shortages in the training queues. This statement may not be universally true, and there may be situations where candidate scarcity is a real concern. Occupations about which managers believe that most women or minority candidates are generally unqualified are occupations in which women and minorities would be expected to feel unwelcome; this would cause them to train in other areas and to contribute to furthering a shortage of qualified women and minority candidates. If there are no obvious exclusionary policies at the relevant training schools, then absences of candidates in training generally reflects rational student adaptations to perceived low employment opportunities. The latter are caused by hiring and promotion policies and are demand-side in nature.

Demand-Side Theories of Occupational Sex-Typing: Some Preliminary Dead Ends

Having established that occupational sex-typing comes primarily from the actions of employers, let us now consider some alternative models of how firms decide which jobs to open or close to women. Just because we can think of *some* hypothetical mechanism by which managers determine which jobs are male or female does not mean that that mechanism is exactly what is occurring in the workplace. Before moving to the set of useful theories, let us initially clean out some deadwood.

Tradition. The most common explanation for why certain jobs are male and certain jobs are female is that such divisions are traditional. It has always been that way. Men have always been doctors; women have always been nurses. People are creatures of habit and like to do things the way they have always been done. Therefore, if they have been brought up with male doctors and female nurses, they tend to want to the male doctor/female nurse tradition continued (Caplow 1954; Oppenheimer 1970).

This is correct as far as it goes. It is, however, a *tautological* explanation. A tautological explanation is a theory that explains something with itself. Let us imagine that someone tells you of an obscure village in Portugal where the farmers like to eat their young. You're shocked when you hear this and you ask in amazement, "Why in the world do the people in that village eat their young?"

The storyteller responds, "Well, it's because in that village there is a tradition that the farmers eat their young."

Technically, the storyteller has answered your question. He has explained why the babies are eaten. However, this is the most unsatisfying explanation in the world. You and everyone else who hears this of course want to know, "*Why* do the farmers have a tradition of eating their young?" The storyteller has no answer to this question.

Explanations of occupational sex-typing that invoke tradition have the same problem. It is not enough to know that a given job has a tradition of being male or female. You want to know how the tradition got started and what the larger logic behind it was.

Let us go back to your conversation about the Portuguese village. On hearing about the baby-eating, the other question you might want to ask is, "Why doesn't someone change the tradition? Why don't the police break this up? What about the parents of the babies involved? Why hasn't the Catholic Church or the National Geographic done a big exposé?" For any given institutional arrangement, there are always people with an interest in seeing it changed. For a traditional argument to hold, one needs to have a compelling explanation of why people who would have an interest in seeing the tradition changed have failed to alter the status quo.

The same applies to traditional theories of job composition. The obvious people who would benefit from a change are the people who are excluded from employment. They may be too powerless to have much of a say about their being hired. A second set of people who might benefit from a change, however, are capitalists who would gain from having the largest supply of labor possible (producing the greatest degree of wage competition and the lowest overall levels of salaries and personnel costs). Why capitalists do not change the status quo on hiring decisions is always a very live theoretical question and one that requires a compelling and specific answer. Theories that just invoke tradition and then go home don't explain half of what needs to be explained about why some jobs are male and some jobs are female.

Sex-Role Theories. A more carefully developed approach that goes beyond the limits of simple tradition is sex—role theory. Sex-role theory argues that companies simply do not hire women for certain types of jobs because everyone in society, male and female, agrees that there are appropriate roles for men and appropriate roles for women. For example, women work as schoolteachers and day-care workers because they are naturally suited to work with children. Women work as waitresses because they serve food in the home. Women work in textile factories because they sew and make clothing for their families at home. Women work as light assemblers because they have a natural tolerance for boredom and their small fingers facilitate delicate work. Men work as executives because they are rational and goal-oriented; women are more likely to be emotional and process-oriented. Men work in blue-collar jobs because they are robust and physical; women work in white-collar jobs because they are more delicate and fragile (Ireson 1978; Oppenheimer 1970; Epstein 1970).

The trouble with this type of explanation is that for every single gender rule one can think of there are always many exceptions that contradict the rule. Consider the argument that women take jobs similar to those performed in the home. In 1990, only 48 percent of all cooks were women even though women do most of the cooking at home.[3] Domestically, baking is generally done by women; commercially, only 46 percent of all bakers are female. At home, most messy cleanup jobs are given to women. However, only 31 percent of janitors are women. Despite women's traditional association with child care, only 57 percent of secondary teachers are female. Women's domestic responsibilities for children hardly stop when the children turn twelve. In medicine, women are disproportionately likely to be pediatricians. This job, however, has never been a female sex-typed occupation.

The same incongruity appears in textiles. That women sew has been used to explain women's concentration in spinning mills and clothing factories. Nevertheless, only 48 percent of all tailors are women. Although the making of a slipcover for a chair is most likely to be a woman's job, only 23 percent of all upholsterers are female.

It is difficult to find social-psychological correlates of male or female jobs. Although women are traditionally associated with nurturance, they have not always held jobs that involve care or sensitivity in dealing with people. Nursing and social work have generally been female jobs. However, psychiatry is a male occupation. Only 10 percent of all clergy are women, even though this occupation specializes in the most profound emotional and spiritual concerns of human life. It is true that some religions have made use of women in specialized capacities; the Catholic Church has always permitted spiritually inclined women to serve as nuns. Nuns, however, have generally been confined to a narrow range of duties. Resistance to ordaining women has been high both within Christian denominations that preach biblical inerrancy (fundamentalist Protestantism) and those that preach that communion involves physical transubstantiation (the various forms of Catholicism). Although other denominations have been more open to formally permitting the ordination of women, there has been substantial resistance to the actual hiring of female clergy in significant numbers (Chaves 1997).

Nor is it easy to link women with delicacy in working with the hands. Women's supposedly superior coordination and manual dexterity have been used to explain their concentration in textile and electronics manufacture. Yet only 12 percent of camera and watch repairers and 34 percent of precious-stone workers are women. Furthermore, surgery continues to be a heavily male specialty.

Note that many of the jobs with female "culture types" cited in this discussion have actual occupational sex types that are mixed, commonly slightly less than 50 percent female. If I substituted 1970 data for 1990 data, almost all these jobs would have been primarily male. Traditional roles did not put women into jobs with feminine properties, even in periods before the 1990s when orthodox sex roles were taken more seriously than they are today. If these feminine properties were what was driving sex types, these domestic-style jobs should have been more female in 1970 than today, not less so.

Statements of fundamental gender principles that determine sex types are often smoke screens for different processes that don't have much to do with culture. A good example can be found in restaurant work on the Mexican border. In Texas, there are a number of dual cities (such as El Paso/Ciudad Juarez) that are really one city with the U.S.-Mexico border running through the middle. Occupational sex types are often different on each side of the Rio Grande. In restaurant work, for example, on the U.S. side, food is generally cooked by men or women but served nearly exclusively by women. In Mexico, restaurants are all-male affairs, and the wait staff are men. I have asked many Mexican informants, some of them sophisticated social scientists, about this unusual situation. I am consistently told that in Mexico no man would let his wife or daughter be a waitress because it is intolerable for a woman to take requests from strange men off the street.

This may easily be true. Yet it is hard to understand why on the U.S. side there would be so many Mexican women happily working as waitresses, if these cultural notions prevailed. This is especially hard to understand considering that the U.S-Mexican border is somewhat porous. Mexican women frequently show up on the U.S. side to work as waitresses until they are discovered by the immigration authorities. A further problem with this explanation is that these same Mexican cities have many street vendors selling cold drinks or hot snacks. Some of these street vendors are women, even though vendors, like waiters, must take orders from the general public. Other Mexican women work as domestics, a job that puts them into the bedrooms and bathrooms of potentially predatory male employers.

It is unclear exactly what causes this U.S.-Mexican sex-type split. One serious possibility is that on the Mexican side there are many female jobs and not many male jobs. The Mexican side of the border has the famous maquiladora factories, assembly plants that almost exclusively hire female labor. Men who show up on Mexico's northern frontier find their job prospects inferior relative to women, who are very much in demand. The men may drift into waiting on tables as a last resort because most of the local manufacturing positions are closed to them. By contrast, on the U.S. side, there are all sorts of interesting blue-collar opportunities for Mexican males. Truck driving, agricultural work, construction work, and manufacturing are generally more lucrative than waitressing.[4] Women are the gender that would be less in demand, increasing the importance of opportunities in food service.

The moral is that cultural statements about principles that guide which kinds of jobs are male and which are female need to be taken with more than a few grains of salt. People will frequently espouse principles they don't follow. They will act in congruence with the cultural precept when that gender rule makes economic sense. They will drop the precept when it does not make economic sense. Simple rationalizations like "I would never do this in Mexico, but America is different" allow for the jettisoning of cultural prescriptions that may never have been held all that tightly anyway. If one wants to understand the forces that determine which kinds of jobs are male and which are female, one needs to move beyond simplistic arguments of cultural determination.

Physical Strength. A third dead end is the argument that women are excluded from certain forms of employment because of their lack of physical strength. Usually physical strength is used as a reason men work in blue-collar or manual jobs and women work in white-collar or mental jobs. Sometimes physical strength is used to explain why women work in light assembling, such as electronics or textiles, while men work in heavier manufacturing, such as auto and steel factories. Supposedly, physical strength is the reason men work as truck drivers, work on loading docks, or work as policemen or security guards.

There are two separate problems with physical strength explanations. The first is that it is not at all obvious that all women are weaker than all men. For the sake of argument, let us grant the traditional formulation that, on the average, men have greater arm and upper-body strength than do women. Let us also grant that even if, on the average, women have greater stamina and endurance than men, this stamina has no commercial value in the marketplace. (The latter is a somewhat stronger assumption.) All this notwithstanding, it is not at all obvious that one would hire men and not women to do one's physical work. Intragender differences in physical fitness are fairly dramatic. There are substantial numbers of athletic women in superb physical condition. There are also substantial numbers of male wimps whose strength and endurance are suspect at best. The present author spent most of his young life as a ninety-seven-pound weakling—the kid who was perpetually beaten up on the way home from school. Nevertheless, I had no problem getting a job handling heavy crates in a shoe warehouse. At that time, it would have been impossible for a woman, even a rugby player, to get a job in that shoe warehouse unless she was willing to work as a clerical worker. It is hard to see why (if physical strength is necessary for certain forms of employment) employers don't simply hire by objective strength instead of using a gender screen.

The second problem is that it is not clear how much strength many supposedly physical jobs really require. In modern work settings, machinery is used to reduce the demand for physical strength. In the shoe warehouse where I worked, most of the heavy lifting was done with dollies and forklifts. In cargo settings with heavier loads, people use cranes. I have trouble changing my tires by hand because I can't get the lugs off. A professional tow-truck operator uses compressed air. A policeman may benefit from upper-body strength to help subdue a perpetrator. However, police officers have access to one very effective method of physically controlling suspects: a regulation pistol.

Furthermore, many male jobs don't require much physical strength, regardless of the amount of machinery used. How much strength is required to be a cab driver? To work as an attendant in a parking lot? To fly an airplane? To mow a lawn? How much physical strength does it take to sell stock? Or to run a company? Many of the most important jobs in the United States are filled by sixty- or seventy-year old men who could easily be physically subdued by the fifteen-year-old baby-sitter hired to take care of their grandsons.

Physical strength tests can be used as a ritualistic device to exclude women whom employers or workers want to exclude anyway. Some public safety employers, such as police and fire departments, use physical exams to screen workers. These exams are defended because policemen must be able to subdue assailants and firefighters must be able to carry heavy, unconscious victims. Men have often outperformed women in these tests because such tests frequently emphasize upper-arm body strength.

The irony is that many members of the police and fire departments cannot pass their own department's entry tests. These tests are given to young job entrants: workers in their early twenties. Once a police or fire department hires you, and unless you commit gross misconduct, you hold that job for life; this means that many police and fire departments are heavily staffed with older officers, many of whom are first-rate professionals. These are experienced veterans, safety officers who bring years of experience and savvy to the department. However, because many of them are forty or fifty years old, some of them have lost the physical strength it would take to pass their department's entrance exam.

The police and fire example illustrates the point of the somewhat arbitrary quality of physical fitness entrance exams (along with many written entrance exams). Most jobs involve skills that are learned by experience. Outside professional athletics, initial physical attributes are not all that important. People who are not physically fit learn to perform strength-related jobs either by using technology and skill or by simply muscling up. I was a lot more physically fit at the end of my summer in the shoe warehouse than I was at the beginning. Between individual variablity, the presence of machinery and skills, and the ability of workers to grow stronger, it is hard to imagine a job that could not hire women on the basis that no woman, ever, would be strong enough to perform it.

Demand-Side Theories of Occupational Sex-Typing: Buffering Models

Tradition, sex roles, and physical strength do not provide compelling explanations of the gendered distribution of jobs within our economy. Labor cost buffering, however, provides some intriguing possibilities. We saw from the previous chapter that differentiating by big firm/poor firm or rich firm/small firm doesn't tell us very much about the use of women. However, differentiating occupations and industries by whether their cost structures encourage or discourage economizing on personnel expenses tells us a great deal about gender in the economy.

Remember the labor cost buffering model of the previous chapter? I argued there that men, being generally sexist, have a preference for hiring men. Yet when the economics of their operations prevent them from hiring men, they are willing to save money by hiring women.

Whether or not sexism is economically viable is determined by the capital intensity of the workplace. In a capital-intensive work setting, the largest component of the budget is capital. The opposite of capital intensity is labor intensity. In a labor-intensive work setting, the largest component of the budget is labor. Capital refers to the nonhuman components of production; these are generally raw materials, equipment, and money. Labor refers to the human components of production; this generally refers to workers.

An automobile assembly line is a typical example of a capital-intensive work setting. Automobile manufacturing uses massive quantities of raw materials. Assembly lines are massive constructions in themselves, not to mention the presses, cranes, forklifts, welders, paint sprayers, and robotics, that are standard automobile factory gear. Managers of automobile factories have to buy a whole lot of "stuff"; this "stuff" takes up a huge share of their budgets. Labor may cost money, but it is dwarfed by massive spending on raw material and machinery.

By contrast, most offices are labor-intensive. Consider a county automobile registration office. Workers stand behind windows; taxpayers drive up or walk up, show their registration, and write a check. The clerk takes the check and hands over a decal and, sometimes, a license plate. Raw material and technology costs for this operation are trivial. All of the expenses go to pay the clerks who are standing behind the windows, or running around in back keeping the records in order. As a result, the supervisor of this office has a budget comprised nearly entirely of labor.

From a financial standpoint, it is far more important for a labor-intensive workplace (as opposed to a capital-intensive workplace) to economize on labor. For a labor-intensive operation, every extra increase in salary has an immediate impact on the total budget. To be efficient requires reducing one's personnel expenses to the minimum, because these are the only kinds of expenses there are.

In a capital-intensive setting, labor savings are nice, but they are not essential. If a manager is particularly proficient at getting the most out of available capital, either by obtaining raw materials cheaply or by maximizing the cost efficiency of technology, he or she could keep overall costs low, even with a relatively expensive labor force. In some work settings, such as refineries and nuclear reactors, the contribution of personnel costs to the financial viability of the enterprise may even be trivial. In some highly automated settings such as refineries, and nuclear reactors, the costs of raw material and equipment are so overwhelming that labor costs can be virtually irrelevant to overall profitability.[5]

Consider now the fundamental observation that women work at a lower salary than do men. If a sexist employer wanted to hire an all-male labor force, he would have to tolerate a higher level of personnel costs. In a capital-intensive work setting such a policy might be feasible because he could cover his inflated labor expenses with competent handling of the capital expenses in his budget. In a labor-intensive setting, the male workforce would be nonviable. If he uses the men, his expenses swell uncontrollably with no possible counterweighing factors in sight. Unless he finds some way to reintroduce cheap labor, his operation will be uncompetitive and he will be put out of business.

The simplest application of this theory is that it helps to explain why women tend to be associated with white-collar work and men with blue-collar work. Most of the alternative explanations as to why women do mental work while men do manual work are not very compelling. Some people say women don't work in factories because the work is dirty, or physical, or both. However, women routinely do dirty and physical work. At home, women are more likely than men to change a baby's dirty diaper. They are also more likely to do the more unsavory housekeeping chores, like cleaning toilets or mopping up spills. In the work world, they take jobs as cleaning ladies. They work in the helping professions, tidying up after the elderly and the infirm. They even work as lab technicians, professionally processing samples of urine and stools. If women can be entrusted to work to clean toilets and handle urine, it is hard to see the cultural objection to hiring women in a factory setting and exposing them to grease or dust.

We also saw from the previous section that physical strength is not a good explanation of why women work in offices while men do manual work. Individual women and men have widely differing strengths with some women being stronger than some men. Furthermore, many manual jobs are not especially strenuous. One does not need to be an Olympic athlete to be an electrician. Labor cost buffering, however, provides useful insights on this issue. Office settings by their very nature tend to be labor-intensive; they have few physical materials and even less machinery. Offices, schools, sales rooms, and banks are all settings where people are practically the only cost of production. Male clerical workers or school people or cashiers or bank tellers will all noticeably increase the cost of production and will be difficult to reconcile with budgetary restraint. Factories, by contrast, are filled with different kinds of capital; raw materials and technology can absorb the costs associated with using men.

Buffering theory also explains why it is that women are more likely to work in light rather than heavy industry. Women work in light assembly, in settings such as textile factories or electronics factories. In the maquiladoras, for example, factories on the Mexican side of the U.S-Mexico border, Mexican women are hired to sew blue jeans, or make computer components by sitting at benches with soldering irons attaching electronic components to printed circuit boards. In Asia, women might make running shoes. The equipment used in these factories is often very modest. There is a simple shed, a set of benches, and a set of sewing machines or soldering irons. There is little other permanent investment. Likewise, the raw materials are very inexpensive. In contrast, men are more likely to appear in automobile factories, in steel mills, or in chemical plants: work settings filled with vast quantities of metal and machinery. The heavier the industry, the more nonlabor-cost items exist in the budget; this can reduce the centrality of cutting salary expenses.

Capital intensity is not the only consideration that can buffer from labor costs. Some lines of work are so profitable that costs don't matter. Some "gold mine" products have potential revenue flows so large that all that matters is making the sale. In Hollywood, one blockbuster hit can salvage a financially ailing studio and more than compensate for five or six box office duds. *Titanic* was one of the most expensive films ever made: It more than repaid every cent of its investment. In this kind of industry, producers throw money at pictures in trying to maximize their chances of getting a hit. Studios pay exorbitant salaries to their stars and producers; they could conceivably hire female rather than male cameramen, or use female rather than male directors.[6] In the grand Hollywood days of the 1930's 40's and 50's, such a move would have been rare, and could have saved the studios a substantial share of their camerawork and directoral salaries. However, in the final accounts for a big success like *Gone With the Wind*, the salary savings would have been barely noticeable on the bottom line, blown away in a hurricane of ticket receipts.

A smaller version of this phenomenon can be found in the restaurant business. Staffing practices in restaurants vary enormously from country to country and with types of restaurants within each country. In the United States, generally women work as waitresses and serve the food; men work as chefs and cook the food. An ambiguous area called food preparation, which can be done by men or by women, involves low-skill assembly jobs such as cutting ingredients or assembling salads. That said, who works in restaurants doing any type of job changes with the price markup of the restaurant. Restaurants vary enormously in what they charge for a meal; these prices do not reflect true costs. Consider a Jack-in-the-Box hamburger, a hamburger at a full-service restaurant such as a Bennigan's, and a Tournedos Haché à la Sainte-Anne-de-la-Reims at the most exclusive restaurant in Washington, D.C. These are all chopped-beef sandwiches for sale at $1.69, $5.49, and $65.00, depending on the location. Obviously the quality of the meat is better for the tournedos than for the Jack-in-the-Box, and one gets more elegant garnishes and a fancier sauce. Furthermore, as one moves more upscale, one sits in a nicer room, one that represents some capital investment. That said, the cost of raw ingredients and capital for the hamburgers in question do not translate into a ratio of $1.69 to $5.49 to $65.00. Management is taking more of a markup on the burger at Bennigan's than at Jack-in-the-Box, and more still at the Washington elite spot than at Bennigan's.

This markup buffers the upscale restaurants from having to minimize their labor costs; they can consider hiring people other than the cheapest possible employees. In the first two settings, one is likely to have one's food served by women. At the Jack-in-the-Box, a high school girl works the counter or window; at Bennigan's, a college girl serves you at your table, but has her salary supplemented by tips. At the elite spot, it is possible the entire wait staff will be male. The waiters, who are full-time professionals rather than part-time students, are expected to be highly knowledgeable about the cuisine. Even though, in terms of traditional sex roles, women know more about cooking than do men, men will be hired for these elite positions. Given the markups associated with the food, the cost savings associated with using women rather than men are from a financial standpoint relatively trivial.

A research lab may be another setting where labor costs are an unimportant component of production. In research, all that matters is making the key discovery that will justify the existence of the lab. Furthermore, physical research often involves raw materials and equipment; these add an extra level of capital labor intensity. It is easy to see how scientific laboratories could become heavily male; labor cost savings would be almost irrelevant to their success.

These considerations also help to explain why engineering continues to be a male occupation. Obtaining a steady supply of inexpensive labor may be fairly important in manufacturing, where few decisions remain to be made and costs are replicated week after week. In engineering, however, the point of the enterprise is to develop some fundamental and huge innovation that will produce enormous revenues or savings for the firm. The cost of the engineers involved is small relative to the anticipated financial consequences of the substantive innovations they bring to the firm. Add to this the capital budget associated with the engineers working with prototypes and one can see that the labor budget for engineering workers themselves is not an important component of the viability of a technical office. Under such circumstances, it is easy to see how capitalists could come to tolerate (or even approve of) all male engineering forces.

Such tolerance in the business world would promote a culture of male superiority in things technical that would be reflected in engineering schools and in math and science education. Engineers, like all other professionals, control entry into their occupation through professional schools. If engineers in the work world are encouraged to maintain a male environment, engineers who leave such an environment to found or administer engineering schools will carry on this same ideology. Parallel developments would occur in math and science training, as scientists from all male laboratories come to set policy for science departments in universities and to design curricula and teacher training programs for elementary and high school math and science teachers. Norms from all-male technical workplaces would thus diffuse into the educational process at a very low level, creating elementary and secondary science teachers who truly believe that boys are inherently better at math and science than are girls; these beliefs produce gender socialization guiding girls into humanities and boys into technical occupations. The key here is that these cultural systems have their origins in workplace practices, and workplace practices have their origins in the economics of the occupations in which they originate. Because scientific and technical tasks are buffered from labor costs, patriarchal ideologies and policies are allowed to go unchecked because there is little financial incentive to introduce female labor. Once the culture is created, it can permeate into other institutions and produce lasting society-wide beliefs about male and female competencies.

Empirical Studies of Buffering and Sex-Typing

The evidence in the previous section has been largely impressionistic. However, the arguments of that section can be supported by more rigorous empirical tests. Some of the best have involved statistical analyses of the occupational structure in the United States. Michael Wallace and Arne Kalleberg (1981) as a part of a larger investigation of the structure of dual labor markets estimated the determinants of the percentage female among 68 industries. They found that capital intensity was negatively correlated with the percentage of females in an industry. Furthermore, capital intensity was the only variable in their model that achieved standard levels of statistical significance.

Bridges (1980, 1982) obtained similar results in analyses of 80 primary and secondary industries and 320 "industry strata." In a 1980 analysis of industries, capital intensity was the only variable that consistently predicted the percentage of women. In 1982, he used occupation rather than industry as the unit of analysis. In this study, he included two measures of capital intensity: a variable called "classic capitalist organization" combining standard indices of capital intensity in industrial studies; and white-collar/blue-collar, a simple measure of capital intensity at the occupational level. These two variables dominated the analysis and were the key predictors of what jobs were male and female.

Cohn's *Process of Occupational Sex-Typing* (1985), an analysis of the history of clerical work, provides further support for the buffering thesis. Clerical work is one of only a handful of jobs to change sex type from nearly all male to nearly all female. In the nineteenth century, office work was done almost entirely by men. A typical Victorian office would have looked like the office of Marley and Scrooge in which Ebenezer

Scrooge and Bob Cratchett worked in Charles Dickens's *Christmas Carol.* The office was all male, with the male owner of the company doing most of the substantive business and a male clerk doing all the clerical work. The clerical work would have involved keeping all the books, filing all the letters, and copying all the correspondence by hand. In 1870, the all-male office began to change both in the United States and in Britain. In both countries, the post office began to hire women for a variety of clerical and postal jobs; this innovation spread rapidly, first to other government offices and then to the private sector. By the 1920s, the vast majority of clerical workers were women, a pattern that has persisted to the present day.

Why did clerical work switch from all male to all female? Labor cost buffering has much to say about this. In early nineteenth-century enterprise, it did not matter very much if firms used male or female clerks. Firms were generally fairly small affairs and hired very few clerical workers of any type, period. Managing a business was simple; cost accounting had not been developed. The owner of the company generally carried in his head most of the details of the running of the firm. Formal records were minimal, usually just a small number of financial ledgers. Few items were copied because everything had to be copied by hand. Bookkeeping was primitive. Cost accounting—the key tool of modern strategic management—had not even been invented, thus much of the perceived need to keep elaborate financial records did not yet exist. With this level of minimalist paper processing, a handful of clerks could serve the needs of all but the largest firms. The costs of most enterprises went into raw materials, machinery, or blue-collar labor, with office staff being a trivial afterthought.

However, as technology developed and Britain and the United States expanded economically, large firms developed that could not be managed informally by one owner. The sheer scope and complexity of a steel mill or an insurance company required far more elaborate record keeping than had been attempted previously. Furthermore, once cost accounting was invented and became popular, firms began to need more and more elaborate financial analyses in order to manage their affairs. The modern corporation became administratively intense. Where companies had once required merely a room full of clerks at their headquarters, now they needed an entire office building, or later on, an entire skyscraper plus multiple branch offices; these growing office staffs began to weigh on the budgets of corporations overall. It soon became evident that, unless some economies were produced in the salaries paid to office workers, expanding clerical forces would become uneconomical. This realization produced a search for cheaper labor and a feminization of most clerical occupations.

The firms that were in the vanguard of this transition were among the most labor-intense of employers; the firms that resisted female clerks and attempted to continue using men were the least labor-intense of employers. The early innovators were government offices. In Britain and the United States, the post office was the first major employer to use female clerks, followed by other divisions of the civil service. The public sector is distinctive in that it is almost entirely labor-intensive. Governments do almost no manufacturing, but they do pay for a lot of clerks and bureaucrats.

In the British case, there is another little twist. The year that women clerks were introduced to the post office was 1870. 1870 was also the year of the Trevelyan reforms, the first great civil service reform program. Before 1870, most of Britain's government jobs were filled by political patronage. It didn't really matter whether the job candidate was qualified or produced enough to justify his pay. Getting into the civil service depended on having the right connections and supporting the right politician in some election. In 1870, all this changed. Candidates were required to be qualified for the positions they filled. More important, offices were expected to be run efficiently rather than as dumping grounds for political flunkies. Budgets were now watched. Labor costs had been irrelevant before 1870; after 1870, labor costs were a serious matter that had to be minimized. Once government bureaucrats had to do real jobs and were scrutinized for the waste of public funds, they began to hire women instead of men. No more suggestive evidence can possibly exist for the claim that discrimination only flourishes where concerns for market efficiency aren't important; when managers have to watch their costs they become more receptive to diversity in hiring.

Clerical feminization proceeded into the financial sector and then into offices generally. It appeared last in heavy manufacturing and transportation. Railroads were noticeably reluctant to use women clerks. In Britain, by the beginning of World War II, when clerk was a female job virtually throughout the United States and Europe, only one out of four railway clerks were female. A similar situation applied to the United States. Railways were overwhelmingly capital-intensive. They owned miles and miles of track, all the bridges and tunnels along their routes, and all the locomotives and railway cars that ran along those routes. If this was not enough, they also built all their locomotives and railway cars from scratch; thus they ran some of the biggest factories of their era. All this capital would have been more than sufficient to make them hire male railway clerks, but there was an additional consideration as well: Most of their workers were not clerks. The railways hired locomotive engineers, firemen, conductors, guards, freight loaders, signal guards, yardmen, locomotive repairmen, right-of-way maintainers, and all the workers in the locomotive and rolling-stock factories. Although they hired a large number of clerks in absolute terms, clerical workers were a trivial percentage of their overhead. Not surprisingly, it was easy for them to hire men, because clerical labor costs were a trivial percentage of their total budget.

Note that some of this tradition survives to the present day. It is not uncommon in railways for the executive secretary to the president of a railway company to be a man. This is a throwback to the earlier history of male railroad clerks. Furthermore, managers are still likely to hire men for clerical positions that are located in factories and warehouses. In the census, these jobs appear under the job titles "Traffic, Shipping, and Receiving Clerks" and "Stock and Inventory Clerks." In 1990, the former job was only 29 percent female; the latter job was only 37 percent female. Every other clerical occupation was over 90 percent female. The argument for male shipping and inventory clerks is that they have to lift heavy boxes. I've worked as a shipping clerk in two separate companies; most of what you do is fill out forms. Occasionally, you use a dolly to move a shipment around. It does not take very much strength to use a dolly. Factories and warehouses, however, are capital-intensive operations. Furthermore, the clerical staff represents a small percentage of total staff and total budget. If the warehouse supervisor believes that only a real man can work in his warehouse, it does not cost the company very much to humor his sensibilities, at least on the shipping-clerk positions.

The final piece of empirical support is a piece of negative support, a sort of exception that helps to prove the rule. It represents a setting where cultural factors were dominant in determining occupational sex types—because labor costs were more or less irrelevant in determining the profitability of the firm. Winifred Poster (1997) did an analysis of the staffing of managerial and sales positions in a U.S. multinational firm in contemporary India. The company was relatively progressive and egalitarian with an explicit commitment to affirmative action and to providing opportunities for women. In the United States, this company filled many of its most important sales and managerial posts with women, although men did have somewhat preferential access to top positions.

In India, the company deferred to traditional Indian sex roles. Indians tended to believe in the isolation of the genders. Women's business activities were limited by two considerations. The first is an unwillingness to include women in potentially acrimonious negotiations. Women were kept away from settings such as dealing with the customs authorities, where a certain level of belligerence and willingness to play hardball was viewed as necessary to success. Aggressiveness and assertiveness were not viewed as being appropriate female traits. Second, women were kept from business dealings that had a social component. Business socializing was considered inappropriate for women, possibly because of the chance of engaging in "low" forms of entertainment or discussion. Note, however, that in many third world countries, including India, nearly all serious business negotiation occurs after courtships that have involved extensive socializing. To be excluded from business entertaining is to be excluded from most major deals.

As a result, in the company's Indian offices, women were restricted to inside jobs that involved contact with other workers in the company. When the company had a position involving dealing with Indian outsiders, such jobs disproportionately went to men. This is in contrast to the firms' policies in its U.S. offices, where no "inside/outside" distinction existed. (Individual U.S. managers could be very disparaging of the skills of female managers, but they had no problem letting women deal with significant figures outside the firm). Note that the Indian women themselves did not particularly share the belief that they should not hold positions with outside contact. While they were aware of what the cultural rules were, they were entirely willing to use the U.S. firm as a chance to break traditional boundaries and show off to the world what Indian women could accomplish. The Indian men, however, would have little of this and did their best to restrict women to in-house roles.

Note that from the standpoint of corporate economics, the use of men for outside positions was relatively cost free. The goal of the Indian branch was to break into the Indian market. Establishing a beachhead for the firm's brand name, and establishing the long-term popular demand for its products was substantially more important than saving money in the first few years of operation. This was a start-up operation where creating market share and a good corporate reputation were critical for the firm's success. These were long-term strategic priorities that made short-term cost cutting relatively unimportant. Furthermore, the firm was a relatively high-tech operation, selling a product that by virtue of the desirable and unique features associated with the company brand name could be expected to be sold at a substantial profit. It was a physical product that required manufacture. Raw materials and technology, the company's capital, were important components of the budget. Within the labor budget, sales and managerial workers were important, but they were buffered somewhat by the presence of the on-site manufacturing staff. Furthermore, labor costs in India are generally low to begin with, to the high surplus of both unskilled and educated labor.

Poster's firm was thus conspicuously buffered from labor costs. Wages were generally low even for males; the profitability of the product more than covered for these expenses; wages were buffered by the presence of capital budgets; managerial labor was buffered by the presence of blue-collar labor, and if this was not enough, the company was in a market-building strategic phase where cost cutting was not essential or even important to organizational success. It should not be surprising under these circumstances that local sensibilities became important to determining occupational sex type and that a traditional Indian division of labor was implemented.

*   *   *

The British General Post Office and Poster's Indian firm provide a nice contrast between two very different types of work setting, each of which exists in the United States today. These settings hire the cheapest workers possible and will not tolerate discrimination getting in the way of firm efficiency. One setting is driven by the need to economize on labor costs; the other is driven by factors other than labor costs. Nobody needs to bother to bring in cheap workers. Managers are allowed to have any gender or racial ideology they want. Culture matters in companies like these, but only because the economics of the firm prevents culture from being made irrelevant by market competition.

There is one occupational regularity, however, that none of the previous discussion speaks to. In the United States, in Britain, in India, and nearly everywhere else, women are more likely to work in low-paid jobs with relatively little power and status, and men are more likely to work in more lucrative jobs with relatively greater power and status. The male-female splits are not nearly as strong as those that exist for race; they nevertheless do exist and require explaining. It is to the question of status segregation that we must now turn: Why are women concentrated in low-status jobs?

Notes

1. In the United States, male Irishmen could be employed for very low wages.

2. Their ability to act on these preferences has been restrained in the light of recent judicial challenges to race- and gender-based university admissions policies.

3. All the statistics for this section come from the 1990 census, in particular Supplementary Report CP-S–1–1: Detailed Occupation and Other Characteristics from the EEO File for the United States (1992).

4. Actually, only truck driving and construction work are all male; manufacturing and agriculture have openings for women as well as men.

5. This may explain how Homer Simpson is able to keep his job for Mr. Burns.

6. For skeptics who doubt that studios could save money by using female talent, note that even in today's liberated, politically correct film industry, male movie stars still earn substantially more per picture than do female stars.

4 Why Women Are Confined to Low-Status Jobs

We saw in Chapter 1 how women are confined to relatively low-status jobs. Status segregation by gender is not as extreme as status segregation by race, and the problem is becoming less marked over time. Understanding why women are more likely to be confined to jobs with low income and promotion prospects is important. From a theoretical standpoint, it is important to know how these forces shaped the history of women's work and produced the occupational distributions we observe today. From a practical standpoint, you, the reader, need to understand this phenomenon if you or someone in your family intends to participate in the labor market. Women need to know what limits their upward mobility so they can either choose relatively egalitarian workplaces or manage the forces of discrimination in workplaces where gender obstacles are a problem. Men need to understand these issues for two reasons. First, they may need to deal with the issues should they become a source of overt conflict in their workplaces. Second, they may be part of a two-earner family where the female earner is experiencing discrimination in her career.[1]

There are many explanations for status segregation, the most important of which will be discussed in this chapter. *Human capital theory* has attempted to explain women's concentration in low status positions in terms of female domestic obligations preventing them from obtaining the skills they need for superior jobs. The *synthetic turnover model* would explain this phenomenon in terms of the need to encourage turnover in settings where long job tenures raise costs for management. *Differential visibility theory* explains status segregation in terms of organizational pressures on minorities; these pressures impede objective performance and make minorities less objectively qualified for promo-tion. *Employee discrimination models* explain women's concentration in low status positions in terms of the superior capacity of male skilled workers to use worker power to exclude women. Human capital theory is extremely problematic in this regard. The other three theories make some contribution and they also apply to specific times and places. Overall, however, employee discrimination is the most universally ob-served phenomenon and probably the most important contributor to maintaining gendered status differentials.

Human Capital Theory

Human capital theory argues that employers' decisions to hire men and women for a given job are motivated by concerns over conserving train-ing costs. The theory argues that women are kept out of many high-status positions because their domestic obligations force them to leave jobs prematurely. Their rapid turnover prevents them from obtaining the skills they need to qualify for high-status positions. In economics, this is the most common explanation for women's low pay and occupational status, and it appears frequently in sociological writing as well (Polachek, 1981; Blau and Ferber 1986; Oppenheimer 1970). Although the theory is popular, it makes a number of questionable assertions about both women's and employers' behavior; as a result, its predictive power when empirically tested has been poor.

Human capital theory starts with some reasonable assumptions.[2] It argues that workers are more productive if they have received training. The effect of training is very similar to the effect of providing a worker with equipment, or capital. Just as a worker with a bulldozer is more productive than a worker trying to move dirt with his or her bare hands, a worker with skills is more productive than a worker who can't apply knowledge to the job and is forced to use raw sweat and guesswork. The productivity-enhancing powers of skills induce economists to refer to them as "human capital." "Capital" is anything that increases the yield produced by labor power, and the "human" means that skills are located within people and not out in some storage shed like a rototiller.

Skills, however, are not cost free. What are the costs associated with human capital? These depend on exactly how the worker is expected to be trained. Some jobs involve classroom training. In this case, someone will have to pay for the classroom, the teacher, the books, and the stu-dents' time. Training in other jobs involves senior workers instructing junior workers at the workplace. In these cases, time is taken from the senior worker, who generally could be more productive doing some-thing else. Still other jobs involve letting workers muddle along until they figure out how to do whatever it is they are supposed to do. This involves little direct instruction, but runs up significant costs in scrap and wasted work. A new sales representative who blows his pitch can cost his firm substantial money in lost sales.

In an employee's ideal world, the company wouldn't pay for any of this. Therefore, if he had his preference, he would have workers pick up the entire cost of training themselves and only start paying them when they were fully trained. Workers, however, are just as rational as employers; in their ideal world, they would have the employer pay the entire cost of training without their having to invest a dime.

What determines who wins this game of "who picks up the check" is based on the utility of the skills involved to other employers. Imagine that the skill involved is useful to many other employers. These skills are called *firm-general skills*. A good example of a firm general skill is literacy; almost every company benefits from having its workers know how to read. Other such skills are knowledge in how to use a word processing program, a command of basic chemistry, or training in nursing. Most employers need workers who know how to word process; many need workers who are literate in basic science, and virtually every city has multiple openings for nurses: in hospitals, doctors' offices, and residential care facilities.

Firm-general skills are generally financed entirely by the worker. Employers are reluctant to pay for firm-general skills because of the risk that employees, once trained, will quit their jobs and go work for someone else using the skills the first employer paid for. Why should Methodist Hospital pay for nurses who are going to work at Beth Israel Home for the Aged? In these cases, the employer makes workers obtain all the training they need before hiring them in the first place. This forces students to attend school at their own expense to obtain qualifications for employment.

A good illustration of the worker in firm-general training is probably you, the reader, holding this book in your hands. Training in the sociology of race or gender, or in social science generically, is a firm-general skill. Many firms need people who know something about labor-market dynamics and intergroup relations. That said, no firm would want to pay for the course you are currently enrolled in for fear they would not gain the benefits of your labor when the course is over. Almost every reader of this book is paying for his or her own college or university education in the hope of getting employment as opposed to having an employer pay for it as part of on-the-job training. This is the typical situation for firm-general skills.

Firm-specific skills are different. These are skills that are of use to only one employer. Running the "It's a Small, Small World" ride at Disneyland or learning how to fly a NASA space shuttle are good examples of firm-specific skills. No one outside of Walt Disney or NASA is ever going to need you to use those skills. Some firm-specific skills are less obvious than these two conspicuous examples. Knowing the internal paperwork processing of one's firm is a firm-specific skill. Only a local would ever need to know when to use a Form Q–21 as opposed to a plain old A–30, or would need to know what Nancy MacKenzie did with the Bolger Enterprises file in 1996. Local politics and diplomacy are often firm-specific as well. Knowing how to play Andrew Tamagachi to get the maximum budget for your operation is firm-specific (and Tamagachi-specific). More common firm-specific skills are knowledge of your firm's proprietary technology, familiarity with your firm's products, and an understanding of your firm's distinctive strategies, finances, and corporate culture. A good IBM executive does not always fit in at other computer firms, and outsiders often can't make an acceptable transition to IBM.

Firm-specific skills are paid for by the employer; this is because no one in their right mind would pay to obtain firm-specific training without an ironclad guarantee of future long-term employment by the one firm that profitably uses that training. Would you pay $10,000 to learn to fly a space shuttle knowing full well that, if NASA did not hire you or NASA fired you for whatever reason, your $10,000 training would be worthless in getting a job with another company? Because few workers would volunteer to undergo these risks, employers who want workers to obtain "one-firm-only" abilities are forced provide and pay for all their own firm-specific training themselves. A good example of firm-specific training is the preparation of sales agents. Sales representatives who go to company headquarters for briefing on the properties of the new product line they are to sell invariably do so on company time; the firm pays for their transportation, their expenses, and the costs of the staff person making the presentation.

Given that employers pay for the obtaining of firm-specific skills, they do not want to lose workers who have those skills. Any time an employee with firm-specific skills leaves the company, the firm has to shell out for a new training program for the replacement worker. Given that the company does not want to pay for endless training programs, the firm's preference is that its workers stay forever and never quit. If men were to have longer careers than women, then by the logic of this model it would be more appropriate to hire men for the jobs involving firm-specific skills and divide the jobs without firm-specific skills equally.

Such a policy if fully implemented would confine women to low-status jobs. Most superior positions involve a substantial level of firm-specific skills. Supervisors are expected to be knowledgeable about the technology used in their firms, about the workers in their labor forces, about the particular needs of clients and higher management, and about the particular financial constraints relevant to their operations. These are all local particularistic matters. There do exist some high-status firm-general positions. A doctor can move from one hospital to the other with relatively little loss of efficiency. A Hollywood actress can move from one studio or project to the next with relative ease. However, most typical manufacturing, financial, or managerial positions involve an understanding of local people, constraints, and technologies. This is all firm-specific.

The logic of human captial theory assumes, of course, that women have shorter careers than men; otherwise there would be no reason to exclude them from jobs with firm-specific skills. Why do human capital theorists argue that such gender differentials exist? Women are more likely to quit because of their domestic obligations. Historically, some women have withdrawn from the labor force on the occasion of marriage, although they are substantially less likely to do so today. Currently, many women withdraw from paid employment when the first child is born. There is a systematic tendency for women with children between the ages of 0 and 5 in the household to have lower rates of participation in the labor force (Killingworth 1983). Other women may stay in the labor force but leave to follow a husband who is relocating for his own career. Still other women may decline opportunities for promotion if this were to mean they would have to relocate their families or become part of a commuting relationship. Note that these last two considerations may not necessarily reflect gender conservatism on the part of the woman. If women earn less overall than men, and maintaining a two-location household is expensive, it may be fully rational for the lower-paid woman to follow her husband in his location decisions, thus allowing for the family as a whole to maximize the prospects of obtaining a truly high income. If women were indeed to be quit-prone, then it might be rational to exclude them from jobs involving training; this would have the consequences of producing status differentials between the genders.

Problems with Human Capital Theory

Human capital theory does not do a very good job of explaining the confinement of women to low-status positions. The logic that employers organize all personnel policy around minimizing training costs is dubious, and the claim that women are naturally quit-prone is controversial. Before considering these claims, however, let us start with a consideration that kills human capital theory in the bud. Human capital theory cannot possibly explain the division of occupations into male and female sextyped jobs!

Human capital theory argues that the world consists of two types of workers: low-turnover men and high-turnover women. Jobs are divided into male and female based on these propensities to leave the firm. But in actuality, turnover does not divide the labor force into two sets of workers, one male and one female. It divides them into two different pools, younger women in prime reproductive age, and others, meaning men and women past the age of childbearing. The primary reason that women supposedly drop out of the labor force is to provide for the care of children at home. This is not a relevant concern for a fifty-five year old woman. Women over the age of forty-five are completing or have completed raising their families and have few reasons not to stay in the labor force until they retire. A woman who is hired at forty and works until she is sixty-five will have a career of twenty-five years. Very few workers of any gender stay with one firm for twenty-five years. Furthermore, there are very few jobs that would require more than twenty-five years of continuous service to justify training a worker for the position. Older workers are an excellent source of stable, loyal labor. Workers of both sexes over forty have substantially lower turnover than do younger workers; this lower turnover is due to the older workers' greater maturity, financial obligations, and traditional values. Furthermore, older women will have lower turnover than older men because of their better health and lower rates of morbidity (Preston 1976).

The logic of the previous paragraph suggests that employers would divide their jobs into two pools: jobs involving no training, which would be given to women, and jobs involving high training, which would be given to men and to older women interchangeably. In real life, no such phenomenon occurs. There are no jobs that go just to men and older women. Jobs are either male or female, period. When mixed jobs occur, rarely are younger women excluded from them because of the problems associated with child care. Because turnover considerations would not predict comparable treatment for older and younger women, it is hard to use this to explain the real-world phenomenon where both older and younger women are excluded from high-status jobs.

Furthermore, it is not at all obvious that women have higher turnover than men in the first place. Turnover is one of the most studied phenomena in human relations, with the literature on same being enormous (and dry). The relationship between gender and quit rates is commonly examined in such studies. The literature is divided, with three different kinds of results showing up in roughly equal proportion. About one third of the studies actually support human capital theory and show that women have higher quit rates than men. About one third of the studies, however, reverse human capital theory and show that men have higher quit rates than women! The remaining third of the studies show men and women have the same quit rates, a nice moderate conclusion, but one that completely contradicts the central premise of human capital theory's teachings on gender (Anderson 1974; Price 1977).

The more detailed and sophisticated studies help to uncover the reason results vary so much from dataset to dataset. Kip Viscusi (1980) investigated the determinants of turnover in a large corporation. When one superficially compared the turnover rates of men and women, he found that women were more likely to quit the firm than were men. Viscusi argued, however, that such a contrast is extremely misleading and masks the actual gender dynamics at the firm. Because the firm had only recently feminized, most of the female employees were recent job entrants; most of the male employees were veteran workers with long experience.

Workers are typically far more likely to quit in their first year of employment than they are at any other time. In the first year, incompetent workers and bad hires are discovered by management and are put under pressure to pack their bags and leave. In the first year, too, workers decide whether they like the corporate culture of the company; the misfits typically seek other employment rather quickly. The first year is also when one loses the professional job-hoppers. Some superstars bounce from company to company very quickly as rival employers bid for their services. Workers with more seniority tend to be those who have made a commitment to the firm; those who do their jobs well enough to be rewarded; those who share the company style and world view; and those who want to build a future in one place rather than sign up for the job of the week. Because the firm had only recently begun to hire women, there were a disproportionate number of women in the first-year cohort, which is typically quit-prone. Among the first-year people, men and women had identical quit rates. Furthermore, among the more experienced workers, men and women also had identical quit rates. The seeming gender differential in stability was the spurious result of the historical timing of when men and women were hired.

Furthermore, Viscusi found that in some ways the women were more loyal than the men. Viscusi calculated, using some sophisticated econometric techniques, how much money it would take to keep a male worker and a female worker from leaving the firm. In general, highly paid workers are more likely to stay with a company than poorly paid workers because the well-paid workers know they have a good deal with their present firm; they know that it would be hard to improve on their conditions by going outside the company. Viscusi contrasted the quit rates of workers with high and low salaries to see how much reduction in quit rate the company could purchase with a $1000 salary increase. Women were far more responsive to the pay increases than men. For the same amount of money, the quit rates of women declined dramatically; the reduction in quits for men was much more modest. This makes sense when one considers that good jobs for female workers are difficult to come by, giving a woman with a good salary a strong incentive to stay. Viscusi's study implies, however, that if a company wants to spend the least amount of money to keep its employees from quitting, the best policy would be to hire an all-female labor force, because the pay required to avoid turnover would be far less than the pay required to keep a comparable set of men.

Another problem with the human capital model is that it assumes that firms obsess about the costs associated with the loss of firm-specific capital. No company ever wants to get rid of a skilled worker because of the presumably prohibitive expenses associated with training a replacement. Such a claim would seem to ring hollow in the face of the massive layoffs and downsizings of the 1980s and 1990s. Modern U.S. capitalism has been driven by a logic of "mean and lean," using the smallest possible number of workers to obtain the greatest amount of productivity. In the campaign for cost savings, skilled and unskilled workers have been released in record numbers, an occurrence that flies in the face of human capital theory (Gordon 1996).

Why are employers so willing to shed workers with firm-specific human capital? To be sure, it is expensive to train a new employee; however, it is more expensive to pay for two people when one person can do both jobs just by putting in longer hours. Training costs are only a small proportion of total costs; these other costs may mandate a gendered division of labor that is wholly different from what would be predicted by firm-specific skill.

Add to that the consideration that often a company can hire "almost-trained" workers from the outside with endowments of firm-general skills that make them practically as productive as locally trained workers; the company can then top off its firm-specific skills in a short time. Many managerial hires are made from outside the firm because many upper-level administrative skills are common to a large number of different settings. As of this writing, the CEO of IBM (Lou Gerstner) was the former CEO of RJR Nabisco. Running a cigarette and food company is very different from running a computer company, and certainly different from running IBM, which has a complex and unique corporate culture. This is not an atypical phenomenon. Many CEOs are hired from outside, as are managers from up and down the corporate hierarchy. These managers are not trainees who are allowed to be unproductive for a year or two; new managers are expected to get results immediately—using their stock of firm-general capital. This suggests that firm-general capital may be more important than firm-specific capital. Basing the entire gender division of labor on firm-specific capital may be like explaining corporate survival in terms of minimizing postage costs.

Empirically, human capital theory has not done well when tested as an explanation of occupational sex-typing or gender differences in job holding. The standard test for a human capital explanation of anything is to assess whether that phenomenon can be explained by differentials in education and experience. Human capital theorists argue, frequently with justification, that skills come from schooling and from experience on the job. Sophisticated tests differentiate between experience in the current firm and experience in other firms in the labor market.

In general, neither education nor experience noticeably reduces observed gender differences in job access or promotion. Both Polacheck (a supporter of human capital theory) and England (an opponent of same) have attempted to predict sex types from demand for firm-specific skills. When either Polacheck or England compares occupations that require extensive firm-specific human capital with occupations that do not, the sex types of the two are nearly equal, disconfirming human capital theory (Polacheck 1981; England 1982, 1984). Although it is true that many female jobs require the acquisition of little human capital and are thus consistent with dropping out of the labor market for childbearing, a lot of male jobs have the same attribute. A future mother could easily work as a parking lot attendant, or as a construction laborer, or as a hospital orderly—yet these jobs are predominantly male.

Similar findings have been obtained by other researchers. Reskin and Ross (1992) included education and experience as control variables in their study of decision-making power among Illinois executives. Despite these human capital controls, gender differences in power persisted. Nesbitt's (1998) study of gender differences in careers of clergy found that very little of the gap between male and female ministers could be explained by differential education and experience. Kay and Hagan's (1998) study of Canadian lawyers did all this and more; it took into account levels of education and experience and adjusted for interruptions in firm-specific training that could derive from career interruptions such as pregnancy leaves. Parental leaves actually *increased* the likelihood of promotion, exactly the opposite of what human capital theory would expect. Kay and Hagan suggest that top lawyers tended to superperform after they returned from maternity leaves as a sign that they continued to be serious employees. This superperformance more than compensated for any skill deterioration during the leave. If this is the case, it casts serious doubt on the claim that maternity leaves are necessarily crippling either to skills acquisition or to corporate performance. If the company maintains competitive pressure on workers to maintain standards, workers can juggle domestic and professional obligations without any loss of firm-specific skill; such balancing undercuts any need to avoid hiring women for jobs with firm-specific training.

Synthetic Turnover

Human capital theory argues that women are kept out of high-status positions to prevent the loss of personnel. However, sometimes women are confined to low-status positions to accelerate the loss of personnel. The use of women to accelerate quit rates is referred to as *synthetic turnover* (Cohn 1985).[3] The phenomenon is very rare in the contemporary United States. However, this played an important role in women's employment historically and is still found in some parts of the third world.

There are times when it is advantageous for firms to shed workers and replace them with new trainees. The most important example of this is the firm with hierarchical series of tenure-based salary scales. Many firms use regular pay increases as their primary tool for motivating workers; such a system is extremely common in white-collar employment. Students who come from middle-class backgrounds may not be aware that there is any other structure of compensation.

Payment systems that do *not* use hierarchical series of tenure-based salary scales are often found in blue-collar employment. In many factories, workers are paid by piecework, or are paid a standard rate for working a certain type of machine; if they change machines, their wage rate changes. Under this system, which does not use tenure-based salary scales, everybody working the same machine at the same speed gets paid the same rate. A six-day newbie can, in principle, be paid the same amount as a thirty-year veteran. Blue-collar workers often get seniority benefits, but they do not show up as more pay for doing the same work. Seniority benefits appear as a) protection for workers against being laid off and b) workers' rights to choose their own work assignments, allowing them to pick machines that inherently pay good rates.

By contrast, in the white-collar world, where tenure-based salary scales are common, workers doing the same work are often paid at different rates.[4] Most white-collar workers receive seniority-based pay increases, often on an annual basis; one obtains such increases merely by continuing to perform adequately. No particularly special or heroic productivity is required. Generally, white-collar job classifications allow for a fixed number of seniority increases, allowing workers to take between two to ten years to rise to the top of their grades.

Above and beyond seniority increases are pay increases associated with promotion. Jobs are typically clustered into multiple classifications, the move from a lower classification to a higher one being associated with a significant promotion. Unlike annual increases, promotions to a higher grade are not semiautomatic; these have to be earned. Workers will generally perform heroically to obtain promotions, working late hours and weekends to outcompete potential rivals for advancement.

A key feature of these promotions is that they are not always associated with a change of job duties. Some promotions produce radical shifts in work assignments, particular in corporate cultures where "moving a worker around the company" is an essential component to being groomed for high positions. In these settings, eighteen months in finance followed by eighteen months in marketing followed by eighteen months in European operations may not be uncommon. In other settings, however, notably the civil service, promotions are often nominal and financial rather than substantive. Capable workers start expanding their job duties and doing more and more work that would otherwise be given to the boss. If the boss is pleased with this assumption of new duties, and upper management permits the funding of a promotion, the junior worker gets a new job title and a raise. Although new duties may be associated with the change, often this is merely a formalization of the advanced job duties the worker has been performing at a lower pay level.

A consequence of hierarchical tenure-based salary scales is that workers become increasingly more expensive over time. Promotions to produce workers performing new tasks that are inherently more productive than the work they were doing before do not particularly pose any cost problems. The higher salary associated with the superior position can be justified with the greater value the promoted worker is producing for the company. Increases based purely on seniority and reclassifications not associated with noticeable shifts in job duties, however, have the effect of making the company pay more for the same level of worker output it had before. Companies are often willing to pay for such "unproductive" pay raises because the presence both of seniority increases and hard-to-get promotions motivate employees to work harder. If a battle for a promotion to Associate District Manager makes four workers really exert themselves, the company gains from the intramural competition. The cost, however, is that the pay increase for the winning worker is permanent.

An excellent example of nonproductive promotions can be found in Japanese heavy industry. Large Japanese corporations typically pay workers by seniority. All twenty-year-olds get paid a twenty-year-old salary. All twenty-one-year olds get paid a twenty-one-year old salary, which is higher, and so on and so forth until the system caps out at age fifty-five. In the younger years, when workers are genuinely learning their craft, these seniority pay increases are compensated with higher rates of worker performance. However, in the later years, Japanese workers are not likely to learn that much extra. There is probably not much difference between the productivity of a thirty-six-year-old and thirty-seven-year-old worker. Nevertheless, the Japanese pay the thirty-seven-year-old worker more. The steady and unproductive aging of the Japanese workforce has been one factor increasing the cost of Japanese products in the 1980s and 1990s and lowering the ability of Japanese firms to compete on price.

When workers become more expensive over time, without becoming more productive, there is an enormous financial incentive to get rid of veteran workers and replace them with trainees. In such cases, the cost of retraining is relatively low compared to the savings in being able to move from an upper-level to an entry-grade salary. Firms who wish to stimulate the circulation of personnel often intentionally hire workers who are relatively quit-prone.

Fast-food restaurants are a good example of this. Most fast food restaurants provide pay raises as an incentive system. They also have a vast number of jobs that are essentially unskilled. The raise system becomes viable because workers flow in and out of fast work all the time. For McDonald's, it would be a catastrophe if all of the workers who were employed there at one time decided that they never wanted to leave and that McDonald's was going to be their lifetime career. To insure that enough workers quit to provide vacancies for entry-level workers, McDonald's hires a large percentage of teenagers. Juvenile workers are the most turnover-prone workers in the labor force. Some quit because they lack work discipline. Others quit because they decide they like other kinds of work better. Many quit to pursue their education. In the contemporary U.S. economy, dividing work between older and younger workers is a strategy for differentiating between staffing positions in which one wants the jobholder to stay and those in which one wants the jobholder to work for a while and then leave.

In earlier historical periods, and in other countries today, gender is the marker that differentiates between positions the company wants to staff with short-term as opposed to long-term personnel. Men were assigned to permanent positions, which tended to include all the high-status jobs. Women were assigned to positions that, it was hoped, would be temporary; these tended to be on the bottom of the status hierarchy. Women did not always follow the game plan. Some women became dedicated careerists who remained longer than their employers would have liked. In these cases, employers often had to encourage or prod their women to leave so that vacancies for cheaper workers could open up. Many of the turnover differentials that existed between men and women were not a product of women's traditional values or domestic obligations, but were created artificially by male employers with psychological pressures, bribes, or, when necessary, by women-only layoffs.

A good example of this process can be found in the British General Post Office, the pioneer of women's employment discussed in the last chapter. One of the first positions for which women were hired in the British General Post Office was telegraph operator, a very highly skilled occupation. In the late nineteenth century the telegraph was the most important technology used for business communication. Although a small number of companies might have had their own private telegraph lines, the overwhelming majority of companies used public telegraph providers. In the United States, the provider was Western Union, a private corporation. Nearly everywhere else in the world, post offices provided telegraph service as an extension of providing mail.

Worldwide, there was a vast demand for telegraph operators. Between 1870 and 1900 business boomed. As the volume of business messages rose, and as more and more companies went "online" by using electronic communication, the need for telegraph service became extraordinary. The ability to transmit messages, however, was constrained by the limited number of telegraph operators. To be able to send a message required the ability to tap out text in Morse code. (A = dot dash, B = dash dot dot dot, etc.) The trick was that you had to be able to do this with your fingers, and you had to be able to do it very, very fast. Because messages had to be sent out letter by letter, a slow operator could seriously tie up an intercity line. It also did not help that telegraph machines were not standardized, so you had to learn how to handle each of several technologies, *plus* the machines tended to break down all the time from the constant repetitive contact. Repair people were scarce, so telegraph operators had to know how to fix their own machines—once again using several different technologies.

The post office needed an enormous number of such workers; furthermore, the post office did not want to pay very much. They found, not surprisingly, that they could not find enough men to fill their positions. Out of desperation they turned to women. Women showed up in ample numbers, took the training enthusiastically, and, beginning in 1870, became a substantial percentage of Britain's skilled telegraph force.

The post office, like civil service employers generally, paid their workers using a hierarchical series of tenure-based salary scales. All workers got seniority increases. Furthermore, jobs were graded into formal ranks, with promotion from one level to the next being a key incentive for motivating employment. According to post office management, one of the key reasons for hiring women (besides the obvious one that they were the only workers available) was that women's quits would facilitate the smooth operation of the promotion chain. Women would naturally want to quit when they found a young man and became married. Female marriages would create openings that could then be filled with other workers.

By always bringing in new people with relatively low seniority, the post office could provide regular promotions to all senior workers and reduce the absolute number of promotions it actually had to give. The expenses of rewarding experienced staff were mitigated by keeping the percentage of experienced staff rather small. When the first Controller of the Telegraph Services, Francis Scudamore, had to explain to Parliament precisely why he was taking the radical step of hiring women for positions as telegraphists, he used this logic in his testimony, explaining explicitly and in detail how high rates of female quits would save the public treasury money by financing seniority increases for the remaining men.[5]

Scudamore's dream of high female quits was not meant to be. After the post office had filled its telegraph offices with women, they made an alarming discovery: The women enjoyed the high pay and the responsibility of telegraphy; very few wanted to leave. The quit rates in the first ten years were disappointingly low, with both men and women showing all the signs of making their telegraph positions the jobs they wanted to hold for the rest of their lives. The workers were becoming more and more experienced and more and more entitled to promotions. The post office had no idea how it was going to finance promotions for men and women alike.

One of the first moves was to cut the number of advancements that women would be entitled to. Within the telegraph service were two types of offices, those that transmitted within cities and those that transmitted between cities. Intercity transmission was much more difficult because long cables made connections tenuous; these difficult transmissions required workers to use sensitive and fragile equipment. Furthermore, because of the heavy volume of intercity communication, much of this work was done at night when the utilization rates of the lines were lower. In the original staffing of the telegraph service, men and women worked in within-city and intercity offices and were equally skilled at low-skill and high-skill transmission. Then one day by fiat all the women were moved out of the intercity offices and limited to simple within-city messages. Some men were allowed to stay in within-city galleries, but many were transferred to intercity lines.

This maneuver served two functions for the post office: Suddenly, most men who had been working day jobs in within-city offices found themselves doing intercity work; the newbies were generally given the midnight shift. Naturally, the men howled in protest, but this change did give the post office a free promotion. Those who worked sufficiently well could be "upgraded" to daytime hours (an improvement it cost the government nothing to give.)

The post office then used the technological complexity of intercity work to justify confining most of its promotions to men working in those offices. Women now "lacked the skills" that would justify their advancement in the service. Because all the women who had just been transferred to single-city offices had been operating intercity apparatus entirely adequately, the female operators thought this policy was outrageous. Many became discouraged and quit, which of course was the whole point of why this division of labor had been started in the first place.

Even with confinement to low-status jobs, the female quit rate was still not high enough to finance the necessary flow of male cash promotions. Because the post office found itself under pressure to find other measures that would induce women to cut short their careers, it developed the policy of a marriage bar. This was to become an extremely influential institution; it was imitated throughout the British economy and was paralleled in many other nations.

The post office passed a policy requiring all women to resign on the occasion of their marriage. Neither superior performance nor the approval of one's supervisors could be used as an exemption from mandatory severance. The post office typically hired new female job entrants at sixteen years of age; the average age of marriage in Britain at this period was twenty-eight. This new postal policy insured average careers of twelve years. This was long enough to remunerate the civil service for the cost of training women in telegraphy. It was, however, short enough to allow for no more than one or maybe two promotions for the average woman before she voluntarily took her exit and allowed for replacement with an entry-level worker.

A problem that remained, however, was that a woman who was dedicated to her career might opt for keeping her position by foreswearing marriage. Some women chose to work all their lives, even if this required remaining single. Being a spinster was not a socially valued role in Victorian England. Above and beyond the deprivation of both male companionship and children, there was the further burden of the stigma of being an "old maid." For some women, this was a cheap or even attractive price to pay. For other women, such a penalty would have been prohibitive. Many women who were ambivalent, or who just wanted a few more years of pay before taking on domestic life, could choose to defer marriage. A career woman could chose to work until age thirty-four, instead of age twenty-eight, and then start her family late.

The post office anticipated this problem and proactively arranged to make this option unattractive. A policy was instituted of giving women marriage dowries. Women (but not men) were given a month and a half of free salary when they announced their engagements. In today's currency, this could represent a payment of $2000. For a woman vacillating between the attractions of love and money, a $2000 bribe to choose love could have been compelling. The policy of marriage dowries is a vivid illustration of the value the post office placed on female resignations. Obviously, quits must have been worth more than $2000 to the civil service; otherwise they never would have instituted the policy.

Marriage bars, such as those imposed by the British General Post Office, were common in Europe from the inception of women's employment up through the middle of the twentieth century. A 1946 survey of major British employers found that every company in their sample, private and public sector alike, required women to retire on the occasion of marriage. Every one of these companies also had a marriage dowry program by which women received bonuses to encourage them to marry and leave. The sample included such prominent employers as the Bank of England, Cadbury Chocolate, British Overseas Airways, the British Broadcasting Company, and every major railway in the country. The study also found marriage bars and dowries in the civil services of Australia, Canada, and New Zealand (National Whitley Council 1946).

An International Labor Office study of discrimination against married women in 1962 also found an impressive array of marriage bars. Married women were generally barred from employment in Japan, the Netherlands, Finland, Ireland, and Italy. Within other nations, marriage bars existed in specific industries. Married women could not work as nurses in Australia or Belgium. They could not work as bank clerks in those countries, or in Greece, or in South Africa. They could not work in textile factories in Portugal, or in chemical factories in Belgium. Furthermore, some occupations had marriage bars virtually worldwide. Nearly every country imposed limits on married women working as teachers. There were comparable restrictions on married women working as flight attendants (International Labor Office 1962).

In the United States, outside of teaching and the airline industry, marriage bars were less common. In most historical periods, economic growth in the United States has been somewhat more vigorous than that observed in Europe; labor has generally been scarcer. (The booming supply of jobs in the United States and stagnant labor markets of Europe was the reason that all those immigrants came from Europe to settle in the United States in the first place.) The perennial shortage of laborers in the United States made employers much less likely than their European counterparts to engage in policies that would limited their access to qualified help.

When labor in the United States was in surplus, however, employers on their own developed policies of synthetic turnover similar to those that were used overseas; the high point of marriage bars in the United States was during the Great Depression. Not hiring married women was justified not only for its cost-saving potential, but out of a moral imperative to make jobs for married men (Scharf 1980). A 1936 survey by Purdue University found that 50 percent of the factories in the study and 61 percent of the offices surveyed had some sort of restriction on the hiring of married women. Forcible resignation was rarer, but existed nevertheless in 20 percent of factories and 31 percent of offices (Best 1938). A 1940 survey found limits on the employment of married women in 13 percent to 43 percent of all establishments, depending on the type of business (Shallcross 1940).

The most sophisticated and detailed analysis of synthetic turnover in the United States comes from Claudia Goldin (1990). Goldin reports that the approximately 55 percent of all school districts in the United States fired female schoolteachers when they married. In office work, approximately 25 percent of all clerical employers forced women to resign at marriage. The likelihood of a marriage bar was highest in the insurance industry, public utilities, and manufacturing; the lowest was in banking and investment.

In the United States, discrimination against married women declined precipitously in the 1950s. In 1951, only 9.4 percent of school districts would not retain single women when they married. Only airlines maintained any strict form of marriage bar, and this only for the occupation of flight attendant. Goldin points out that female labor was in high demand and that young female workers were hard to find. Due to declining fertility, the cohort of women aged from 16 to 24 was relatively small in the 1950s (Oppenheimer 1970); employers simply could not find enough young single women to meet their needs. With employment booming and vacancies waiting to be filled, companies had few choices other than to accept the widespread use of married women in female sex-typed jobs.

Today in the United States and Europe synthetic turnover is practically nonexistent; furthermore, there is no real prospect that synthetic turnover could emerge as a force in the United States in the next century. The demand for female employment that was spurred by the occupational changes of the 1950s and 1960s has remained with us. As modern economies de-industrialize, and increasing emphasis is placed on services rather than manufacturing, the occupational structure of advanced capitalist nations will favor the creation of female rather than male employment. The continued expansion of traditional female sex-typed jobs, along with the relaxation of gender boundaries in some traditionally male jobs, continues to create significant demand for female labor. Under these conditions, it is hard to see how employers could return to a status segregation system that involves the intentional shedding of qualified female labor.

In contrast, synthetic turnover continues to be important in the third world. Underdeveloped economies have a substantial supply of

surplus labor. Shedding qualified labor is not problematic, because vacancies can easily be filled with unemployed or underemployed workers
of any gender. In settings where traditional sex norms remain accepted,
it is easier to legitimate treating men and women differently based on
patriarchal ideologies.

Synthetic turnover will be most noticeable when surplus labor exists
with large bureaucracies that use seniority or tenure-based systems of
payment. Japan and South Korea represent prime settings for marriage
bars. In Japan, workers are generally paid by their age, rather than by
their narrow job title. Workers enter employment with a young person's
salary. Every year up to age fifty-five, they receive a pay increase based
on their calendar age. This represents an archetypical tenurebased
salary system, with obvious potential for steadily increasing personnel
costs over time. These policies become more expensive in the light of
Japan's long history of lifetime employment. Because Japanese workers
are rarely laid off, except for gross malfeasance or nonperformance of
duty, it is hard for employers to avoid paying the steady stream of seniority increases that are due to their labor force. Without some form of temporary unstable labor force, many Japanese firms would become economically nonviable.

In Japan, historically, and still to some degree today, there has been a
gendered division of labor, with men receiving lifetime employment and
women leaving employment when they marry; such a labor division allows for the provision of extensive training to male workers in a wide variety of technologies useful to the company. The supertraining of Japanese male workers, and their resulting high productivity, is a well-known
feature of the Japanese economic miracle. By contrast, women are confined to very low-status positions involving negligible skills. Their rapid
turnover keeps them cheap and suitable for easily replaceable positions,
that is, those involving only firm-general skill. High female turnover is
produced by marriage bars. Before the 1980s, Japanese companies had
explicit policies requiring the resignation of women upon marriage;
those policies have since become illegal. Marriage bars, however, continue to exist informally and are widespread. Japan's long-standing tradition of weak unions and negligible enforcement of workplace regulations make it feasible for firms to continue discriminating against
married women regardless of whatever laws may be on the books.

A similar condition exists in South Korea. South Korea is generally less
well-developed than Japan, giving it a larger pool of surplus labor. Its
large corporations share the Japanese policy of lifelong employment.[6]
Furthermore, a very large percentage of the economy is concentrated in
these large firms, where problems of overseniority and rising labor
costs are very real. In South Korea, informal marriage bars are generally

widespread. Female labor force participation in South Korea drops off extremely precipitously after marriage, a differential that reflects the official policies of the large Korean conglomerates (Brinton, Lee, and Parish 1995).

There is an exception that proves the rule: This exception is Taiwan. Taiwan is a rapidly developing economy with extensive opportunities for married women. Both countries are underdeveloped, but Taiwan has unemployment rates that are only half those observed in South Korea. Although neither country is rich, there is less surplus labor in Taiwan than in Korea. More important, however, Taiwanese employment is more likely to be located in small family firms. Small family firms do not have tenure-based salary scales or inflexible systems of remuneration that reward seniority. Workers' salaries are decided by managerial behest, with no guarantees and little bureaucracy. Furthermore, relatives of the owner, both male and female, can work unpaid or for very little. The greater flexibility and freedom from bureaucracy of Taiwanese firms eliminate any wage pressure from seniority-based systems. Thus, the motivation to engage in synthetic turnover is negligible. Married female labor-force participation in Taiwan is high and marriage bars are relatively rare (Brinton, Lee, and Parish 1995).

Synthetic turnover has been a historical factor of some importance in the West; it plays a role in some underdeveloped countries. Yet it is hardly the dominant force creating status inequities between men and women in the modern United States. If glass ceilings are not caused by human capital theory, and not caused by synthetic turnover, then just what does cause male-female status differentials?

Differential Visibility Models

Differential visibility models were developed by Rosabeth Moss Kanter to explain the differences in promotion and advancement among men and women executives in contemporary large U.S. corporations. Her *Men and Women of the Corporation* (1979) is one of the great classics of the sociology of gender, and rightly so. The book is one of the most profound and nuanced discussions of the promotion process ever written; it is filled with unusual and intelligent insights about corporate life in general and the struggle to get ahead in particular.

Rosabeth Moss Kanter's primary observation is that minorities have difficulty advancing in large bureaucracies. By minorities, however, she does not mean African Americans, or Hispanics, or ethnic groups per se. She is referring to anyone who belongs to a group that represents less than 50 percent of the people at the job site: being the only Texan in a New York workplace, being the only New Yorker in a Texan workplace, being the only white in a black workplace, or being the only opera lover in a country-and-western-lovers' workplace. Anything that makes an individual stand out represents a risk.

The risk exists because minorities are conspicuously visible. Whenever there is a group of people, everyone notices and pays attention to the one who is different. In a typical corporate "diversity" public relations photo, people look at the African American or female executive. In a rock and roll band of five guys and a girl, everyone looks at the girl. At political conventions, both parties schedule a lot of speeches by women and members of minorities, not only out of an attempt to self-interestedly appeal to those particular blocs of voters, but because people of all races and genders tend to pay more attention to the atypical speaker.

Visibility used well can be an enormous asset. However, it also represents a very real risk. Visibility is wonderful when you are performing well. Everyone takes note of your accomplishments and spreads tales of your triumphs to the highest circles. Often one of the laments of the nameless, faceless bureaucrat is that no one pays attention to what he is doing and that his great contributions go unacknowledged, soon to be lost to oblivion.

However, visibility is not so wonderful if you are not prepared to perform and everyone is watching you two weeks too early. Think about the phenomenon of undergraduates in a class where a paper is due, but they haven't written it yet. No one wants to be seen by the professor no matter that the profesor can figure out in two seconds who has or has not turned in a paper. Students cut class if this is practically possible; if they don't, they slide into the classroom invisibly, sit towards the back or off to the side, and they certainly don't engage the professor in conversation after class.

This aspect of life does not change when you enter the business world. Although there are fewer solo term papers and a lot more team projects in the corporate world, business is still a lot like school: It gives better rewards for good grades and worse punishments for flunking. Your superiors dump extraordinary amounts of work on you, with incredibly short deadlines, and you try to get it all done as best you can. Some of the jobs are well within your capacity and you can handle them with elan and flair. Other jobs are somewhat of a stretch, and you make a stab at them, even though this is an area where you may not be very good.

Visibility is advantageous when one always meets or exceeds one's target. Margaret Thatcher, the Tory prime minister of Britain, thrived on visibility. She was a woman with a forceful personality and a knack for winning elections; her high profile allowed her to rise quickly to the highest ranks of Britain's Conservative Party, an organization that is no bastion of politically correct feminism. Visibility is more problematic when you fail while everyone is watching. Few lawyers have been raked over the public coals as severely as Marcia Clark, the district attorney who lost the O. J. Simpson case.

What is ideal is not visibility but control over visibility. When one is not ready to perform, or is facing a bad objective performance, one wants the ability to hide, the ability to take one's mistakes and make them on the smallest, darkest, and most obscure stage. When one has an impending triumph, one wants the world and the universe to be fully aware of one's great accomplishments. White men have some control over their visibility by having the ability to disappear into the woodwork or come out into the limelight, depending on the circumstances. Women and minorities are always on center stage. If they can perform perfectly, this central placement guarantees them a rapid rise to the top. In some respects, this visibility gives them an advantage over white men. However, if they fail, their failure will become well known and their ability to engage in impression management will be quite limited.

Unfortunately, further considerations make minority members likely to fail, namely, the boundary heightening activities of majority members. In the chapter on occupational sex-typing, we reviewed the concept of homophily. People like interacting with people of their own kind, and this is especially the case when they are nervous about performance and need reassurance that they are doing the right thing.

When an outsider with a distinctive culture or style comes into a workgroup, this represents a potential challenge to the interactional style of the incumbents. A woman enters an office that is previously 100 percent white male. The men may wonder, "Can we continue spending all our free time discussing football scores?" "Will it be okay to tell dirty jokes?" "What about commenting on the physical attributes of workers in other departments?" "If she's feminist, what kind of things might we say that might get us into trouble?" If it is a black man instead, the football discussions might be viewed as being safe. However, there might still be plenty for the white men to worry about: "Will we be able to have candid discussions of politics?" "Are we about to be tagged as being politically incorrect?" "What if this new black guy screws up on the job? If I criticize him, will he call me a racist and complain to my boss?" Usually, with the passage of time, most of these interactional problems can be dealt with. Most people with functional social skills learn eventually how to maintain working relationships with a wide variety of people. However, at the beginning, the introduction of the new worker poses a problem for the office.

Majority members frequently react to such a stimulus by *boundary heightening* (Kanter's term). Boundary heightening means exaggerating the characteristics of a majority group as a way to make the new member feel as different as possible. When a woman enters the workplace, talk about sports goes up and not down. Sexual jokes and comments become overt rather than repressed. In some settings, the physicalization of the workplace can begin to approach sexual harassment. Derogatory comments about women or minorities are made publicly and loudly. The point is to see how the new member will react, and what they will do. If the new entrant quietly accedes and plays along with the group, he or she has demonstrated a position of little opposition. In doing so, however, the new entrant may have publicly accepted a subordinate position within the office hierarchy. If the new entrant becomes antagonistic, the group can avoid this person in the future because he or she is clearly combative and not one of the in-group. Self-respect may be maintained, but only at the cost of making enemies. There are diplomatic ways of handling such intentional abuse while maintaining both self-respect and good relations. Pulling off such a victory however, is nontrivially difficult.

The primary cost of boundary heightening is that it isolates the new entrant. Being without friends is not particularly a professional problem at college, where even the most solitary nerd can study for exams and write term papers without help. Being without friends *is* professionally dangerous in the commercial world. In business, information does not come from the library; it comes from people. If one does not have a wide-ranging network and receive input from lots of different people, one is at danger of being blindsided by new organizational developments.

Consider the hypothetical case of an office clique with some of their members having links to upper levels; these members get word that company headquarters is about to start a big burst of cost cutting. Everyone in the office has proposals due, and all the members of the social network are cutting their expenses to the bone. The social isolate is writing a technologically perfect proposal. In pure effectiveness, this proposal is vastly superior to anything his or her office mates are producing. When the entire office makes its presentations, the cheap, mediocre proposals of the network members are all well rewarded. The techie who wrote the effective but expensive proposal gets publicly dressed down by the divisional vice president. Not being well integrated into social networks undercuts one's political ability to get policies implemented. Deprived of information, one is likely to make poor choices and accidentally find oneself on the wrong side of a powerful alliance.

Network isolation increases the likelihood that a new worker will fail. The initial handicap from isolation may be relatively small. The trouble is that in business, small disadvantages cumulate. One of Kanter's most insightful discussions is about the importance of reputation in business. People who are reputed to be on the way up find all their obstacles eliminated. People who are reputed to be dead-ended find the obstacles they face multiplied. The absence of obstacles makes one a more effective worker and increases one's odds of further success. The presence of obstacles encourages pathological behavior, which gives further objective evidence for the perception that one is a loser.

Consider the subsequent history of an individual who is well connected into social networks and has received signs of promotion to high places. Kanter refers to such individuals as "fast-trackers" or "water-walkers." Everyone wants to help out a fast-tracker. When a superstar advances, he is likely to have the opportunity to take along members of his team. If you are indispensable to the future company president, when he gets promoted, you are likely to become a vice president. Therefore, employees work really hard for the fast-tracker and give him their best and most devoted performances. Furthermore, with a shiny future assured, the fast-tracker can afford to make compromises. The fast-tracker knows that he will continue to have significant input into all sorts of decisions and is therefore generous in making promises to other people in return for their cooperation. The human resources person whose one goal in life is to implement a cafeteria-style benefit plan knows that helping the water-walker may result in a friend of cafeteria-style benefits in the future.[7] With subordinates and peers cooperating every step of the way, the water-walker becomes objectively effective; because of good performance and accomplishments, the water-walker has become a serious and deserving candidate for further promotion.

Now consider a social isolate, a female supervisor, who has had one noticeable public failure (or, for that matter, consider a minority member, a female, whose prospects are dim because she is a member of the wrong group). There is no reason for subordinates to do more than the bare minimum for this supervisor, who is not advancing any time soon; her workers can count on no particular reward for doing a good job. The minority member discovers that her subordinates aren't doing anything, so she has to give them bad evaluations and criticize them. She gets a reputation as a screamer and for being a hard boss to work for, which further lowers the morale and productivity of the workers underneath her. Peers in other offices have no motivations to make concessions on her behalf. A sacrifice on a political issue on behalf of the minority member is not likely to produce a parallel benefit when the minority gets into power because the minority may never get into power. Thus the woman in question may find nothing but stonewalling and noncooperation from other offices in the company. Because the poor performance of her subordinates and the lack of support from other offices is draining away her organizational power, she is forced to cling to whatever legal remnants of authority she has remaining. In interoffice disputes, she must be extremely defensive of turf. She cannot afford to share information because that would support the work of rivals who will rise over her head and undercut her own projects. All of this generates a reputation for the woman as being a difficult person to work with and an obstacle to getting things done. The woman is now objectively a bad team member and a bad corporate performer. At this point, her lack of accomplishments is now objective on the record. She is legitimately a poor performer and deserves nonpromotion or firing.

Kanter's argument about how perceptions of future promotion affect present day productivity is intelligent and important. The argument gains further force when Kanter discusses the role of past hires on future hires. One of the problems with being a minority member is that people judge the performance of your entire group on your personal performance. Because they have seen a zillion white men, they know that all white men are different and that each performance reflects only the attributes of an individual. Hiring the first black vice president of finance, or the first female football coach, is a precedent-setting act. No one has done anything like this before, so everyone is watching to see if the new hire works out. If the first female football coach is a success, this opens the door for many other women to become football coaches at other institutions. If the first female football coach bombs, everyone is going to throw that example in the face of the general manager who dares to suggest hiring a second.

Thus when minority managers fail as a result of an inability to avoid visibility or the heightening of boundaries by members of the network, their failure becomes part of corporate mythology. The objective features of their underperformance provide credible support for discriminatory workers who want to argue that women and minorities are not qualified for high-status positions. It is possible to argue against such objections. Everyone knows that performance is an attribute of individuals and not entire groups. But that said, the presence of a bad precedent slows down the rate of future promotion of other people in that group.

So how do women and ethnic minorities break into the higher ranks of management? Kanter argues that to some extent it is a numbers game. Although minority workers are handicapped in their attempts to compete with white males in management, this handicap is not an absolute barrier to success. Over time, ultimately, some woman or minority will be the conspicuously successful example that becomes part of corporate mythology; black and female hires will become acceptable again.

Furthermore, the continued hiring of women and minorities at low levels, even by managers who have no intention of promoting them, can help provide support for future advancement. As the numbers shift from 99–1 to 80–20 or 70–30, the minority members can provide enough of a critical mass to form their own social networks. They can pool information among themselves, collect tips they have been able to gather from individual contacts with superiors, and map out survival strategies for the group. Joint support allows them to compare what works and what doesn't work as far as dealing with boundary behavior; joint support also allows them to provide a "safe place" where workers can relax and be frank without having to manage more fragile intergroup relationships. Furthermore, when by simple law of averages some members of the minority group are able to advance, they can use their clout to improve conditions for the rest of the group (within the limits of the high visibility and extreme boundary-heightening activities that will be manifest every time a minority member enters another new domain).

Kanter's theory is not only stimulating but it has empirical support. Kanter herself was a qualitative rather than quantitative scholar. Her data came purely from anecdotes from one particular Fortune 500 corporation, but her predictions have been borne out by more scientific tests. Cohen, Broschak, and Haveman (1998) studied the career advancement of female managers in California savings and loan associations. This has been a relatively favorable environment for women managers; it has undergone dramatic feminization in the reaches of upper management. Their first finding was that the odds of a woman being promoted to a managerial position depended on the percentage of women that were already in that very job title. If there were no women in a given position, or only a few, it was difficult to get another woman promoted to that position. Once a large number of women had already reached that rank, however, the odds of further promotion of women vastly increased. In the no-female settings, all-male managers preserved homophily. In the low-female settings, the presence of one or two tokens did little to help other women. It was only when a critical support mass of women existed and the deleterious effects of early nonperformers could be erased by later performers that jobs for women opened up at these ranks.

The odds of a woman being promoted depended on the percentage of women working in the level above the focal position. This was a curvilinear relationship. Women were unlikely to be promoted if the next level above the one they wished to be promoted to either was staffed by very few women or was staffed by many women. The best situation was to have a noticeable minority of women supervisors, ideally about 20 percent. Cohen et al. argue that if the number of female supervisors is too low, women simply don't have the clout to get women hired into the lower position. However, once the percentage of female supervisors gets too high, women stop behaving as a strategic interest group furthering each other's needs and begin to act in a gender-neutral fashion.

Female promotions are more likely to occur when there is a limited minority of female supervisors, who out of a concern for defensively protecting the interests of women are likely to hire other women who could be possible allies.

Konrad and Pfeffer (1991) report similar findings for women and minorities in university administration. Konrad and Pfeffer did not do the nuanced contrasts between small and large minorities that can be found in Cohen et al.'s analysis. However, they did find that the percentage of women in a given job, the percentage of women in higher administration, and whether the previous occupant of a job was a woman all predicted whether any given hire in higher educational administration was a woman. When they replicated the analysis for nonwhites, all the findings repeated; relationships were even stronger than those found for gender. It is hard for women and blacks to get hired where there are no women and blacks.

Further support for Kanter's reasoning comes from Kay and Hagan's (1998) work on Ontario lawyers. Kay and Hagan examined the rates at which male and female attorneys were promoted to partner. In general, the majority of Ontario lawyers do not make partner. Superior performance is generally required. They found that average-performing men were more likely to be promoted than were average-performing women. Men with mediocre performance were more likely to be promoted than women with mediocre performance. Women with exceptional performance, however, were more likely to be promoted than men with exceptional performance. This is consistent with Kanter's discussion of differential visibility. When average or mediocre women generate average or mediocre results, this becomes generally noticed; because women are visible, it is harder for them than for men to hide disappointing results, and this lowers their promotion rates. By contrast, everybody notices an outstanding woman. The female superstars parlayed their visibility and performance into rates of promotion higher than those enjoyed by male superstars because news of their triumphs was immediately publicized and well known.

Differential visibility is an appealing theory. However, it cannot be a general explanation of low female occupational status. It narrowly refers to how the exclusion of women from high-status jobs keeps women from obtaining future high-status jobs. It does not tell us why women were excluded from these positions in the first place. Furthermore, the barriers to advancement in these theories are relatively permeable. All one needs is one success or a handful of allies and the negative impressions associated with minority status begin to evaporate. This may reflect the improving prospects of women and minorities in management in the contemporary environment. Yet such an approach makes it hard to explain why the exclusion of women from good jobs was such a permanent and enduring feature of industrial employment for such a long time. To deal with the deeper questions of how women came to be excluded from high-status occupations, one needs to invoke other theories of gender dynamics.

The Simplest Theory: Employee Discrimination

The theories we have discussed in the last three sections are relatively complex. Sometimes, however, life is simple. Women are excluded from high-status positions because high-status men have the ability to exclude them. Low-status men would like to exclude women as well, but they simply don't have the power to restrict women from their occupations.

There are lots of reasons why men could want to oppose women entering their occupations. It is plausible to argue that men view work as an expression of masculinity, just as home and child care can in some contexts be expressions of femininity. The introduction of women threatens the identity of men as men by invading the province that defines their gender (Hartmann 1976; Rose 1992). Parallel arguments could be made about technological competence and craft: Men would have no objection to women working but would object to the feminization of the manly skills that define their special masculine competence (Cockburn 1988). One can also follow Rosabeth Moss Kanter (1977) in arguing that the introduction of women to a male workplace threatens homophily and creates the potential for social disharmony. There are some workplaces where clearly all this occurs.

In general, though, it is wise to treat status-based arguments with some skepticism. Men do not need to exclude women either to display masculinity or to manifest power. Males are more than capable of demonstrating masculinity in mixed-sex settings. Consider that there is no shortage of macho and gender display in the average dance hall. Furthermore, the introduction of women to the U.S. armed forces has had almost no effect on the masculine "rough, tough" image of the modern soldier (Williams 1989). It is equally easy to create patterns of status and dominance-submission within work settings even with mixed-gender groups at both top and bottom. There is no doubt as to who are the members of the board of directors and who are the underlings, even if the board is split fifty-fifty by gender.

The simplest and most compelling arguments about the exclusion of women don't involve status. They involve money. From a selfish financial standpoint, many reasons exist for men to be opposed to the feminization of their occupations, even if the men are feminists themselves.

It is always in the interest of any small set of workers to restrict entry into their occupation so long as that set of workers has the power to compellingly enforce their preference. Wages are set in the market by the forces of supply and demand. To the extent that there is a large supply of workers who can do a given job, those workers will compete with each other and bid each other's price down, producing a relatively low market wage. If the supply of workers who can do that job is instead limited, then the current officeholders will have a relative monopoly on their jobs. The reduced number of competitors will produce only minimal market pressure to lower wages. The employer will find him or herself having to choose among a small number of qualified job candidates, all of whom are demanding a top salary. Scarce labor makes wages rise.

Note that while it is in every worker's interest to maintain such an exclusionary position, most workers do not have the power to enforce these preferences on their employers. Entry to most jobs is controlled by management, not by labor. It is in management's interest to hire from as broad a pool as possible. In many cases, management will ignore workers' self-interest demands for restricted recruiting, find the qualified candidates they want who will work for the least, and hire those candidates, be they red, green, or purple.

Few workers have the ability to keep an employer from hiring an employee they don't want. In general, in the United States, management controls who is hired and fired by most firms. Most workers in the United States are not unionized. With no viable strike threat, the leverage they have over their employers is negligible. Unionized workers rarely have any input into hiring concessions. Even relatively powerful unions, such as the United Auto Workers, are limited in their bargaining power to discussions of pay, fringes, and working conditions. In a pinch, the union may be able to obtain preferential hiring rights for formerly laid-off workers. They are in no shape to dictate what genders or ethnic groups will be considered for outside hires. [8]

There are, however, three exceptions to the rule that workers do not control access to their occupations. The first exception is professionals. Professionals, such as doctors, lawyers, and university professors, can determine who is or is not allowed to work in their occupations by using two separate mechanisms. The first is through guild control of training. In most occupations, either outsiders or capitalists control the training sites where skills are obtained. Some skills are obtained in public schools, which are run by school teachers rather than by workers. Others are obtained on the job, where management controls the overall training process. Professional skills are taught in professional schools where members of that profession determine who is or is not qualified to practice. Doctors run medical schools. Lawyers run law schools. Engineers run engineering schools. If the occupation were to choose not to admit a given group into their training schools, that group would be permanently barred from the profession. Certain occupations add another level of craft control of entry with standardized exams. One can't practice medicine without passing a state medical exam or practice law without passing the bar exam; exams become another screen by which professionals determine who works in their professions (Caplow 1954; Form and Miller 1964).

The most important control over employment, however, occurs in the actual hiring process. Professional firms are run collegially: Members of the firm vote on whom to hire or not to hire. Sometimes, as in academic departments, everybody votes (or at least everybody on tenure track). Sometimes only the top members of the firm vote (such as law partners). Note, however, that voting for job candidates is different from the normal process in business where a manager or a small set of managers hires with full individual discretion without having to subject the matter to a vote. In the upper professions, workers basically administer themselves as opposed to normal industrial employment, where managers control the workers underneath them. [An intermediate case consists of semi-professions such as librarian where, despite librarian control over library schools, hiring is done in a bureaucracy by a boss.] Worker control facilitates hiring policies based on maintaining the wage levels of incumbent workers rather than finding the cheapest source of labor possible. Professional settings thus encourage discriminatory hiring when this can be made consistent with maintaining a scarce supply of professional labor.

The second occupation that can control entry into its own ranks is, ironically, management itself. Executives hire other executives. They do not have an interest in obtaining the cheapest possible managers because this would dilute the overall supervisory labor pool and ultimately lower the salaries of the very officers who brought in inexpensive managers in the first place. Managers are thus faced with a conflict of interest between reducing the overall costs to their firms and acting to increase the overall pool of managerial salaries. Hiring women and minorities would allow them to obtain top-level administrators at 59 cents to the dollar and reduce personnel expenses. Hiring only white men maintains the demand for white male managers and insures robust salaries for these executives. It should not be surprising that the same executives who vote themselves generous stock options, golden parachutes, and multimillion-dollar incentive schemes would also attempt to restrict the supply of possible competitors to maintain higher-than-market levels of remuneration.

The third and least common example is highly skilled craft workers. Some artisanal workers have been able to maintain control over their apprenticeship programs and thus control entry into their occupations. Classical musicians fit this description, as do some construction workers such as electricians and plumbers. This control over apprenticeship is fairly fragile, however. If outsiders can learn how to play the violin or to install plumbing without obtaining the approved training, and the public is willing to pay for these outsiders' services, the power associated with apprenticeship control is limited. Country and western fiddle players are not especially constrained by their lack of training at the Julliard Conservatory, even though that or a similar credential may be needed to play in the Philadelphia Symphony Orchestra. Likewise, although some construction jobs specify union labor, many homes get built by nonunion workers, who may or may not be as qualified as those with proper union training.

The evidence that men have tried to exclude women from entry into their occupations is copious. There have been extended battles over the introduction of women into textiles, carpet making, printing, cigar making, papermaking, clerical work, bar tending, automobile assembly, furniture making, medicine, nursing, and many other settings. To read in the history of women's work is to read tales of women being introduced to an occupation, encountering male resistance, and then being either thrown out of the trade or forced in by the use of managerial power. Alternatively, women are already in an occupation, men decide they want them out, and after a successful campaign, women's work is restricted or eliminated (Kessler-Harris 1982; Baron 1991; Cobble 1991; Rose 1992; Gabin 1990; Cohn 1985).

A typical example can be found in medicine. An excellent discussion of the issues involved can be found in Mary Roth Walsh's outstanding history of the history of women physicians: *"Doctors Wanted: No Women Need Apply"—Sexual Barriers in the Medical Profession 1835–1970* (1977). Until 1900, fewer than 5 percent of all physicians were women. That number had only risen to 7.2 percent by 1970. (Note that after Walsh's book was written, the occupation rapidly feminized. In 1997, 25 percent of all doctors were female. However, for one hundred and seventy years the percentage of women physicians was extremely low. The main point of her analysis is to explain this historical exclusion).

Doctors have had excellent means for controlling entry into their occupation. Today, they have absolute control over membership of the profession through licensing. If one does not pass the appropriate state medical examinations, one may not legally practice medicine in the United States. In the nineteenth century, licensing requirements were substantially looser. In many states, anyone who wanted to could just open up an office, call themselves a doctor, and treat any willing patient (or victim) who walked through the doors.

Even in this laissez-faire environment, physicians had ways of restricting access into their field. They could refuse entrance into local medical societies. Membership in medical societies was an important credential of quality, and doctors outside those societies would have encountered obstacles in attracting clients. They could refuse entry into medical schools. In the nineteenth century, more than a few doctors were self-taught or had rudimentary training. The current tradition of doctors displaying their diplomas on their office walls dates back to the nineteenth century when patients really did examine all the certificates on the wall to see if their doctor was any good. Doctors also refer patients to each other for further treatment. Even today, doctors can severely hamper or restrict the practice of someone they don't like simply by not sending the outcast any patients. This is especially lethal for specialists such as surgeons, who get most of their patients by referral from general practice physicians.

Historically, doctors have made use of all these means to restrict competition from female physicians. In the early nineteenth century, the use of such devices was not especially important. There was a rough division of labor in the early nineteenth century between allopathic male doctors and female midwives. Allopathic means using mainstream scientific techniques; most of the normal medical doctors and surgeons in practice today are allopathic. Women tended to train for midwife rather than allopathic positions because the intimate female nature of midwifing duties gave the women strong marketing advantages in this area. In the mid-nineteenth century, however, the science of obstetrics and gynecology made dramatic inroads, making allopathic doctors much more effective in providing childbirth services. Female midwives found themselves being driven out of business. This was not out of any particularly sexist exclusion by the doctors themselves, but because women as consumers preferred allopathic doctors whose new techniques promised safer, more risk-free deliveries.

The trouble emerged when women practitioners sought to follow the market trends and train as allopathic doctors rather than as midwives. The male medical profession put up every conceivable barrier to maintain this market for themselves. Women were systematically denied entry into most of the major U.S. medical schools. For a woman to obtain medical training, she had to be foreign-born, or had to travel overseas to get an education. Zurich and Paris became particularly important locations for the training of women doctors from the United States, but the openings in these locations were limited (Bonner 1992). There were a number of women's medical colleges in the United States; these institutions had real problems attracting qualified faculty (meaning many men wouldn't teach there). As a result, many of these schools earned a legitimate reputation for providing substandard training, further limiting women's capacity to obtain necessary skills.

Some of the antifeminist campaigns were more colorful than others. When, in 1869, some feminist male doctors invited female colleagues to attend clinical lectures at Philadelphia's Pennsylvania Hospital, male medical students objected. During the first class, the male students waited until the last hour of lecture and then showered the women with a nonstop barrage of paper airplanes, tinfoil balls, and tobacco quids. After all attempts to maintain order failed, the hospital canceled any further attempt to coeducate clinical sections. The story illustrates both the intensity of the antifeminist feelings of Philadelphia's medical students and the lukewarmness of the sympathies of feminist doctors, who did little to support the women and backed down at the first sign of male resistance.

The same exclusionary treatment that women received in medical schools was repeated in state medical societies. The Massachusetts Medical Association, for example, did not admit any women to its ranks until 1884, although qualified women doctors with testimonials from the most prestigious male doctors in the state had been trying to obtain entry for the previous thirty-two years. Even after that, it had maintained a policy of admitting only a small number of exemplary female physicians to its ranks to differentiate them from the large mass of "unqualified" female doctors.

Although it is hard to tell, there probably were similar exclusionary patterns in referrals as well. Walsh's book is replete with examples of prominent doctors who had worked with female physicians, or even supported their admittance to medical schools or medical societies, nevertheless making speeches or publishing articles condemning the unsuitability of women as physicians. The most common argument used was that women's menstrual cycles made them unfit to be doctors because during their premenstrual days they would not be rational enough to treat patients. The discussions of female hormonal cycles in this literature tend towards the gothic with purple prose descriptions of the incapacitating effects of menstruation on all aspects of female functioning. A national convention of the American Medical Association (AMA) in San Francisco devolved into a shouting match when advocates of the monthly menstrual incapacity of female physicians were countered by a male physician who noted the daily cycles of incapacitation experienced by men doctors who drink.

The twentieth century actually produced retrogression rather than progress. The handful of medical schools that had opened to women in the nineteenth century reduced their offerings in the early 1900s. At Tufts, the faculty found that their top medical students were all women and that the men were forced into shyness and awkwardness through having to compete with females. The faculty's solution was to ban women from the main medical program and put them in an inferior, underfunded female college. More commonly, medical schools opened up their ranks de jure to women but in practice maintained strict quotas limiting female admissions. Some medical schools, Yale and Emory among them, cited explicit discriminatory policies against women in their promotional literature. In other cases, the evidence for these comes from the oral testimonies of actual deans. Among some of the quotes Walsh provides from midcentury medical school deans are the following:

"Hell, yes, we have a quota.... We do keep women out when we can." (1961 Dean)

"We have a six percent quota for women and we give priority to men." (1946 Dean paraphrased for use here)

"Yes, indeed, we take women, and we don't want the one woman we take to be lonesome, so we take two per class."

(Actual quote, anonymous medical school spokesman, no date)

Why did male doctors do this? Some of this may have been due to a principled belief in male supremacy. Some of this may have stemmed from Kanterian bad experiences with one or two highly visible female doctors. However, much of this is likely to have been an economically motivated attempt to restrict the occupation of physician to the smallest number of applicants. Walsh provides damning examples of male doctors' fears that they would be supplanted by female competition. The Tufts story is a conspicuous example of protecting men from better-performing female rivals. Walsh also provides cartoons from the 1870s with strongly economic themes. In one, a prosperous lady doctor in a horse and carriage stops on the road next to a male doctor whose bad fortune has reduced him to walking. The caption reads: "Miss Manbury M.D. to her unsuccessful competitor: Doctor, let me give you a lift." Note as well the name the cartoonist gave the lady doctor. Another cartoon titled "Ten Years Hence" shows a rich woman physician riding down the street on a fine steed while her impoverished foot-bound competitors watch. Even more galling, behind the lady doctor rides her well-dressed black servant. The unsubtle message of the cartoon is that if women doctors prosper, male doctors will be reduced to a status lower than Negroes.

Consider as well the following satiric Scottish poem that appeared in the *Boston Medical and Surgical Journal:*

An' when the leddies git degrees,
Depen' upon't there's nocht'll please
Till they hae got oor chairs an' fees,
An' there's an en / o' you an' me.

Fortunately, Walsh's book is now somewhat outdated. The prospects of women physicians improved dramatically in the 1970s, 1980s and 1990s. The driving factor was affirmative action. It became illegal for medical societies and medical schools to bar women candidates because of gender. Furthermore, as Walsh herself notes, large medical research hospitals became increasingly dependent on federal research dollars. Because participation in federal funding is contingent upon compliance with affirmative action, medical schools began to aggressively promote female advancement.

Note that just as the original justification for keeping women out was economic, so was the rationale for bringing women in. Restricting women's role in medicine reduced the overall supply of doctors and thus maintained high fees and salaries for men. Such policies may have come under challenge with the increase in competent foreign-trained doctors in the United States and with the growing concern among corporations for stemming increased health care costs. The financial incentives to medical centers to obtain federal research dollars, however, also helped promote affirmative action, a consideration that may have been important to the financial health of many hospitals but that would have had different repercussions if seen narrowly as a question of regulating labor supply. The linkage of the incomes of elite doctors to considerations other than the mere number of doctors in the labor market helped to undercut the medical profession's own financial incentives to restrict women (or at least the incentives of the subset of doctors who control entry into medical training). Furthermore, as I mentioned before, a changing legal environment weakened the ability of doctors to control entry into their craft by eliminating the most blatant forms of gender exclusion.

Conclusion

Thus the medical case clearly supports the larger conclusions of this chapter. Women's confinement to low-status jobs is primarily a function of employee discrimination. The exclusion of women from medicine had an economic motivation; it was also linked to the degree to which doctors had power to control entry into their occupation. Human capital considerations are not likely to be relevant in this case. Most medical knowledge is firm-general rather than firm-specific. Doctors can carry their knowledge wherever they go. Medical partnerships do not pay for training; doctors pay for training themselves, eliminating any financial incentive not to hire women. Synthetic turnover cannot explain the exclusion of women from employment because doctors are not paid with tenure-based salary scales, so there is no problem with "over-senior" workers in medicine. Differential visibility may have had some impact in reducing female access to medical training. Walsh, however, cites ample examples of prominent women doctors who were universally acclaimed by male and female observers alike (even if the sexists claimed such women were exceptions). Differential visibility of female incompetence would also seem to jar with the evidence from the Tufts story, where women were barred from medical school because they were *too* competent, rather than not competent enough. Employee discrimination, with its emphasis on economic motivations and worker power, seems to resonate with all aspects of the experience of women in medicine. If this theory were to prove generally correct, it would also explain women's lack of access to other high-status professions, to skilled blue-collar work, and to the upper ranks of corporate management.

Notes

1. Of course, politically committed readers who are interested in equality for its own sake need no further justification for talking about theories of inequality.

2. The argument in the following seven paragraphs is drawn largely from Becker (1971).

3. This section is a condensed version of a longer discussion in Cohn (1985).

4. The description that follows closely parallels what Richard Edwards refers to in his *Contested Terrain* (1979) as superbureaucracy. Although the label given here is more accurate, the dynamics of promotion and incentives are drawn almost entirely from Edwards's discussion.

5. United Kingdom, House of Commons Sessional Papers, Vol. XXXVII, 1871, pp. 703–852.

6. In the 1990s this policy has been weakened although not eliminated.

7. Cafeteria-style benefits are a compensation package in which workers don't receive a fixed set of fringe benefits but may choose individualized options from an elaborate menu.

8. The best discussions of unions' capacity to discriminate are written in the context of race rather than gender. However, the same strength based argument applies to both groups. An elegant statement of the position in this paragraph can be found in Ashenfelter (1971), and a more discursive account of the same logic can be found throughout Marshall (1965).

5 Why Are Women Paid Less Than Men?

It used to be said that women are paid 59¢ to the dollar. In the 1990s, women are paid nearly 75¢ to the dollar. The basic principle, however, still holds: Women are paid less than men. Understanding why women are paid less than men gets at the heart of the economic basis of gender differences. If females were paid the same as males, it would matter much less whether they worked in the same types of jobs as males. Even if they were systematically deprived of organizational power, they would earn the same incomes as men, and therefore not be as dependent on men in their domestic lives. The financial basis of patriarchy in the home would be significantly reduced (although not eliminated, because gender differences might still persist in unemployment).

This chapter will lay out three standard explanations of gendered pay differentials and one nonstandard explanation. All these factors probably contribute in some way to accounting for why women are paid less than men. That said, the best single explanation is probably one of the standard ones, the *overcrowding hypothesis*. The logic of the overcrowding hypothesis is compelling, and it is backed by strong empirical support. The other two standard explanations, *human capital theory* and *comparable worth theory* have logical problems that make them less than fully satisfactory. They do have some support within the data, however, and as such cannot be dismissed in their entirety.

The nonstandard explanation developed here within the feminist neoclassical tradition, is called *production constraint theory*. Production constraint theory argues that men are paid more than women because men systematically lower women's productivity. Note that the claim is not that men systematically undervalue women's productivity; that argument is traditional comparable worth theory. I am saying that men lower women's real, physical, objective productivity. Women are placed in structured situations, which makes them less useful to their employers. They end up being paid less through no fault of their own. Traditional neoclassical wage theory argues that wages are linked to the productivity of workers. Productivity does not explain 100 percent of what occurs in wage setting, but the output of workers is not irrelevant in determining how much workers get in their paychecks. As such, any patriarchal arrangement that prevents women from producing economic value with their labor will affect their salaries adversely. In the crudest sense, men earn more than women because they sabotage the competition.

The discussion deals with the three standard explanations first. These are the most famous, the most important, and often the least well understood, even by professional writers in the field. The overcrowding hypothesis often fails to get the respect that it is due, yet at the same time people gloss over the more glaring problems with human capital and comparable worth theory. We then turn to the juicier stuff of feminist neoclassical theory and discuss how men solidify their own relative economic positions by limiting and expropriating the products of women workers.

The Overcrowding Hypothesis — *either women's wages will be driven into the ground, or be ridiculously high*

The overcrowding hypothesis is one of the oldest theories of gendered pay differentials. It was first put forward by Millicent Fawcett in 1918, and then restated in more neoclassical form by F.Y. Edgeworth in 1922. Most of the social scientific writing on gender from the 1910s and 1920s is now hopelessly outdated and inconsistent with modern evidence. The ideas of Fawcett and Edgeworth have survived well.[1]

The overcrowding hypothesis is a variation on traditional economic models of supply and demand. Because taking an economics course is not a prerequisite for buying this book, it is useful to review the basic mechanics of the interaction of supply and demand before moving to the twists added by Fawcett and Edgeworth.

The supply of labor is more or less the number of workers willing to take a job and the demand for labor is the number of workers that employers are willing to take to fill jobs.[2] Wages will be determined by the difference between the supply and the demand for labor. When there are a zillion workers and only fourteen jobs, those zillion workers will be desperate to get one of those fourteen jobs. If one worker offers to do the job for $5 an hour, one of his competitors will offer $4.95. The next one will offer $4.90; the next $4.85, and so on and so forth. The wages will continue to drop until they reach a level that is so low that only fourteen people in the labor force will take the job. That said, the fourteen workers working for 0.5¢ an hour are happy (well, maybe not ecstatic, but they know they got the best deal available); the employer has his jobs filled. The situation has reached a stable equilibrium.

Now reverse the situation. A zillion jobs need to be filled, and only fourteen people in the world who are willing or qualified to do them. Now it is the employers who are desperate and will have to pay any price to attract candidates. The bidding war of salaries to attract the fourteen workers goes up and up until finally equilibrium is reached when the fourteen most desperate firms pony up $20 million a year for each worker, and no one else wants to match that price.

The general principle should be clear: Assuming the same number of workers, the more jobs that exist, the higher the pay. Assuming the same number of jobs, the more workers that exist, the lower the pay.

Now consider a world where men and women want to work and have jobs. Biologically, there are almost an equal number of men and women, so the supply of labor of both sexes is the same; As a result of occupational sex-typing, however, men can work only in men's jobs and women can work only in women's jobs. How would this affect men and women's wages?

If the number of jobs open to men and women were the same, occupational sex-typing would have no effect on wages whatsoever. The labor market would be split into two halves, one masculine and one feminine. Within each one, the ratio of workers to jobs would be the same, and, therefore, the equilibrium wage would be the same.

Now let's change the assumptions. In this world, men are allowed to work in 80 percent of the jobs and women are allowed to work in 20 percent of the jobs. The number of men is equal to the number of women. Now enormous gender disparities are created in wages. In the masculine sector, 50 percent of the population is being sought after by 80 percent of the employers. The employers will bid up male wages to a high level because, overall, male workers are comparatively scarce. In the feminine sector, 50 percent of the population is competing with each other to obtain a scant 20 percent of the jobs. There is a vast oversupply of labor. The employers are thus enjoying a buyers' market: They can negotiate wages down to a bare minimum. In this world, men will have high wages and women will have low wages—a reasonable fit to contemporary data.

Of course, the real world is not nearly as tidy as the simplified world of the overcrowding hypothesis. In the real world, not every man and every woman wants to work. Some observed withdrawals from the labor force are gender neutral. Some severely disabled people are not interested in holding full-time jobs; disability, however, affects men and women equally. Some lazy people are not interested in holding full-time jobs; laziness is common to both sexes.

The one cause of withdrawal from the labor force that is not gender neutral is childbearing and child care. When a baby comes into a family, the woman is more likely to stay home and take care of it than is a man. To be sure, this difference can be exaggerated. If women had superlative opportunities in the labor force, and if men were constrained in their upward mobility, the gender differential might be reversed. In societies with no history of traditional family values, it might also be possible for more men than women to stay home. In most capitalist and precapitalist societies, however, economic opportunities for men are better than for women. In addition, these same societies usually have some cultural tradition of female domesticity. Thus, although it is absolutely the case that not all women want to stay home with their babies after childbirth, it is also the case that more women want to stay home than do men. At any given time, the size of the female labor force will be generally smaller than that of the male labor force.

Fertility-based withdrawl from the labor force provides a nontrivial complication for overcrowding theory. It makes all the difference in the world exactly how much larger the female labor force is relative to the male labor force, and it makes just as much difference exactly how much larger the female pool of jobs is relative to the male pool of jobs. In a world where 100 percent of all men want to work, but only 90 percent of all women, and where 93 percent of all jobs are reserved for men, but only 7 percent for women, then severe overcrowding would exist. This 100 percent of men could pick from 93 percent of all jobs; the 90 percent of women could pick from only 7 percent of all jobs. The feminine sector would be catastrophically overcrowded and female wages would plummet.

Imagine, though, another scenario where 100 percent of all men want jobs but only 10 percent of all women want jobs. Furthermore, 55 percent of all jobs are reserved for men and 45 percent of all jobs are reserved for women. One hundred percent of all men are trying to pick from 53 percent of all jobs and 10 percent of all women are trying to fit into 45 percent of all jobs. The 10–45 discrepancy means a vast undersupply of female labor will put women workers in extraordinary demand. In this world, the overcrowding hypothesis would suggest a huge wage advantage for women!

So what is the situation in the real world? It is actually hard to tell. We can roughly estimate the jobs open to men and women by observing the gender of the jobs that are currently filled. This is not a perfect measure because some jobs might be open to workers of either sex; that said, the measure is probably good enough. The main problem is estimating the size of male and female labor forces: Many people who would otherwise work become discouraged and drop out of the labor force because they believe no jobs are available to them. In one of the earlier scenarios I described in which 90 percent of all women wanted to work but only 7 percent of jobs were open to them, the overcrowding of the female labor market was catastrophic.

The vast majority of women in this setting are not going to find work. It is unrealistic to expect that the surplus women will spend their time reading the want ads and going to job interviews when the odds of their finding employment are pathetically small. Most workers under these conditions will stop looking for work and find something else to do with their time. They will have children, or go back to school, or take up painting, or become active in church, or engage in some form of activity that is not related to paid employment.

If you ask these women why they are engaging in these activities, they will not tell you they are doing this only because they could not find jobs. Most people react to life's disappointments by coming up with some positive reason for why they are glad events worked out the way they did. Few men will say they married Marilyn because Abbie rejected them, even if Abbie was the love of their life. Few accountants will say they chose bookkeeping because Hollywood wouldn't touch them, even if in reality they would drop it all to become movie stars in a New York minute. We always praise our current lot and deprecate alternatives we can't have because it is no fun to live life as a frustrated loser. That said, these statements of preferences are merely sour grapes. If the world were to change, our interest in Abbie, Hollywood, and table grapes would reemerge instantaneously.

Women's statements of disinterest in employment need to be viewed in this light. In societies where female opportunities are scarce, some women really don't want jobs. Other women do want jobs but have learned it is better not to want what you can't have. It is virtually impossible to know whether any given woman is one type or the other.[3] Given that, we will never know how many women would work if the labor market offered them attractive employment possibilities. Without knowing the true number of women workers, we will never really know if female overcrowding exists in any real economy.

So why under these circumstances is overcrowding considered to be a useful theory? First, because it is logically compelling, and second, because it works empirically.

From a theoretical standpoint, overcrowding theory is appealing because it is based on the commonsense operation of supply and demand. Few authors would want to challenge the argument that when workers are relatively scarce, the pay of the average worker goes up and when workers are relatively plentiful, the pay of the average worker goes down. I am currently writing this essay in the middle of a town undergoing an economic boom and where the number of jobs is growing far faster than the rate of population growth (Austin, Texas: late 1998). Salaries have gone sky high not only for technical workers, much in demand by the computer companies, but for all sorts of unskilled labor as well. Entry-level supermarket stockers are earning between $8 and $9 an hour, a rate that would have been unheard of several years ago. These salaries are obviously linked to the huge number of job openings and the scarce supply of available candidates. It is unlikely that the new salaries have come out of the goodness of employers hearts, or that employers have suddenly decided to reward long-term performance, or that supermarket stocking jobs in Austin suddenly involved a dramatic increase in the skills associated with the position.[4] When Ph.D.'s in the humanities find themselves in acute oversupply because of low demand for university jobs, and brilliant Ph.D.'s are forced to accept untenured teaching positions at low wages, doing the same work or more than they would be doing as highly paid tenure-track professors, their reduction in wages would seem to be linked to their oversupply, not to any reduction in the skills required for scholarly work, or even to an increase in mean-spiritedness on the part of university deans.

Another appealing feature of overcrowding theory is that it helps to explain the paradox of how most women end up suffering economic disadvantages even though many men are not sexist and do not personally participate in discriminatory practices. Let us consider an alternative theory of gender gaps. Men just hate women and want to pay them less to keep them in their places. This theory would seem to run into problems immediately, because not all men hate women. Many feminist men, and many who may not be feminist, out of a spirit of fairness believe in paying everybody the same wages for the same amount of work if they deserve it. Not every male on the face of the planet is a misogynistic patriarch who personally discriminates against every female he encounters.

If simple gender hatred drove gendered pay differentials, we would expect women-hating men to pay men more than they pay women, and fair-minded men to pay the two sexes at the same rate. We would find male-female pay differentials only in firms that were notoriously sexist, and in which men self-consciously and publicly depreciated female labor.

The overcrowding model, however, permits the widespread existence of gendered pay differentials, even in firms where men are basically fair-minded and nondiscriminatory. In the overcrowding model, all that matters is that *some* men choose to restrict female opportunities. If *some* males limit female employment, then *all* women experience labor market opportunities that are adverse when compared to those of men.

This is because the actual women who are victimized by the initial discriminatory male core find themselves thrown into the labor market to compete with the remaining women for the population of jobs left that are administered by nondiscriminatory males; this increases the labor supply for all positions, both discriminatory and not, and will lower all women's wages throughout the economy. All that matters is that the nondiscriminatory employers maximize profit and pay the prevailing market wage. As long as all employers pay the lowest wage possible while still obtaining a qualified candidate, women overall will be paid less than men overall.

Note that overcrowding allows for a compelling explanation of pay differentials in Firm A in terms of the behavior of employers in Firm B. Most discussions of discrimination assume that differentials at Firm A must stem from patriarchal attitudes or behavior at Firm A. Even if no one can find any evidence of gender prejudice at Firm A, the presence of systematic wage inequality makes some investigators assume some sort of local sexism must be active. There are, in the real world, wonderfully progressive feminist firms that pay women less than men. Overcrowding at least provides a theoretical hint as to how this could occur; other theories have a hard time with this phenomenon.

Getting evidence to support overcrowding has always been difficult. One needs to compare multiple labor markets that differ in their extent of overcrowding. This on a practical level has been difficult to do. International datasets that use statistics from different countries tend to be too small to support the sophisticated econometric techniques required to properly test the theory. Longitudinal data from the United States has a similar property of overly small case bases. One observation per year for forty years will not allow the use of a methodology that requires three hundred or five hundred cases. As if this were not enough, both kinds of analyses suffer from all sorts of technical problems stemming from different definitions of occupations across nations and periods.

Finally, in 1998, a clean, large sample test of the overcrowding hypothesis was performed. A team of researchers from the University of Maryland analyzed the determinants of the female-male earnings ratio in 261 cities (Cotter et. al. 1997, 1998). In each city, they calculated the demand for female labor, defined as the percentage each occupation has of the total number of jobs in the city, multiplied by the national percent female of that occupation.

Their primary findings were that the greater the demand for female labor, the lower the gap between female and male earnings and the greater the demand for male labor, the greater the gap between female and male earnings. These findings are exactly what would be predicted from the overcrowding hypothesis.[5]

Further evidence for the role of overcrowding comes from longitudinal analyses of the gender gap. Over the last few decades, the male-female wage gap has been declining; at the same time, indicators of occupational sex segregation have been decreasing as well. As one would expect from overcrowding theory, these two phenomena are not unrelated. Note, however, that this correlation is not entirely tidy. An analysis of the 1967–87 period shows that during this time of rising gender opportunity, women's wages did not particularly rise. Instead, male wages fell (Bernhardt et al. 1995). The collapse of male earnings was a result of the downsizing and rationalization trends of the Reagan years. Employers moved jobs overseas, deunionized jobs, and reduced head counts. As a result, the demand for male labor fell precipitously and with it, male wages. The overcrowding hypothesis was validated, but only in an unpleasant way. Because male labor market opportunities were decimated, male earnings were decimated such that they approximated the levels previously associated with women workers. Relative market size mattered because women were somewhat insulated from these adverse trends.

The same researchers who analyzed the cross-city variations in gender gaps also studied changes in the gender wage gap between 1980 and 1990. They found that 36 percent of the rising equality between men and women can be explained by changes in the level of occupational segregation, the primary variable evoked by the overcrowding hypothesis (Cotter et al. 1995). Thirty-six percent is a lot of change. On similar data, human capital variables show an inferior performance. The authors rightly note, however, that for a variable this important, one would have wanted to see a higher number. Note that, in the light of the previous Bernhardt et al. studies, demand for male labor was going down as a result of job cuts. Because men were being thrown out of the labor force, lost demand was appearing as increased unemployment rather than increased occupational gender mixing. Overcrowding logic would expect this unemployment to help reduce the gender wage gap above and beyond what would be expected from occupational sex segregation indices alone.

One last confirmation for overcrowding theory comes from the work of Petersen and Morgan (1995). In an analysis of two 1970s-era wage datasets, they ranked several factors for their contribution to gender gaps and discovered the following:

A. Segregation by occupations is very important in producing gender inequality.
B. Segregation by establishments, with women working in poorer establishments, is somewhat important in producing gender inequality.

C. Gender inequality within the same occupation and within the same firm is very rare. Most firms pay men and women doing the same work roughly the same wage. (Actually some gender differences still exist for same-firm/same-occupation contrasts, but compared to a and b, they are remarkably small.)

This last finding is extremely important. It somewhat discredits simplistic male hatred accounts of gender inequality and supports the commonsense observation that most firms try to be somewhat fair. The issue is that women are limited as to which occupations they can enter, and this limitation causes them to earn lower wages than men. The centrality of occupational segregation is once again reaffirmed, and with it the role of free market forces and relative labor market size as a key determinant of male and female economic differentials.

Human Capital Theory

women are paid less than men because of their intermittent labor force participation.

Human capital theory shows up everywhere in gender studies. We discussed it extensively in the last chapter on status segregation and argued that it was not a very good explanation for why women are concentrated in low-status jobs. It does better as a theory of women's wages, although it still has serious problems.

Human capital theory argues that women are paid less than men because their intermittent labor force participation reduces their supply of human capital. Because women plan to leave the labor force to have children, they invest in less firm-general human capital. Because firm-general human capital is financed by the worker and not the employer, a worker who plans to be employed only for a short period would have less financial incentive to invest in firm-general training. Why pay for schooling that will only provide a benefit over a limited period? Furthermore, women's exits from the labor force cause their firm-specific and firm-general skills to deteriorate. Work-related abilities need to be maintained by practice. During women's years out of the labor force, they supposedly lose many of their occupational skills, both from disuse and from not participating in training opportunities available to their working male peers. As a result, men tend to accumulate a larger body of occupational knowledge, which makes them more productive for their employers; this results in their receiving a higher market wage.

One can raise a lot of questions about this model. It is not obvious to what degree women who are temporarily out of the labor force experience any permanent loss of skills. Many graduate schools accept students who have been in the work world and out of school for a while. Presumably their studying and test-taking skills would have deteriorated while they were holding real jobs. Nevertheless, most adult graduate students adapt relatively quickly to the academic regime and find that their seminar and test-taking skills come back fairly quickly. You, the reader, may want to think about some older woman you know who has gone back to work after significant time off for family or personal obligations. Ask yourself how long it took that woman to readapt to the work routine. Most of the women of my personal knowledge make the back-to-work transition in less than a month; the experience of the people you know may be different.

One can also ask whether all those men who are working continuous long careers are actually obtaining skills all the time they are working. The learning curves for most jobs show diminishing returns to experience. One learns a whole lot the first year one is on a job. One learns somewhat less the second year, and even less during the third. Finally, the job gets old and stale; the occupation can present few new surprises or twists. How much does one learn in one's third year of being a supermarket cashier? Or in one's eighteenth year of being a doctor? Ultimately, all jobs lose their capacity to provide significant on-the-job training, making further continued job-holding not likely to increase productivity.

The human capital model also assumes that burnout does not exist. There is no worker fatigue, and no bureaucratic deadwood. All workers maintain their vigor and enthusiasm through the entire span of their careers. In a world with burnout, increased on-the-job experience can produce lower rather than higher productivity. I ask the reader to reflect on the teachers he or she had in high school. In my case, there were one or two brilliant, wise old sages, veteran teachers who were absolutely excellent. These exceptions aside, most of the live wires in my high school were the younger teachers, kids just two or three years out of education school with lots of new ideas and bursting with enthusiasm. Many of the older teachers were just going through the motions, waiting for retirement. The older teachers were paid more than the younger teachers; it was not at all obvious, however, that they were more productive or doing a better job. There was a strict seniority system, and as long as you had the years in my home town school system, you could be nearly dead and still make a top salary.

Sociologists and institutional economists have long been aware of the phenomenon of seniority systems that are out of synch with productivity. They developed an alternative theory of wages to account for this, a theory known as the *internal labor market theory* (Piore and Doeringer 1971; Osterman 1984). Advocates of internal labor markets argue that wages are determined by bureaucratic logic rather than by productivity per se, and as a result are highly arbitrary. Salaries are often the result of empty, formalistic credentialing procedures. Workers are rewarded for the number of academic degrees they have regardless of whether this allows them to perform better. Workers are also rewarded for years on the job. Education and experience are stratifying principles that are easy to justify, and simplify managers' choices as to whom to reward. Some authors argue these bureaucratic procedures facilitate training (Thurow 1975). Others argue that they encourage productivity by insuring rewards for loyalty or by creating tournaments where workers can compete for promotions (Edwards 1979). Regardless of which model or explanation one prefers, the bottom line is that these systems divorce pay from individual skills; the fit between human capital and wages is, as a result, quite poor.

Scientific evidence for the reasonableness of internal labor market claims comes from the work of Medoff and Abraham (1981). Medoff and Abraham studied the pay and productivity of a set of executives in a New England corporation. Unsurprisingly, they found that executives with more experience were paid more than executives with less experience and that executives with more education were paid more than executives with less education. The shocker is that

Executives with more education were less *productive than executives with less education, and executives with more experience were* less *productive than executives with less experience!!!.*

The italicized paragraph is not a typo. Educated, experienced executives were less productive than their less educated, less experienced peers. How can this be? First, the executives who got their jobs without any educational qualifications had to talk their way in on the basis of merit. These tended to be superperformers at lower ranks who fought their way up on the basis of exemplary command of the jobs associated with the company. This gave them a productivity edge over the empty shirt who got the job merely because he had an M.B.A. from Stanford (and if you have any doubts that there are empty shirts within the ranks of graduates from Harvard, Wharton, or Stanford, ask anybody who has attended any of those fine institutions). The finding on experience mirrors the previous burnout discussion concerning teachers. It may be that the longer you stay, the more you learn; the longer you stay, however, the more jaded and bored you become. The two factors can cancel each other out.

These findings help to explain the half-empty/half-full nature of human capital theory's predictions about gender differentials and wages. The human capital theorists are correct to argue that education and experience make a difference in wages. They are incorrect in claiming that these differences affect actual skills or ability to do the job. Labor market interruptions hurt women's wages because bureaucratic rules concerning pay reward continuity in service per se. It is not that the discontinuous workers are objectively worse performers. It is that if you skip two or three years of annual increases, your salary is two or three annual increases behind, regardless of your ability to do the job.

The best analysis of these issues comes from Kilbourne et al. (1994). The Kilbourne team analyzed the wages of men and women in the National Longitudinal Survey. They found that gender differences in education and experience explained from 25 percent to 28 percent of the wage gap between men and women. A wage gap of 25 percent to 28 percent is quite a lot. The performance of the education and experience variables chould be viewed as a superficial confirmation of the human capital model. However, the Kilbourne team also had evidence on the actual skills of the workers involved. For every worker, they were able to assess that worker's skill holdings in each of four separate subskills: cognitive skill, physical skill, authoritative skill, and nurturant skill. Gender differences in skill had almost no effect on gender differences in wages; skill could at the maximum account for only 2 percent to 5 percent of the gap in wages. Education and experience mattered; skill did not account for this relationship. Overall this finding is highly consistent with the internal labor market view that bureaucratic procedures rather that firm-specific or firm-general skills are the critical determinants of wage rates.

The finding that education and experience can explain a substantial proportion of the gender gap has been replicated in many studies; supporters of human capital theory can take some comfort in this. In fact, Kilbourne et al.'s estimate of from 25 percent to 28 percent runs towards the low side. More typical are the results reported by Wellington (1994). In an analysis of two years of data from the Panel Study of Income Dynamics, one of the most commonly used national samples in the social sciences, human capital variables were able to explain, depending on which year was being considered, from 37 percent to 42 percent of the wage gap. She was unable to include any data on actual skill. For any theory, though, this would be considered a commendable performance. A theory that explains 42 percent of the gap, however, leaves 58 percent of the gap unexplained. The critics of human capital theory, and these are many, keep asking what accounts for the other 58 percent of the gap. This is a reasonable and good question.

This 58 percent of the gap matters, a point made forcefully by Sørensen and Trappe (1995) in an analysis of gender inequality in the former East Germany. East Germany was a communist country that was dedicated (on paper) to the elimination of economic differences between men and women. Educational attainment for males and females were virtually identical. Occupational experience for the two genders was also nearly identical. Communist ideology mandated that all able-bodied adults work. Extensive state-run day care facilities were made available so that women would not have to stay home with young children. As a result, the human capital attainments of East German men and women were virtually identical.

What happened to the gender pay gap? It continued to persist. The level of gender inequality was not noticeably different from that observed in many Western European countries where equality of education continues to persist. Furthermore, Sørensen and Trappe broke down their sample into age groups where there was absolutely no human capital differential and age groups where some gaps still existed from the old pre-Communist regime. The two groups showed the same level of gender inequality. Removing gender differences in education and experience did not remove gender differences in pay.

East Germany was a quintessential internal labor market. Wages were set bureaucratically rather than by the market because communist economies by definition have no free market that can set wages. The gender differences in pay that existed in East Germany survived by managerial fiat. In capitalist corporations, gender differences can also survive by managerial fiat if internal rules and regulations, rather than market pressure, are responsible for wage profiles overall. But if this is the case, what is the logic of bureaucratic action that would produce systematic gender differentials in pay? Comparable worth theory represents the most systematic attempt to answer this question—grounding women's pay disadvantage purely in the dynamics of internal labor markets per se.

Comparable Worth Theory

employers underestimate the value of women's labor

Comparable worth theory claims that women are paid less than men because employers systematically underestimate the value of women's labor. Employers ostensibly pay workers the value of their output. In the bureaucratic world of the internal labor market, however, there is no systematic force to insure that anybody, male or female, will actually get paid his or her true worth. If men systematically believe that women's labor is not worth much, they won't pay women very much for their labor. The obstacles to women's receiving higher pay are not economic but cultural, not market based but psychological.

In theory, comparable worth discrimination manifests itself as occupations that are heavily female and paying both men and women less than occupations that are heavily male. Women's jobs are viewed as being feminine and womanly; because of their gendered aspect, they are devalued by employers. As such, the work pays anyone, male or female, in those occupations a poor wage.

Comparable worth theorists also argue that the consistent tendency for a gender gap in wages to persist after human capital variables are controlled also supports their theory. This residual suggests a penalty for being female that is consistent with an undervaluation of women's work (England 1992; Treiman and Hartmann 1981; Sorensen 1989).

Certainly plenty of evidence supports these last two claims. We saw in the human capital section how gender differentials persist after human capital variables are controlled. Many analyses show that occupations hiring a large percentage of women pay both men and women lower wages than do comparable occupations that are staffed by men (Treiman and Hartmann 1981; Kilbourne et. al. 1994; England 1992; Tomaskovic-Devey 1993). Without question, comparable worth discrimination contributes to the ongoing gender differential in pay; whether this is the primary cause of the gap or a logically compelling explanation of the gap is subject to significant doubt.

The primary claim of comparable worth theory is that employers lower women's wages by psychologically devaluing their work. If this is true, why don't managers devalue everybody's work, too, by underestimating their worth? Why don't all employers turn into Ebenezer Scrooge and say "Bah, humbug" to *all* their workers and pay them *all* 2¢ an hour because that is all they are worth? If sheer meanness alone can lower people's wages, it is hard to see why the capitalist class doesn't save itself a bunch of money by simply turning sarcastic and cynical, thus doing to the entire population what they have already done to women.

Neoclassical economic theory argues this doesn't happen because women can shop around among employers until they find one that does value their true productivity. The actions of unprejudiced employers will put market pressure on discriminators to raise the wages of their women or risk losing their services entirely. This, of course, is the position of Gary Becker. We argued in Chapter 2 that discrimination persists because some employers are buffered from labor costs. Not all employers enjoy this protection from market forces, however, and so a significant subset of firms really do have to pay appropriate market wages. A world with a mix of discriminating and nondiscriminating employers would produce data that shows some firms with significant male-female pay differentials and other firms with male-female pay equality. There would be no tendency for female occupations to pay men or women less than male occupations because employer attitudes, rather than occupation, would be the prime determinant of pay.

The latter prediction flies in the face of the data. One empirical regularity that the comparable worth advocates have shown time and time again is that occupations with a high percentage of women pay both sexes less than do occupations with a high percentage of men. This is what the numbers show, and it would be foolish to hold to a worldview that is inconsistent with those numbers.

If there is any kind of labor market at all, however, the only way these differentials could maintain themselves in the face of workers changing employers to jockey for the most favorable deal would be if all employers shared a common prejudice against women's work. All employers would need to equally undervalue women's contribution to the labor force. Some feminists argue that this is exactly what occurs, but I am a little bit more than skeptical of this claim. Is it obvious that feminist employers undervalue women's work? Is it obvious that women employers undervalue women's work? Is it obvious that the undervaluation of women's work is shared by all employers over all occupations in all industries and all labor markets?

In the world of gender attitudes, there is a whole lot of disagreement. People disagree about abortion. People disagree about whether mothers with infants should work. People disagree about how much gender discrimination exists in the workplace. It is implausible in the face of all this disagreement that everyone has the same cultural idea that women's work is worth less than men's and by the same amount and that this applies across all regions and firms.

Put differently, if individual views about women's productivity were the only conditions that produced women's pay inequality, then gendered pay differentials would be too easy to escape. Women could in principle simply "shop around" for unprejudiced employers. Women's pay is so low because they are forced by their own lack of power to accept inferior wages. In reality, women cannot escape low wages by "shopping around" because their position in the labor market is weak. Overcrowding and occupational sex-typing insures that a glut of women on the labor market will always exist. This glut lowers the wages for all women. It also weakens women's capacity to avoid prejudiced employers because the surplus supply of female labor reduces the number of job possibilities for all women; such conditions force them to accept a variety of work-based disamenities, such as part-time status, reduced access to organizational power, and sexual harassment from peers and superiors.

Note that overcrowding will produce a labor market in which jobs that are disproportionately female will pay both their male and female jobholders a relatively low wage. Jobs that hire a lot of women are easily filled by workers with a labor market disadvantage—the disadvantage of overcrowding. This means that if a worker chooses to quit and the employer has to find a replacement, the odds are high that the employer can find a qualified individual who is under labor market pressure due to the reduced job opportunities available to women. This means the employer can afford to offer all women the pay given to a candidate with limited counteropportunities because there will be many viable candidates who are subject to this burden. The employer can also offer these lower wages to men; if the men don't like the low pay, the employer can replace the fussy male with a woman. Thus, the lower wages associated with occupations that have a high percentage of women is not necessarily evidence of the undervaluation of women's work. It may indicate the lower bargaining power associated with women overall.

If this were the only evidence supporting comparable worth theory, the status of comparable worth would be tenuous indeed. However, there is other, more suggestive evidence that supports the claim that comparable worth theory has merit. The best of this comes from Paula England (1992), who has done an exhaustive analysis of the pay differential between male and female jobs. Using the 1980 census, she statistically considered no fewer than fifty-six different variables that could each explain why male jobs pay more than female jobs. These include percent female, the preferred variable of comparable worth theorists, and a host of control variables. The controls include such indicators as the racial and ethnic composition of the job, the amount of cognitive skill involved, the amount of various physical skills that might be involved such as strength, hand-to-eye coordination or mechanical aptitude, the presence of social amenities, such as making a societal contribution, prestige or the ability to control the speed at which one works, the presence of disamenities such as stress, monotony, toxic fumes or personal safety, the extent to which the government employs workers in the occupation, the extent to which wealthy firms employ workers in the occupation, the extent to which the occupation is unionized, etc. etc. etc.

Many of her side findings are fascinating, although not always easy to explain. The more dangerous the job, the less you get paid, a factor that should lower men's pay relative to women's. The more you have to violate your conscience, the more you get paid. Neither heat, nor cold, nor working in the wet significantly influences pay. Giving workers medical insurance neither raises nor lowers their pay. (Don't let your employer tell you that if he gets you health insurance, your wages will have to drop). Working in a job where you make a societal contribution raises your wages. Note that women are more likely to hold such jobs than are men, so this actually lowers the gender gap in pay. Working in a job staffed with many blacks does not lower pay, but working in a job staffed with many Mexicans does. Men are more likely to work with Mexicans, a factor that lowers the gender pay gap. England does not always provide detailed interpretations of these side findings, which is understandable given their counterintuitive nature. Their existence, however, serves as a salutary warning that many things determine men's and women's pay besides overt gender dynamics per se.

Given all the auxiliary factors that reduce the gender pay gap, what produces the gap that we actually observe in both 1980 and contemporary census data?

Paula England included several measures of the gender content of jobs showing the extent to which different occupations incorporate male or female cultural aspects. The two male measures she used were authority, that is, whether your job gave you actual power over people and whether your job involved physical strength. The female measure was nurturance, that is, whether your job involved caring for people or being emotionally sensitive to their needs.

These three gendered attributes were important determinants of male and female pay. Working in an occupation that involved either authority or physical strength raised the wages of both men and women; working in a job that involved nurturance lowered them. It is not surprising that occupations involving authority are better paid than those that do not. After all, one of the functions of authority is to set pay scales; bosses are usually very good about rewarding other bosses and themselves.

The other two findings, concerning strength and nurturance, are definitely more unsettling. Given the low status associated with manual work, it is surprising that men and women who do physical jobs are rewarded for that physicality. Male and female marines, male and female ditchdiggers, and male and female lifeguards all get a premium that takes everything into account for strength associated with their work. In other words, they are rewarded for behaving like men. People who work in nurturing jobs are penalized for acting like women. Male and female child care workers, male and female nurses, and male and female clergy all receive pay cuts, net of their education or qualifications, for doing jobs that involve emotions and sensitivity. If you want to be rewarded in this society, dig a ditch.

The England findings have been replicated on other datasets (Kilbourne et al. 1994), so we cannot dismiss these results as a methodological fluke. These findings make it hard to deny that stylistically masculine work is rewarded and stylistically feminine work is punished. This is consistent with the presence of a societal gender role system that rewards maleness per se. So how can one reconcile the strength of these findings with the general weakness of the other aspects of the comparable worth model? How does one take a model that makes radical assumptions about the primacy of internal labor market forces and align it with a real world in which market factors continue to have some, albeit limited, effect?

Production Constraint Theory

When sociologists discuss wage differentials, they tend to omit the most important theory of all. In neoclassical economics, it is argued that wages equal marginal productivity. Ignore the "marginal" for this discussion. "Marginal" refers to the niceties of what happens when one increases the amount of labor while holding capital constant, a dynamic that is not important to the study of gender differentials per se. The main idea is that wages are somehow equal to workers' true productivity (Hicks 1964).

It is easy to see why wages would have some relation to productivity in principle. An employer could not afford to pay workers more than their productivity over any stretch of time. The cost of the worker would be greater than the cost of what they produce; the employer would ultimately go bankrupt. It is easier to pay workers less than their actual productivity. Karl Marx argued that this is an endemic feature of capitalism. The bourgeoisie extract surplus value from the proletariat, meaning that the owner of capital extracts some value created by the worker and kept it for himself. Unless a capitalist is the only employer in his labor market, however, there are limits on the ability of managers to pay less than true productivity. This is because ripped-off workers maintain the option to negotiate a better or fairer deal elsewhere.

The labor market is not a magical fairyland where everybody's salaries are automatically set to the market value of what they produce. Seniority systems, internal labor markets, minimum wage laws, union contracts, occupational custom, firm tradition, and plain old managerial sloppiness all determine wages, too. For any one worker, the odds that his or her paycheck will exactly reflect his or her true productivity is probably next to zero.

However, for large groups of workers, and over time, these factors can random out, providing wage productivity links that are roughly correct. Seniority systems may reward old incompetents over young stars, but the global scale can be set so that the average worker receives an average pay that is more or less in line with productivity. Managers may toss cash at a team of workers without having the slightest idea about which individual worker is contributing what. That said, the pay for the team may roughly reflect what the team produces, even if the internal division of pay within the team is wacky. Unions may raise wages over productivity in the short term (and in fact all the statistical evidence suggests that they do.) However, over time, new firms and new countries enter the labor market, providing cheaper nonunion labor that challenges old-style union wages. Unless unions can raise their productivity to fend off this foreign nonunion competition, the union wage advantage in the long term is doomed.[6]

Sociologists don't like to address productivity theory because, used in an unsophisticated fashion, it could be used to generate an explanation that no one wants to hear:

? **The gender differential is caused by true productivity differences between men and women** **?**

At first appearance, this would seem to be an unacceptable conclusion. No one wants to claim that women don't work as hard as men, or that women are less intelligent than men, or that women are less competent than men. Most writers would be adamantly opposed to claims that women are lazier than men, or dumber than men, or less capable than men. The way to avoid these black holes is to ignore productivity theory.[7]

If marginal productivity theory truly meant that one had to argue for the inherent inferiority of women, it would be easy to see how neoclassical theory could be quite unappealing. Marginal productivity theory, however, implies none of the sexist conclusions presented above. Women can be less productive than men because *men make women less productive.* Patriarchy can put women into situations where their talents and energies are grossly underused; it can stick women in jobs that are unproductive by their very nature. Women can be forced into occupations where they simply cannot produce economic value for their employers, no matter how hard they try or how much talent they bring to the endeavor. In this case, the social injustice does not come from employers undervaluing the product they produce; it comes from being limited to intrinsically unproductive jobs that by economic logic produce low market rates of pay. If women were placed into the jobs to which men have access, women would produce ever so much more.

To understand the process by which males reduce or restrict female output, it is helpful to consider what causes workers to be productive in general. Effort, skill, and competence are obvious components of productivity. These have a moral component in that an employee could realistically be expected to be insulted should someone suggest that his or her effort, skill, or competence was not up to snuff. There are, however, structural determinants of productivity that are just as important as effort, skill, and competence; such nonmoral factors tend to be omitted in superficial considerations of worker productivity. Structural considerations are frequently beyond the control of the individual worker, and as such, there can be no question here of individual blame.

Among the structural determinants of productivity that tend to be ignored are capital, product price, and the contributions of team members. Let us consider each of these in turn.

a. *Capital.* A worker with access to capital will generally be more productive than a worker who relies solely on his or her own labor power. A man with a backhoe will move more earth than a man with a shovel, no matter how athletic or hard working the man with the shovel may be. You can tear up more pavement with a jackhammer than you can with a pick. Workers who have superior access to high technology and equipment will outperform their rivals who use low tech or their bare hands. As a result, they will generally earn a higher wage, even if they are relatively lazy and unconscientious. Workers in petrochemical refineries earn generous salaries in part because of their access to the vast stock of capital embodied in the refinery itself, which exponentially increases the worth of a day of their labor. Babysitters exclusively use labor, with no capital whatsoever. Their pay tends to be pretty low.

In this regard, consider the finding from Chapter 3 that women tend to be concentrated in labor-intensive rather than capital-intensive industries. Men are associated with high technology, fancy equipment, and big machines. Women do handwork and are given work that is not too mechanically complex. This sorting does not come from culture; it comes from the differential economics of capital-intensive and labor-intensive workplaces, by which capital-intensive workplaces are more capable of discriminating against women because they are buffered from labor costs. A by-product of the concentration of women in labor-intensive workplaces is that women are deprived of the productivity-enhancing advantages of machinery and high technology. They are ghettoized into human-powered occupations, in which labor is the only factor of production. These jobs are intrinsically less productive because an entire second factor of production, capital, is missing. A man on a GM assembly line earns more than a woman in a Mexican maquiladora factory. The woman makes automobile electronic components with a soldering iron and not much else. The man at GM has all sorts of fancy robotics helping him do his job. He produces more in an hour than she does because of the vast technology at his disposal.

b. *Price of Product.* In neoclassical wage theory, wages are equal to workers' marginal *revenue* product. The revenue is an important consideration. Workers are not paid by the number of widgets they make; they are paid by the value of those widgets. Workers who make more valuable widgets earn bigger paychecks.

Sometimes this leads to significant inequities. Consider two hypothetical miners, one mining coal and the other mining diamonds. Both miners have to do physically strenuous work. Both miners undergo real danger from breathing dust and from the threat of collapse. That said, the diamond miner will earn more than the coal miner. The productivity of the diamond miner is extraordinary because of vast monetary value of the diamonds he produces. The productivity of the coal miner is less because coal is cheap, even if he had to risk his life to acquire the coal. The diamond miner is paid more. Life is unfair.

Price is significant in determining women's wages because the price of traditionally female services is low. Comparable worth theorists are correct to argue that employers do not value women's labor. However, customers often do not value women's labor either, and pay a miserable price to women providing female sex-typed services even when the customers are women themselves.

The most conspicuous example of this is day care. Day care workers are some of the most poorly paid workers in the United States. People care passionately about their children. Everyone acknowledges that psychologically healthy children are essential for the well-being of our society and for our own well-being. That said, day care workers are absolutely disrespected. Nobody wants to pay more than the rock minimum for day care. Note the critical point here that women take advantage of day care workers to the same extent that men do. Both fathers and mothers pay their child care providers low wages. More important, customers take advantage of day care workers to the same extent that employers do. Both day care workers who are employees of centers and day care workers who are self-employed receive salaries that are appallingly low. Day care workers cannot free themselves from underappreciation by getting rid of their employers because the public imposes this same level of underpayment on free and independent self-employed care providers.

This last point about customers undervaluing and underrewarding women's work is important: The critical test is to measure the extent to which self-employed women underearn self-employed men against the extent to which employed women underearn employed men. If the gender gap for self-employed and bureaucratically employed were equal, this would suggest external market rather than bureaucratic determinants of women's pay disadvantage. If the gender gap for self-employed people was less than that of bureaucratically employed people, this result would be more in line with comparable worth theory, which blames the discretionary actions of employers for men's wage premiums.[8] To my knowledge, this test has never been performed. (With my luck, such a study will appear seven days before this book gets published.)

A dry run of the test has been done by England in her famous 1992 comparable worth analysis. In that study, controlling for authority did not remove either the salary handicap associated with being in traditionally female occupations or the salary handicap associated with nurturance. Authority is not the same as self-employment. This finding does suggest, however, that women are not underpaid exclusively because they are deprived of organizational power. There is an additional penalty for being in occupations staffed by women and for being in occupations that are culturally female; such a penalty suggests that bureaucratic power is not the entire source of the female handicap; market undervaluation of women's work may easily account for some of the rest of the gap.

Note that day care is not the only female specialty that receives a low price in the free market. Cleaning houses and washing clothing are both female sex-typed jobs. Neither janitors nor dry cleaners are very well paid, even when self-employed. Women in the female "semiprofessions" (an obnoxious term that refers to teachers, social workers, librarians, and nurses) often have low earnings in comparison to men in the male "professions" (doctor, lawyer, engineer). It is not obvious that this handicap is removed when women become self-employed. A freelancing social worker may still earn less than a freelancing psychiatrist. Customers still think that nurses are worth less than doctors, that social workers are worth less than psychiatrists, that florists are worth less than electricians, and that school teachers are worth less than plumbers. If customers insist upon underpaying for female products, it is not surprising that employers do the same.

c. *Contributions of Team Members.* That many jobs are performed by teams in which it is hard to discern exactly how much has been contributed by individual members complicates the link between wages and productivity. Situations where individual output is hard to measure invite injustices based on failure to appropriately credit workers for their input.

Consider a set of advertising executives designing a promotional campaign for "Duzzo" baby food. One person suggests advertising on women's talk shows. Another comes up with the slogan "Duzzo Makes Your Baby Brighter." A third develops the concept of having the pitch made by a family of bears. A fourth develops a happy little bear dance in which the bears dance around in a circle while singing the Duzzo slogan.

For whatever reason, Duzzo sales go up 3 percent nationally. Although it is unclear whether this success was the result of the commercial, people in headquarters think the ad campaign contributed in some way to Duzzo's new market share. How does one reward the members of the advertising team? What was the exact worth of the idea of selling on talk shows? What was the exact contribution of "Duzzo Makes Your Baby Brighter"? What was the exact contribution of using bears as spokespeople or of having them dance in a circle? Nobody knows, and nobody can know.

This implies that potential conflicts exist over crediting for production in most work settings where output is produced by teams. Once the real work is accomplished, there is a secondary task of social construction in which workers stake claims on having been responsible for everything that was successful and disclaim responsibility for whatever actions appear to have produced adverse consequences. In the ex-post-facto accounts, "everybody" contributes in a significant way to organizational success, and "somebody else" is responsible for whatever mishaps occurred along the way. Because the truth of these matters is hard to discern, there is substantial free play both for creative history writing after the fact and for earning one's salary with spin rather than objective performance.

One of the consequences of the retrospective reallocation of productivity is that the strong can steal production from the weak. Line workers who make small beneficial adjustments to work procedures can find that upper management attributes this productivity to the engineers in charge of supervising the facility. Secretaries who correct the syntax and grammatical errors of their bosses find that the better presentation reflects exclusively on their supervisor and not on them. The nurse who deftly covers for the surgeon's errors finds the surgeon's unblemished reputation continues to draw professional esteem, lofty fees, and cheap malpractice insurance; she, meanwhile, labors on in complete obscurity. Even though the financial value of avoiding serious lawsuits may be worth millions of dollars, the nurse is not likely to see this added value appear in her paycheck.

Any position that allows one to take credit for the accomplishments of others is likely to be relatively well remunerated. This affects gender differentials in pay in two ways. First, women have less access than men do to positions of authority. As Marx pointed out in the nineteenth century, ownership and control positions in firms facilitate the extraction of surplus value and the amassing of the work done by others to the advantage of oneself. Even in a bureaucracy where a middle supervisor reports to a higher supervisor, the middle supervisor's ability to selectively report results to the higher-up, combined with that higher-up's lower level of familiarity with the details of day-to-day production, allows for substantial creative working of responsibility for who did what. Paula England reports that authority is associated with higher pay. Part of this is a simple return to rank and status. Part of it, however, reflects supervisors' ability to claim credit for innovations coming from the workers in their operations and, at the same time, avoid punishment for their own bad performance by firing or penalizing underlings.

The second way in which ambiguities in the allocation of productivity to workers adversely affect women is that in a society with patriarchy and sexism, women are disproportionately likely to have difficulty getting credit for their legitimate accomplishments. Often women or minorities, upon achieving high organizational rank, find that enemies attribute their rise to race or gender rather than to talent. If a black receives a promotion, it "must be because of affirmative action." If a women receives a promotion, it "must be because of an office romance or the sexual factor" (or because of "affirmative action" and the company is too intimidated by feminists to judge objectively by talent). Such accusations are not made against all women in all corporations. The potential for backbiting and gossip are always there, nevertheless, and they are particularly likely to affect outsiders trying to crack an organization staffed by male insiders.

Even without sexual or political gossip per se, the lower status of women overall may put them at a disadvantage in the battle for the claiming of credit for accomplishments. Recent work by Cecilia Ridgeway (1997) on the origins of status hierarchies suggests that it is not uncommon for gender to be arbitrarily linked to mythologies about inferior performance, even in laboratory situations where no such objective basis for such a claim would exist.

*   *   *

If the women's wage gap was exclusively the product of women failing to get credit from their employers for their just accomplishments, the comparable worth theory would be the dominant explanation of gender differentials in wages. If one adds differential access to positions of authority as a consideration, the comparable worth argument is diluted because a class element has been added to an otherwise pure gender dynamic. If one adds customer discrimination against female specialties, external labor market factors enter the previously all-internal labor market discussion; comparable worth is diluted further still. If one adds availability of capital to the model, the comparable worth model is still technically correct, but it is being affected by a lot of additional factors more linked to job assignment than employer undervaluation per se.

Overall, in any situation in which one group is being rewarded at the expense of another, one has to ask, "What forces the lower group to accept the inferior treatment that it is receiving?" A theory of differential privilege has to have a compelling theory of power that explains how the superior group maintains its advantage over competitors even when this is not in the competitors' best interests. In this regard, overcrowding theory becomes especially attractive: It explains why women are forced to accept lower wages overall and it is consistent with reduced access to strategic occupations being associated with further labor market disadvantages due to loss of bargaining strength. In addition, the theory is consistent with the data on women's wage attainments, both cross-sectionally and over time. The explanatory force behind overcrowding theory is market competition, the simple law of supply and demand. Market competition is also the force behind marginal productivity theory, a viewpoint that has a lot to say about gender differentials in wages. These insights are reconcilable with modern feminism and suggest empirical relations that appear plausible.

Most gender specialists are reluctant to embrace market explanations of male-female differentials because much of the work that has come from economics departments has invoked human capital models of limited appeal or applicability. The economics profession has undersold its own wares, however; there are many legitimate insights that neoclassical economics provides for studying differentials of all kinds.

Remember that all of these wage dynamics are driven by employers' exclusion of women from particular jobs. If employers did not create occupational sex-typing, there would be no overcrowding of the female labor market. If employers did not exclude women from jobs with intrinsic high productivity, production constraint theory would be inoperative. Wage discrimination against women is largely a by-product of occupational sex-typing. Wage discrimination, however, is one of the key mechanisms by which occupational sex-typing damages women's economic opportunities. To the extent to which market forces can eliminate occupational sex-typing (and we have seen that market forces have some ability to do this but they are not omnipotent), the economic gap between men and women can be made to go away.

Unfortunately, racial differences in employment are not easily subject to market explanations and are thus less open to amelioration by market forces. Racial differences are more likely to be the result of racism, both institutional and otherwise, that seems to defy elimination by market mechanisms. The next chapter considers black-white employment differentials and the decidedly social, rather than economic, forces that perpetuate their existence.

Notes

1. The student seeking a readable and convincing longer treatment of overcrowding should look at Barbara Bergmann's 1986 *Economic Emergence of Women*. Stevenson (1984) played an important role in rediscovering these models and bringing them to more contemporary academic attention.

2. Technically, both supply and demand are relationships between the wages offered by an employer and the number of employees that would apply for work or be hired at that wage that is, supply and demand are curves rather than absolute quantities. For our purposes, talking about them as absolute quantities vastly facilitates the discussion and does little harm to empirical reality. Economics is not the only discipline allowed to make simplifying assumptions.

3. Similarly, some working women really don't want children. Other working women do want children but are forced to develop other preferences because their work life, relationships, or medical situation prevent them having a family. Nothing is sacred or primal about paid employment per se.

4. For readers knowledgeable in labor economics, they will recognize these three results as the predictions made by a simplistic internal labor market theory [Wages are completely divorced from market forces and are determined entirely by internal bureaucratic procedures], training oriented labor market theories [Wages are designed to motivate long term good behavior and training of peers] and human capital theory [Wages represent the value of the human capital associated with the worker].

5. Note that the supply of male and female labor (based on the age and education structure of each sex) did not predict the earnings gap; the researchers measured expected labor supply from age and education, however, not actual labor supply. The actual labor supply of females is likely to depend on the demand for female labor. The more female jobs available, the more women enter the labor market. Exogenous increases in female labor supply stemming from, say, changes in fertility, should unambiguously raise the gender gap. Increases caused in response to employer demand should have an ambiguous effect, however, because the increased number of female jobs mitigates the effect. This is precisely the finding that Cotter et. al. report.

6. For an extended discussion of this issue, see Cohn (1990).

7. When Paula England (1992) attacks marginal productivity explanations of gendered wage differentials, she only considers questions of whether women and men put in equal effort on the job. On this ground, she can refute her limited version of marginal productivity theory compellingly. Her evidence leaves little doubt that men and women work equally hard in their occupations and that gender pay gaps cannot be explained through effort.

8. Actually, such a test would have to control for the types of variables controlled in England 1992. It would in particular have to control for authority because part of the advantage that comes from self-employment is being your own boss. England's analysis shows that supervisory power or deprivation from same is important in its own right, so that the supervisory component of self-employment would need to be removed for self-employment to represent a pure measure of having one's remuneration set strictly by customer prices.

6 Why Are Blacks More Likely to Be Unemployed Than Are Whites?

One of the most unpleasant issues in the study of discrimination is accounting for why blacks are more likely to be unemployed than whites. The figures in Chapter 1 showed that this relationship has applied relatively continuously over the course of the twentieth century and shows no signs of conveniently going away. If this differential persists, most of the promising explanations are unflattering for either blacks or whites. Because of this, bringing up the subject usually gets everybody good and insulted.

Consider the possibilities:

1. BLACKS ARE TOO LAZY TO LOOK FOR WORK. Few social scientists would quite use this language, but this is what is implied by many conservative discussions of the persistence of poverty. Some authors claim that many blacks are members of an underclass that suffers from a "culture of poverty" (Banfield 1958; Moynihan 1965; Lewis 1963; D'Souza 1995). The culture of poverty hypothesis argues that the demoralizing effects of long-term poverty, combined for blacks with the historically destructive effects of slavery, have created a black underclass that has experienced few realistic prospects for advancement. This supposedly has created fatalism within the black community—a belief that all doors are permanently closed to black people and that working hard to advance yourself either in school or the workplace would be pointless.

Some authors blame the destruction of the black family for the persistence of this mentality. Blacks are disproportionately likely to live in single-female-headed families. Because the father is absent and the mother is often away from the house working, children receive inadequate supervision and socialization. They are more apt to go light on their studies or find deviant peers who encourage them to adopt deviant or gang-related life-styles. There is substantial statistical evidence that blacks are more likely to live in single-female households, net of household income, and that children of both races who come from single-female-headed households have fewer years of completed education and lower household incomes than do children from traditional nuclear families (Moynihan 1965; Garfinkel and McLanahan 1986). Thus, the household structure argument is nontrivial and requires being taken seriously.

A related culture of poverty argument involves welfare dependency. Some opponents of big government argue that the presence of welfare allows some blacks to remove themselves from the labor market. Economists would argue, with some justification, that most workers, black or white, have a "reservation wage," and have a wage rate below which they would not accept work. Very few us of would consent to working twelve hours of heavy labor a day for three cents an hour. Welfare can raise the reservation wage by giving poor people an alternative source of nonlabor market income. Some conservatives go further and argue that the presence of welfare undercuts ambition by providing a permanent safety net that can perversely reward idleness (Murray 1984).

Suffice it to say, liberals agree with none of these positions. They tend to argue that unemployment is a function both of an economy that does not generate enough work for all and of racism in the allocation of the supply of jobs that exists. William Ryan (1976) refers to such culture-of-poverty-style arguments as "blaming the victim" because the victims of a larger system of societal oppression are blamed for adverse outcomes not of their own making. Arguments about these positions often break down into polemics that escalate bad feelings on both sides.

2. BLACKS ARE TOO STUPID OR IGNORANT TO COMPETE EFFECTIVELY IN THE LABOR MARKET. If the first proposition wasn't controversial enough, this one can lend fuel to any polemical fire. Some authors have argued that blacks have lower IQs than whites (Herrnstein and Murray 1994; Jensen 1971). If blacks have lower IQs, they would be less likely to obtain the educational credentials required for employment and less likely to perform jobs successfully in the labor market; they would be more likely to be fired or laid off. Most people know this argument is "politically incorrect," but because few people can actually construct strong scientific arguments about why this is an invalid proposition, they are thus fair pickings for any determined racialist who comes along citing bogus numbers.

For those who find the IQ argument unpalatable, there is the traditional human capital argument: Blacks are educationally less qualified than whites. Some scholars argue that blacks get less schooling because their families push their children to a lesser degree than white families do (Murray 1984), an argument hard to justify given the relative similarity of black and white levels of education. Others argue that blacks learn less for every year of education they receive, making the years of education statistics misleading. Low levels of black learning could be a function of family or cultural attributes; it could also be a function of low levels of funding for minority schools, or of discrimination by teachers who present less material to black students than to white students (Jencks et al. 1979; Kozol 1967; Dreeben and Gamoran 1986). Any of these factors could make blacks less prepared with the skills required in the modern labor market, which would make them less qualified employees.

3. WHITE EMPLOYERS DISCRIMINATE AGAINST BLACKS. This explanation speaks for itself. It is an embarrassment to many whites who profess to hold racially tolerant attitudes. Were discrimination to be found to be the primary cause of racial inequality in employment, it would give great force to arguments advocating equal opportunity employment, affirmative action, and other proactive policies designed to limit companies' discretion as to who they may or may not hire. These policies are generally unpopular, both with employers and with whites in general. Because antidiscrimination remedies are often politically charged, there is often a strong incentive to find some more "neutral" approach that promises the hope of equal opportunity in employment without having to directly confront managers' rights to hire whom they choose.

Within social science, there is one "neutral" explanation that allows for the explanation of racial employment inequality without invoking negative attributes on the part of blacks or discrimination on the part of employers:

4. SPATIAL MISMATCH. Spatial mismatch argues that the homes of blacks are too physically far away from jobs. In large cities, most blacks are concentrated in the central city. Most U.S. metropolitan areas consist of a relatively black inner city combined with suburbs and exurbs that are disproportionately white; this is due to a combination of income inequality, which prevents blacks from buying and renting in more affluent neighborhoods, and overt racial discrimination, in which both realtors and rental agents are more likely to steer blacks away from exclusive white areas and towards areas that are already racially integrated (Massey and Denton 1993; J. Farley 1988).

Spatial mismatch theorists argue that the confinement of black residence to the inner city hurts black employment. This is because jobs are steadily migrating from the central city to the suburbs. As cities expand and age, older production facilities in the inner core depreciate and become obsolete. When companies build new facilities, they build these in the suburban ring, where land prices are cheaper, crime is lower, and traffic is less congested. This causes a decrease of employment in the central city, where older plants are closing, and an increase of employment in the periphery, where new plants are opening up. This means that jobs are moving away from concentrations of black population and towards concentrations of white population.

Job outmigration would not be a big deal if everyone had access to automobiles. Blacks would get in their cars and drive out to the suburban industrial parks, look for work—and get work—making racial employment rates equal. Job outmigration only becomes problematic if blacks have less access to transportation than do whites. If minority poverty populations don't have cars, and mass transit links between the ghetto and the suburban periphery are poor, then some African American workers may be incapable of reaching the suburban belt where the new jobs are all locating. This could effectively exclude them from an important sector of the labor market and thus increase minority unemployment relative to whites (Kain 1968; Kasarda 1990).

Spatial mismatch is an extremely appealing notion because it explains racial gaps in employment without using any of the unpopular explanations like employer discrimination or skills differentials. Just because an argument is appealing does not mean it is right, however. For any of these four arguments to have any validity, they have to be consistent with the available evidence. How well do these arguments do when confronted with the facts? Each of the positions given above will be considered fully with a detailed consideration of their strengths and weaknesses. But before this systematic discussion, let us look at some maps that shed some surprising light on the overall problem.[1]

A Cartographic Analysis of Race and Employment

Maps 6.1 and 6.2 show the racial distribution of employment in Detroit and Atlanta in 1980. Maps 6.3 and 6.4 show the racial distribution of residence in Detroit and Atlanta for the same year. The striking thing about both these cities is how much the employment maps and the residential maps resemble each other. In both cities, the labor force of urban firms is heavily black, whereas the labor force of suburban firms is generally white. This difference is particularly striking in Detroit. There is a clear racial line of demarcation along Eight-Mile Road, the northern border between the city of Detroit proper and the northern suburbs. The city side of the line has black employment; the suburban side of the line has white employment. The sole exception to this is a tiny corridor of intermediate black employment in Warren. A less dramatic east-west boundary exists along Telegraph Road, with the only significant black labor force west of Telegraph Road being the Detroit Metropolitan Airport. Employment throughout the city of Detroit is moderately black to heavily black, with the strongest concentrations being in the residential neighborhoods to the northwest and northeast of downtown.

MAP 6.1   Percent of Black Employment Detroit 1980—Central Detail

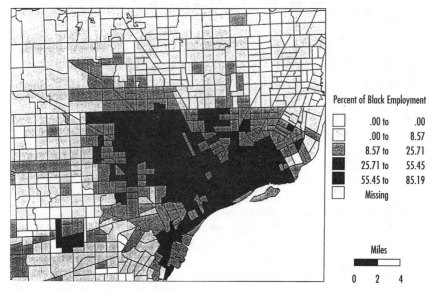

SOURCE: Urban Transportation Planning Package, Detroit, 1980.

MAP 6.2   Percent of Black Employment Atlanta—Central Detail

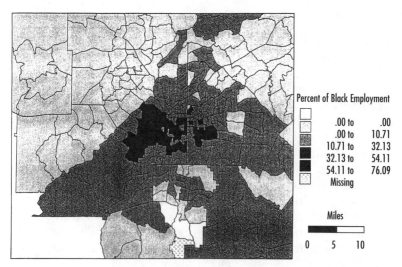

SOURCE: Urban Transportation Planning Package, Atlanta, 1980.

MAP 6.3   Percent of Residence That Is Black Detroit 1980—Central Detail

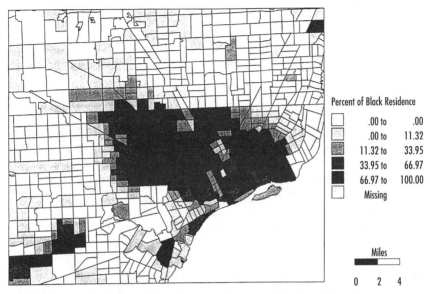

Percent of Black Residence

.00 to	.00
.00 to	11.32
11.32 to	33.95
33.95 to	66.97
66.97 to	100.00
Missing	

Miles

0   2   4

SOURCE: Urban Transportation Planning Package, Detroit, 1980.

MAP 6.4   Percent of Black Residence Atlanta—Central Detail

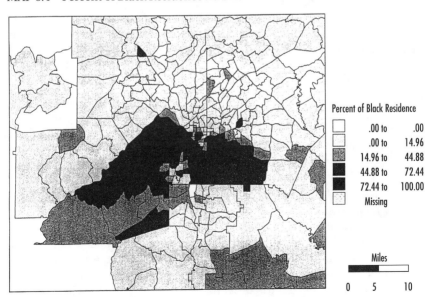

Percent of Black Residence

.00 to	.00
.00 to	14.96
14.96 to	44.88
44.88 to	72.44
72.44 to	100.00
Missing	

Miles

0   5   10

SOURCE: Urban Transportation Planning Package, Atlanta, 1980.

In Atlanta, black employment is concentrated on the south side of the city, in Fulton and Dekalb counties. These jobs are found in two clusters, one in a broad expanse on the west side of downtown running on either side of Bankhead Highway, the other east of Carter Center, in the corridor leading to Decatur. Note the strong color break of employment associated with county lines. In the northwest, black employment stops abruptly at the Chattahoochee River, the border between urban Fulton County and suburban Cobb County. In the northeast, black employment stops abruptly at the border between semi-urban DeKalb County and suburban Gwinnet County. Note as well that Northern Atlanta has a higher percentage of black employment than the suburbs, but less than that of the south side.

These employment patterns closely echo patterns of racial residence. The percent of black residence is shown in Maps 6.1 and 6.2. The city of Detroit is relatively uniformly black. The pattern changes dramatically at Eight-Mile Road, the border between Detroit and the northern suburbs, and the equally dramatic break point for changes in racial hiring. The western border is more diffuse, a pattern also noticeable in the employment map. The northern suburbs are all predominantly white; the primary black suburbs are Inkster and Ecorse, the two suburban centers of black employment.

In Atlanta, black residence is concentrated on the south side of the city with Marietta Boulevard and Route 278 representing the northern borders of the ghetto. As was the case with employment, black residence stops abruptly in the northwest at the Cobb County line; in the northeast, however, black residence only extends part of the way into DeKalb County. Both northern Atlanta and the northern suburbs are predominantly white.

This pattern is not unique to Detroit and Atlanta. Cohn and Fossett have investigated ten other U.S. cities: Chicago, Boston, Philadelphia, Houston, Louisville, Seattle, San Francisco, Phoenix, Fort Lauderdale and Buffalo. This pattern can be found in every city that was investigated (Cohn and Fossett forthcoming) and has been independently confirmed in the MultiCity Survey of Urban Inequality (MCSUI) four-city study of Los Angeles, Boston, Detroit and Atlanta, and in a separate study of Atlanta fast food establishments (Holzer 1996; Ihlanfeldt and Young 1996).

How can one explain that whites work in white neighborhoods and blacks work in black neighborhoods? One obvious possibility is that blacks are discriminated against in white suburbs. There is some statistical evidence suggesting that this may be the case. In the MCSUI study, the investigators analyzed for suburban and inner-city firms, the probability at these establishments that a black would be hired assuming that he applied for work. Black job applicants had a much lower chance of being hired by the suburban employers than by the urban employers.

One possible explanation for this is that suburban firms have white customers, whereas urban firms may have black customers. The race of the customer base was found to have an important role in determining race of hires in studies of San Francisco, Atlanta, and Boston (Holzer and Ihlanfeldt 1996). If white customers were prejudiced and did not want to be served by black people, employers might choose to respect these decisions and only hire whites to serve whites. This would be an indirect form of discrimination, rather than direct, because the employer would be reflecting the sensibility of the market rather than exercising personal preference.

However, it is not likely that customer prejudice is driving this pattern. In the South there has been a long tradition of black people providing personal services to white people. When rich whites had black cooks who prepared food and black maids who brought the food to the table, who would object to a black worker making or serving hamburgers at a McDonald's?

More important, in the MCSUI study, the racial hiring rates were presented for occupations separately. The exclusion of blacks occurred not only in jobs that involved contact with a white public, such as retail sales, but also in jobs with no exposure to white customers at all! Blue-collar back room positions such as operatives, craftsmen, and laborers were subject to the same racial patterns that were applied to jobs with customer contact. This suggests that the issue is not contact with white consumers—the pattern held where consumer contact was absent—but contact with white managers and foremen, and that it is the sensibilities of the managers and foremen that caused blacks to be excluded.

Can spatial mismatch account for these findings? Superficially it might seem so, because blacks work in cities where they live and whites work in suburbs where they live. However, the racial boundaries in Maps 6.1 and 6.2 are much too clean to be accounted for by transport situations. In Detroit, there is a clear race line in employment on Eight Mile Road, with blacks working to the south and whites working to the north. How likely is it that blacks' lack of access to automobiles allows them to reach the south side of Eight Mile Road but does not allow them to cross the street to work on the north side of Eight Mile Road?

Cohn and Fossett considered the role of transportation quite explicitly by actually measuring the race of which workers could or could not reach each job site in both Detroit in Atlanta. For each city, they calculated the percentage of workers of each race that have cars, and used commuting data to calculate how far car owners can travel and how far noncar owners can travel. Given that, for every job in each city they could calculate the percentage of all people within commuting distance of that job who were black or white.

The race of the labor force able to reach suburban and urban jobs was practically the same. The majority of blacks in both cities have cars. At the time of the study, 72 percent of all black households in Detroit and 76 percent of all black households in Atlanta had access to at least one car. Although this number is smaller than the comparable figure for whites, it put practically three-fourths of all black workers within range of any job in either city. Furthermore, this three-fourths figure does not take into consideration public transportation, car pooling, sharing rides, bicycling, or any of the other methods that noncar owners routinely make use of to get to work. Cohn and Fossett adjusted for noncar owner-ship and the distance that walkers, bicyclists, and mass transit users are able to travel. Overall, in Detroit, the distances blacks and whites were able to travel to work differed by only 0.9 of a mile! In Atlanta, the dis-tances blacks and whites were able to travel to work differed by only 1.7 miles. It would be implausible for a suburban manager to say that black candidates were unavailable because none of the blacks in Detroit was able to reach the job site.

It also does not appear that spatial composition of employment can be explained by urban-suburban differentials in jobs requiring educa-tion. Conceivably, if suburban jobs were highly skilled, and inner city jobs were relatively menial, then blacks with low levels of education might be unqualified to take suburban positions. However, jobs in the suburban belt do not have unusually high skill requirements. For every job in Detroit and Atlanta, Cohn and Fossett calculated the educational requirements as can be inferred from the average education of jobhold-ers working in that occupation in the city as a whole. The results are shown in Maps 6.5 and 6.6.

What is striking about both maps is that skill requirements do not show a strong urban-suburban gradient that would concentrate black workers in the central city. In Detroit, there is no statistical relationship between the educational requirements of jobs and distance from the downtown business district. In Atlanta, high-skill jobs are more likely to be found downtown than in the suburban belt! By education alone, one would expect whites and blacks to work in the same areas in Detroit, and for whites to work downtown and blacks to work in the suburbs in Atlanta. This plainly does not occur. Skills and education tell us little about why blacks work in inner cities and whites work in suburbs.

Shiftlessness would seem unhelpful as an explanation. It could be that blacks don't travel very far because they are reluctant to leave the central city. The patterns of data in Maps 6.1 and 6.2, however, are consistent with lazy whites not wanting to leave the suburbs as well as lazy blacks

MAP 6.5   Demand for Education Detroit 1980—Central Detail

SOURCE: Urban Transportation Planning Package, Detroit, 1980.

MAP 6.6   Demand for Education Atlanta 1980—Central Detail

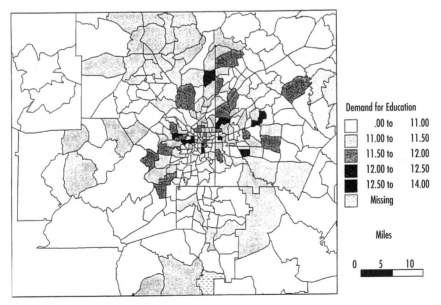

SOURCE: Urban Transportation Planning Package, Atlanta, 1980.

not wanting to leave downtown. That said, there is no statistical evidence that blacks are less willing to travel to go to work than are whites. There is an extensive sociological literature measuring the distance of the journey to work for blacks and for whites. This literature tends to report two kinds of findings, depending on the sample and methodology involved. Some studies find no differences between blacks and whites in their journeys to work (Gordon et al. 1988). Other studies find that blacks travel significantly longer distances to work than do whites (Greytak 1974). There are no studies that find that blacks travel shorter distances to work than do whites.

The Detroit and Atlanta maps are consistent with discrimination-based explanations of employment inequality. They are inconsistent with shiftlessness, human capital, and spatial mismatch explanations of this phenomenon. However, the Detroit and Atlanta data are not the only empirical evidence in the world relevant to the study. What does the rest of the literature suggest about the relative validity of these explanations?

Shiftlessness

The best work on shiftlessness has been done by Marta Tienda and Haya Stier (1991). Marta Tienda has been chair of the sociology department at the University of Chicago, the top-rated sociology department in the United States, and editor of the *American Journal of Sociology*, the most prestigious sociological journal in the United States. She has published extensively on the causes and consequences of poverty. In this particular study, Tienda and a coauthor examined the labor market behavior of a large sample of residents of poverty areas within the city of Chicago. The South Side of Chicago represents the biggest contiguous concentration of black urban poverty in the country. In both area and size, it is this country's largest ghetto. Other sections of Chicago, notably the West Side and some of the western portions of the North Side have poverty problems that are just as severe. Inner-city Chicago neighborhoods tend to have a high rate of joblessness. Tienda and Stier examined this population to determine the extent to which the observed lack of employment was due to shiftlessness or laziness, or other factors.

Obviously, many reasons besides laziness would induce someone to not have a job. One is age. We do not expect four-year-olds to work. We also do not expect eighty-five year olds to work. Tienda and Stier excluded the very old and the very young from their analysis. At another level, if a young, single 25-year-old male chose not to work and not to take welfare, this would not be a central concern of public policy. Anyone who wants to go hungry is free to do so. Poverty debates tend to center around the provision of welfare, and the most controversial welfare programs are those that involve families. Public discussion centers on welfare parents who take public money to feed their children when in theory they could be out working. Therefore, Tienda and Stier concentrated on this population: Parents in a state of poverty who were of prime working age, namely, from ages 18 to 44.

Tienda and Stier asked the following simple questions (loosely paraphrased here):

1. Are you currently employed? (Obviously poor people who are holding down jobs are not shiftless. They're working.)
2. If you are not employed, are you currently looking for work? (Not having a job but actively looking for work represents the standard definition of being *unemployed*. Someone spending time sending out resumes, reading the want ads, and visiting potential employers is hardly being lazy; that person is working at getting a job.)
3. If you are not employed, and you are not looking for work, do you actually want a job? (Here is where we divide the shiftless from the rest of the population. Anyone who is not employed and not looking for work is technically *out of the labor market*. Not all people who are out of the labor market are shiftless. Someone may have been actively been looking for work for six months. After visiting every employer in his or her field over and over again, the worker is instructed by the receptionists not to come back, and when they have something, the companies will call. Realizing that the search is hopeless, the worker stops searching. Now if news were to emerge that work was available, the worker would leap into gear. If a new factory were to open up in town, the worker would be the first person in line. That said, when nothing is going on, the worker isn't searching. This person is technically referred to as a *discouraged worker*, and should not be considered shiftless. This is a person who is not working and is not searching, but if you asked that person, do you want a job, the answer would be an emphatic yes.

   By contrast, one can imagine someone who is not working, and not looking for work, who, if asked if he or she wants a job, would say, "Hell, no!" This individual represents what is meant when we say someone is lazy or shiftless.) Social policies designed to cut welfare to get people back on the job rolls clearly have this second kind of person in mind, the individual happy to take a check rather than put himself or herself out. So shiftlessness in Tienda and Stier's study is defined as answering "No" to all three questions.

TABLE 6.1   Work Status of Chicago Inner City Poverty Neighborhood Parents
Age 18–44: 1987

Currently Employed	57.0%
Unemployed (No Job but Actively Looking)	8.2%
Discouraged Worker (Out of the Labor Force but Wants a Job)	29.3%
Shiftless (Out of the Labor Force and Does Not Want a Job)	5.4%

NOTE: Numbers do not add to 100% due to rounding error.
SOURCE: From Tienda and Stier (1991).

Tienda and Stier found that shiftlessness existed in Chicago's inner city, but there was not as much as one might think. Somewhat over half of the Chicago inner city poverty parents were employed (Table 6.1). Eight percent of the parents were formally unemployed. Slightly over a third were out of the labor force. The vast majority of the parents who were out of the labor force wanted some kind of job, and weren't looking simply because they couldn't find work. Only 5.4 percent of the poverty parents fit the shiftlessness profile: not employed, not looking for work, and not particularly wanting a job.

Note that this 5.4 percent figure probably *overstates* the actual level of shiftlessness. Some of the individuals in that 5.4 percent may have had legitimate reasons for not wanting a job. For example, the sample included parents who were aged from 18 to 44. There was probably at least one, if not more, full-time student in Tienda and Stier's population. An individual attending the University of Illinois-Chicago Circle on student loans, carrying a full course load, and taking care of children at home is technically not employed and not looking for work. Such an individual is hardly likely to lack professional motivation or a work ethic.

Some of the individuals in the study could have been disabled. Some blind or mobility-impaired people can hold down traditional jobs. Others with more severe conditions cannot. One can argue about whether the definition of shiftlessness would apply to individuals with mental health disabilities. Whether a schizophrenic or an individual with dissociative disorders who doesn't want to work is lazy or sick is a judgment call.

However, someone with severe physical impairments would seem to have an excuse for not working and should be exempt from the shiftlessness label.

A third category, which must be considered, is the traditional parent. Some women, often those with traditional religious values, genuinely believe in staying home with their children, and are legitimately concerned with what would happen to them if they were left with inadequate supervision. Whether or not you would call these people shiftless depends on a number of circumstances: Is the woman single, or merely married to a low-income husband? How responsible or irresponsible were the fertility decisions when they were made? Would the costs of child care completely wipe out any wages that would be obtained by working? One can see that this is a huge gray area in which conscientious moral people could strongly disagree about what the appropriate ethical behavior ought to be for the woman involved. (Naturally this discussion finesses on whether big government should be telling these women how many kids to have or whether or not to stay home with them in the first place.)

It is safe to say, however, that there were at least some full-time students, some disabled people, and some responsible stay-at-home mothers in the 5.4 percent of poverty parents who were labeled as shiftless. When you take these people out, the 5.4 percent would become a smaller number. How small it would become is hard to say; we don't know how many students, disabled people, and mothers there were in the sample. But no matter how you calculate this, 94.6 percent of poverty parents were *not* shiftless, and in reality this figure was somewhat higher. This makes it hard to explain unemployment differentials in terms of some widespread laziness or lack of work ethic in minority or disadvantaged populations.

One small concluding note. In 1990, there were 230,647 people aged from 18 to 44 with incomes below the poverty level living in the city of Chicago. Assuming that 5.4 percent of these people were shiftless, this would mean there were 12,455 shiftless poor people. Even though they were a small percentage of the group, 12,455 is an absolutely large number. This means that if a newspaper reporter wanted to do a shock Sunday magazine story on the scandalous poor, he or she could have picked any one of 12,455 cases to report. Any story that had from eight to ten of these people combined with horrible pictures and juicy anecdotes could convey an impressive picture that poor people in Chicago's South Side are a set of irresponsible losers frittering away public welfare dollars. The thing to remember is that these people are a relative exception, and that such a story would misrepresent the 229,192 poor people in Chicago who do not share the work attitudes of the 12,455 minority.

Percentages are important in this kind of issue, and the percentage that matters is that at least 94.6 percent of prime working-age poverty parents are not shiftless. The solutions to their employment problems must be sought somewhere other than in changing their work ethic.

IQ and Human Capital

Human capital differences were once an important explanation of why blacks were less likely to be employed than whites. These differences still play a role today, but their significance and importance is greatly diminished. We saw from the statistics presented in Chapter 1 how educational differences between blacks and whites have declined dramatically over the twentieth century. While the racial education gap was once substantial, whites and blacks currently have nearly equal median education and nearly equal rates of high school graduation. It is only in college graduation rates that any noticeable gap continues to exist. In 1940, educational differences between blacks and whites were substantial; many African Americans would not have been qualified for higher status blue- and white-collar positions. However, as Chapter 1 maintained, despite the reduction in racial education gaps, racial employment gaps have remained virtually unchanged. Educational differences are not the primary explanation of why blacks remain less employed than whites today.

Bound and Freeman (1992) found that increased schooling has been no panacea for black economic woes. Throughout the 1980s, black earnings and employment declined relative to whites. (Black economic prospects are improving as of this writing in the late 1990s.) However, the importance of the 1980s is that it represented the culmination of the 1970s tendency for African Americans to increase their education relative to whites. In the 1980s when these newly educated blacks entered the labor market, there should have been some evidence of relative reward. Bound and Freeman examined the economic prospects of workers who had recently entered the labor market, that is, had nine years or less experience and thus had received their education in the years of increasing educational equality of the 1970s. They found the prospects for African Americans generally deteriorated; worse still, college graduates suffered the greatest declines of any educational group! They had the largest rate of decline of earnings of any educational group and the second largest rate of decline in employment. Black college graduates outearned other black groups, but they still had lower pay and higher unemployment than did whites with comparable levels of education.

One possible explanation—and one that I don't espouse—is that blacks have lower IQs than do than whites, so that even with comparable levels of schooling, blacks are less qualified than whites because they are simply less intelligent. This genetically-oriented argument reappears every decade or so, the most recent manifestation being Herrnstein and Murray's 1994 bestseller, *The Bell Curve.* In this book, Herrnstein and Murray present various statistics showing that whites perform better on tests of mental aptitude than do blacks and Hispanics, and that people who score higher on tests of mental aptitude tend to have more education, better employment prospects, and higher incomes.

The Bell Curve generated a firestorm of controversy in social science, much of which was emotional or nit-picky rather than constructive. However, the biologist Stephen Jay Gould saw exactly what was wrong with Herrnstein and Murray, and his arguments apply with force to anyone who wants to make an IQ-based explanation of black poverty or unemployment (Gould 1994). First, IQ tests are not the only viable psychometric measure of intelligence. Cognitive psychology uses many indices of mental capacity besides traditional IQ, and the other indicators do not correlate tidily with race.

Second, and most important, *even in Herrnstein and Murray's own data,* IQ has no particularly strong relationship either to income or to employment! In the body of the manuscript, the authors present tidy little graphs showing adverse effects of low IQ based on a statistical technique known as logistic regression. They save the actual equations for a statistical appendix. If one looks at the equations in the appendix, the results are damning. Yes, the equations show a statistically significant relationship between IQ, earnings, and employment. However, the effect is trivial. This can be shown with the R^2 statistic, a measure of the explanatory power of a regression equation. This number runs from 0 to 1.00. Generally, for an equation to be considered valid, an R^2 should be at least 0.20; it is preferable to have scores in the 0.30 or 0.40 range. On a particularly difficult estimation, one might settle for 0.15. Their equation, which included IQ, social class, and age, had an R^2 of only 0.01. By most social science standards, this is pathetically low. An R^2 of 0.01 means that the equation with IQ could only explain 1 percent of the differences between individuals in employment. Put differently, 99 percent of the differences between people in their unemployment rates was unexplained by IQ. They repeated the analysis changing the measure and using selected subsamples. Changing the measure to long-term unemployment raised the R^2 to 0.03, still very weak. Using subsamples produced results ranging from 0.03 to 0.10, not even their best equation left 90 percent of individual differences in unemployment unexplained. The situation was similar when they tried to predict poverty status. Their basic equation had an R^2 of 0.10. Analyzing subsamples reduced the R^2 to 0.06 to 0.09. And remember, part of the R^2 they achieved came from the two other variables in the analysis, social class and age. Overall the performance of the IQ variable was quite weak.

This is consistent with other research that has been done on the effect of IQ on adult economic prospects. The definitive study of occupational success is the Wisconsin High School senior study. The University of Wisconsin took a large sample of all Wisconsin high school seniors in 1957 and followed them for twenty years after senior year. The seniors were asked about every aspect of their childhoods, educational and professional lives, including their actual labor market experiences, their attitudes and their relationships with other people. One of the many pieces of information that the Wisconsin researchers had access to was the students' IQ.

The careers of the Wisconsin High School seniors have been exhaustively studied, with several books and over a hundred articles being derived from these materials. One of the topics that received attention was the relationship between IQ and future success in life. This relationship was fairly weak. IQ played some role in schooling experiences. There was a modest correlation between IQ and high school grades, and also between IQ and Teacher Encouragement to Go to College. However, there was no direct relationship between IQ and years of education completed, educational aspiration, occupational aspiration, status of occupation attained in adulthood, or adult income (Sewell and Hauser 1975).

This pattern of findings makes sense. Generalized human capital such as intelligence and education, are far more important in the early stages of the career than they are in middle and late adulthood. The primary function of education is to sort people into occupations. When young people enter the labor market, they have little experience. They do not have an established track record; they do not have concrete accomplishments in an occupation they can point to; they have a relatively underdeveloped set of network connections of friends and associates in the work world who can help them obtain positions. They enter the labor market as relative ciphers. Employers are faced with an army of such ciphers. To help distinguish among essentially identical-looking neophytes, corporations use screening devices, such as years of education and grade point averages. These modestly help to identify who is talented and who is not, even if the relationships between education and future productivity are tenuous or weak.[2]

Education thus matters in determining who enters occupations. Technically, the process described in the previous paragraph only refers to how individual firms decide which labor market entrants to hire. However, companies in an industry tend to use screening rules that are typical of comparable firms in their labor market. If one chemical company on the Texas Gulf Coast insists on their warehouse workers being high school graduates, the others tend to do so as well. If one teaching college in Philadelphia insists on Ph.D.'s for its assistant professors, soon other

Philadelphia colleges of comparable status are insisting on the same requirement. Without the formal education, one does not get an entry-level position. Because IQ and other formal tests of aptitude are used by schools to stratify students, with higher scoring students receiving more encouragement to continue, it is not surprising that IQ would have some relation, even a tenuous one, with occupational status.

These factors become much less important in determining adult unemployment once an occupation has been entered. Adult unemployment depends on two considerations: the likelihood of quitting or losing one's job and the likelihood of obtaining a second job after the first job has been left. Job instability has only a limited relation to education or intelligence. The likelihood of losing one's job is based on the economic health of the company with which one is employed, the presence of other people in the firm who can do the same job as the worker, the alignment in office politics with winners rather than losers, and the presence of union protection or other contractual/legal limitations on the employer's right to fire. When AT&T buys out a competing telecommunications company and announces a 15 percent reduction of upper management, most of the victims will have levels of education comparable to those managers who will remain after the merger. The unemployment of the losing managers stems both from their being in a company that is downsizing and being located in a workgroup that new management wants to replace with outsiders in an occupation with few union or legal obstacles to the implementation of mass layoffs.[3]

Getting a new job after losing a first job is less dependent on education than is obtaining the first job. Because the worker has been in the occupation for a while, he or she has developed concrete accomplishments to talk about. The worker is master of particular occupational skills that can be sold to employers. This type of worker requires less training than do raw labor market entrants. Furthermore, because the worker has been involved in the social interactions of the industry and labor market, he or she has network connections in other firms. The worker hears of jobs before the general public does and can count on acquaintances to facilitate his or her hiring at the acquaintances' home firms. What matters is the mastery of a particular set of occupation-specific skills, and to some extent being sociable enough to develop a web of friends and associates. These aptitudes are not the same as IQ, and they may not even correlate with IQ.

A geneticist might argue that this discussion underestimates the impact of intelligence in the work world. Bright people are more talented. They are more likely to develop workplace-specific skills that make them useful to their employers. Bright stockbrokers become high-volume, high-commission stockbrokers; bright mechanics become the irreplaceable fix-it-alls that are indispensable to the running of their factories. Bright workers may even be more astute at playing office politics, both within their own companies and with allies in other firms. Such multitalented individuals might be less likely to be laid off by their employers and more likely to be hired by competing firms.

However, many occupational skills simply do not require very much raw intelligence. Numerous studies have examined the educational requirements for the U.S. workplace. Since the 1960s, the skill required to fill a 50th percentile U.S. occupation has been merely a high school education or one or two years of college. Some jobs may require more as part of the bureaucratic prerequisite, but external measurements of the job skills involved place the educational requirements at high school or early college level. Note that this figure has not changed between 1960 and 1990, despite the computerization of the U.S. economy (Berg 1970, Rumberger 1982, Mishel and Teixera 1990).

Naturally, good jobs require more than the skill required for a 50th-percentile occupation. But even here, job skill and general intelligence are not the same. Most jobs involve the mastery of a specific and distinctive set of routines. A currency trader trades currency. An allergist administers skin tests and allergy shots. An insurance adjuster adjudicates casualty claims using his company's formal claims adjustment procedures. Once one gets past the rituals associated with education, such as premed exams or underwriting course work, the actual on-the-job routines involve fairly narrow intellectual tasks. Continual daily exposure to the same regular tasks can produce a skilled practitioner, even in the absence of a high IQ per se.

Many good jobs are like playing poker. Poker is a skill. It is a narrow skill. Not everyone who has a high IQ can play poker well. Some expert poker players are idiots at almost everything else in life. However, they play poker; they've played a lot of poker, and they're highly motivated to play poker. Their combination of practice and dedication has made them extremely competent in their field.

The labor market is like that. The person who sells commercial real estate everyday, supervises a set of tile warehouses everyday, or counsels disturbed adolescents everyday can become very good at what he or she does, even without a high IQ. By contrast, many brilliant people with advanced academic degrees do not have a single useful skill in their repertoires. So when the labor market worsens, and unemployment threatens, it is not always the person with a high IQ who will be the most competent nor the person with an advanced degree who will be the most protected from dismissal.

Unemployment is shaped by the state of the economy, the prosperity of one's company, one's social connections, and one's ability to learn very narrow skills. Neither general education nor IQ guarantee competence let alone a good economy or good connections. Therefore, while generalized human capital does reduce one's odds of experiencing unemployment, it is not surprising that this relationship is somewhat weak. Adult unemployment is driven by the immediate experiences of the mid-career, not by one's school experiences of ten to twenty years earlier.

Spatial Mismatch

The spatial mismatch hypothesis has been the subject of extended controversy ever since it was first proposed in the mid–1960s. One of the reasons for its survival is that it contains some elements of truth. It is indisputable, for example, that jobs are increasingly leaving the city for the suburbs (Kasarda 1990). There is also clear evidence from Boston and Oakland that firms located near mass transportation stops are more likely to hire blacks than those that are not (Holzer and Ihlanfeldt 1996; Holzer 1991; Raphael 1998). If blacks have less access to automobiles than do whites, then some black workers will be dependent on subways and busses for getting to work. These workers are more likely to apply to workplaces near subway stations and less likely to apply where travel poses practical problems.

That said, on most other points the spatial mismatch hypothesis looks weaker. One problem, first identified by Fremon in 1970, is that blacks are actually physically nearer to more jobs than are whites. If anything, whites have a spatial disadvantage concerning access to employment because, in most cities, the largest concentrations of employment are located in the downtown areas. The bulk of Chicago's employment is in the Loop; the bulk of Boston's employment is between Kenmore Square and Lechmere, with some spillover into the Kendall Square area of Cambridge. Yes, jobs are relocating to the suburban ring. However, these clusters of jobs are thin. Most cities have a suburban ring freeway or a set of highway spoke corridors that contain substantial commercial and industrial development; but these developments are also thin. They go two or three blocks in each direction from the freeway, then quickly taper off into residential development. In the center city, by contrast, industrial and commercial zoning goes on for block after block after block. Downtown, multiple skyscrapers fill areas of twenty-five blocks. Farther out, industrial zones extend from three to five miles at a shot.

Residential segregation confines blacks to the central city. This ironically puts them at a spatial *advantage* in being able to reach the downtown superconcentration of jobs. Downtown Boston is just across one railroad track from Roxbury, one of the primary ghettos of Boston. The Fifth Ward of Houston, the largest concentration of black residence in that city, borders on both the downtown business district and the Medical Center, the second biggest concentration of blue-collar jobs in the city. The Sears Tower in Chicago is within walking distance of several low-income black neighborhoods. People in the suburbs may have a higher quality of life; however, it is easier for an urban black to walk to work (Fremon 1970; Harrison 1974).[4]

As a result, critics of the spatial mismatch theory have generated a substantial number of disconfirming results. Ellwood (1986), Leonard (1986), and Cooke (1993) in separate studies of Chicago, Los Angeles, and Indianapolis found no relation between distance from jobs and unemployment for minority youth. Raphael (1998) reports a similar nonrelation between proximity to changes in the number of jobs and unemployment for black youth in the Bay Area. Ellwood (1986) Raphael (1998) and Cohn and Fossett (1995) report job accessibility counts (using measures of stock rather than flow) that show blacks are nearer to as many or more jobs than are whites in Chicago, San Francisco-Oakland, Boston, and Houston.

This does not exhaust all the work that has been done on spatial mismatch. A literature exists that supports this theory. Sympathetic reviews of these findings can be found in Holzer (1991) and Kain (1992)—and a hostile discussion of these same materials in Cohn and Fossett (forthcoming). The arguments between the scholars stem over questions of methodology. Should we count the total number of jobs available to blacks or just the numbers that were added in given years? (I say count them all because employment rates count them all; others say just look at net changes because this makes the suburbs look as though they have more jobs than the cities.) When we complain about jobs moving to the suburbs, should we take into account black suburbs that might benefit from such moves? (Early prospatial mismatch literature ignored black suburbs.) The debates over technicalities go on and on. The interested reader is free to read the reviews of this literature and come to his or her own opinion.

The student who wants to get some closure on this issue may want to consider Table 6.2. Table 6.2 ranks twelve major U.S. cities by their levels of spatial mismatch and by the observed gap between black and white employment. The twelve cities represent 100 percent of the cities for which data was available on spatial mismatch at the time the study was conducted. There is almost no relationship between the two lists. Buffalo is the least mismatched city in the sample but has a high racial employment gap. Seattle is the second most mismatched city in the sample but is relatively egalitarian. Atlanta and Fort Lauderdale are at about the same position on both lists; all the other cities move around in crazy ways. Statistically, the Pearson correlation between these two items, a

TABLE 6.2   Rankings of 12 American SMSAs by Spatial Mismatch and by Observed Black-White Employment Gaps

Spatial Mismatch (Highest to Lowest)	*Black-White Employment Inequality* (Highest to Lowest)
San Francisco	Chicago
Seattle	Detroit
Boston	Philadelphia
Detroit	Buffalo
Louisville	San Francisco
Atlanta	Atlanta
Chicago	Boston
Phoenix	Houston
Philadelphia	Louisville
Houston	Seattle
Fort Lauderdale	Phoenix
Buffalo	Fort Lauderdale

NOTE: Spatial mismatch is defined as the median number of jobs within commuting range of black residents divided by the median number of jobs within commuting range of white residents.

Black white employment inequality is measured as the log odds ratios of black to white employment.
All data are for 1980.

SOURCE: Cohn and Fossett (Forthcoming).

measure of statistical association is 0.08; this number is statistically insignificant, and virtually equal to zero, meaning there is no relationship between the two items. Given the poor performance of spatial mismatch in explaining the patterns we saw in the Detroit and Atlanta maps and its equally bad performance in the Table 6.2 ranking exercise, there is reason to be skeptical about the theory overall. The issue remains controversial, and this book will undoubtedly not be the last word on the topic.

Employer Discrimination

Discrimination is a relatively appealing theory because, unlike the other models, there is very little negative evidence disconfirming it; unfortunately, there is also very little positive evidence confirming it. Few employers will openly admit to engaging in racial exclusion given that discrimination is both illegal and frowned upon socially. In most situations, the decision not to hire blacks can be legitimated on a case-by-case basis, with individual objections as to why this particular black or that particular black would not be suitable for the job. Objections can be found to any job applicant. (Think about presidential elections; political parties comb the nation for the one best candidate out of literally millions of people. As soon as the one great candidate is found, that individual is subjected to excoriating, excruciating, and all too often accurate critique.) It becomes hard then to separate out reasonable and bona fide objections from cover stories for a simple preference not to hire minorities. As a result, in contrast to the copious literature on human capital and spatial mismatch theory, there are relatively few studies of discrimination per se.

The strongest and most direct evidence for employer discrimination comes from audit studies. In an audit study, one arranges for two actors, one black and one white, to apply for the same job with a given employer. The actors are given identical vitae and qualifications, save for trivial differences to avoid detection of the experiment. One can then assess whether the white actor is more or less likely to get the job than the black actor. A minor problem with this design is that in most cases, neither actor gets the job. If there are fifty candidates for one position, there is only a 4 percent chance that one of the experimental pair will be selected for the hire. Audit studies compensate for this by contrasting the black candidate's and white candidate's progress through the hiring process. Thus contrasts are made between the likelihood of getting an application (some black candidates are actually denied applications at the outset), the likelihood of getting an interview, the length of the interview, the courteousness with which the applicant is treated, and in the rare cases where one or both test takers are hired, the quality of the job that is offered. (Sometimes black candidates will be referred to a lower-status position or white candidates referred to a higher-status position.)

The best analyses of employer discrimination are the Urban Institute Employment Discrimination Studies of 1989 and 1990 (Struyk, Turner, and Fix 1991). This was a series of approximately nine hundred audit interviews conducted in three cities. The one study measured discrimination against blacks. The Urban Institute found small but persistent tendencies towards discrimination against minorities. In the case of blacks, 80 percent of the time the applicants of both races were treated the same. This sounds like an impressive display of equality, but one needs to be careful here. Equal treatment generally meant neither candidate got the job. As we argued before, if there are two experimental candidates in a pool of fifty candidates, there is a 96 percent chance that neither candidate will be hired and that the applicants will report "equal treatment." This would hold even in a firm that as a matter of policy never hired black candidates and only hired white candidates; by the law of averages, the firm would be highly likely to hire a different white than the one in the study.

The way one assesses discrimination is to observe the cases where the two candidates receive differential treatment. Differential treatment is the normal outcome of a recruitment procedure because, unless there is only one candidate, someone will be hired and the rest of the applicant pool will be rejected, producing unavoidable and natural unequal treatment. Inequality, however, can be racially neutral or racially biased. In a nondiscriminatory world, the black candidate should be equally as likely as the white candidate to get the position. In a biased recruitment process, one racial group would be more likely to get hired.

In the Urban Institute Study, in the cases where blacks and whites received different treatment, meaning one of them was hired, the white candidates were three times more likely to be hired than were the black candidates. The Hispanic experience was similar to that of the blacks. When there was unequal treatment, Anglos were three times more likely to receive a job offer than were Hispanics.

Preferential treatment for whites extended to most of the substages of the hiring process as well, although not all of these differences were large. No white was ever refused a job application. Two percent of blacks were not allowed to apply. More notably, in settings where only one candidate received an interview, it was three times more likely that the interviewee would be a white than a black. Whites were 60 percent more likely to receive a long interview rather than a short interview. They were twice as likely to be have multiple rather than single interviewers, an indicator that the interview was being taken seriously. Blacks were twice as likely to be kept waiting for the interview but almost half as likely to get a long interview once they got in.

The results varied enormously between cities and between industries. Although the sample was too small to allow a careful analysis, it appears that some industries and places were relatively nondiscriminatory while others were highly discriminatory. The most consistently biased firms appear to have been retail stores. This is consistent with evidence from Holzer et al. (1995) that suggests firms are especially reluctant to hire blacks when the firms' consumer bases are primarily white. Some people might interpret this as an indicator of consumer discrimination. However, it is the employer who is refusing to let black salespeople work in his establishment, not the customer. Given the records of African Americans in such verbal occupations as the ministry and entertainment, and the widespread use of African American athletes to endorse merchandise, I leave it to the reader to assess whether blacks are capable of selling products to white people.

Outside of audit studies, the evidence gets significantly thinner. There are a number of surveys of employer opinion (Kirschemann and Neckerman 1991; Moss and Tilly 1996). These interviews tend to be open-ended, loosely structured discussions in which employers are openly encouraged to give their own subjective opinions about black workers. The opinions they give are not flattering. Blacks are almost universally characterized as being lazy, unqualified, lacking interactional skills, and having questionable professional motivation or ethics. The most obvious interpretation of these data is that the employers sampled in these studies were fairly prejudiced. It would not be hard to understand how such individuals might be reluctant to hire black workers.

Whenever I assign these studies to undergraduates, I always get some papers or exams back making the following arguments: "Kirschenmann and Neckerman show that blacks don't get jobs because they are lazy, unmotivated, and unethical. The evidence for this comes from the employers who have hired them." Technically, none of these studies provides any evidence whatsoever on black performance. There is not a shred of data to substantiate the claim that black performance differs from white performance in any way. However, this absence of data is a two-edged sword, and none of the authors can provide any evidence that black performance *was* the same as white performance. People who already believe the two races have equal productivity assume this to be the case. People who already believe that blacks are inferior performers assume that to be the case as well. Technically, the interpretation of employer surveys, and of black work experience in general, is always going to be somewhat indirect and backhanded until someone takes the bull by the horns, objectively measures racial differences in productivity, and settles which set of preexisting assumptions is correct. Because of the technical difficulty of measuring productivity and the highly politically charged nature of such an agenda, it is not surprising there have been few researchers willing to take on such a task.

*   *   *

Debates about the causes of black unemployment will continue well into the next century because so many social and political issues depend on what particular answer is provided to the question. Although the evidence strongly suggests a primary role for discrimination, this body of evidence is small. The killer study that would settle the issue definitively by measuring the impact of all four factors simultaneously has yet to be attempted, and the difficulties involved with such a study are formidable. However, the body of negative evidence against shiftlessness, human capital, and spatial mismatch is sizable, and the number of such studies is steadily increasing.

Notes

1. The analysis that follows is largely drawn from Cohn and Fossett (forthcoming).

2. The position given in this paragraph is generally referred to as *screening* theory or *credentialling* theory. For the evidence showing the weak relationship between education and productivity see Berg (1970) and Medoff and Abraham (1986).

3. Quitting is not dissimilar when it is the product of "jumping before one is pushed," that is, leaving in response to adverse future employment opportunities. To the extent that quitting is truly voluntary, it often represents leaving for better economic opportunities in a competing firm, which then does not produce significant unemployment.

4. There is a parallel perverse advantage that comes from residential segregation. Racism often confines African Americans to the most unsavory neighborhoods. It is unpleasant and sometimes even unhealthy to have to live next to railroad yards, chemical plants, ports, or steel factories. However, these locations do provide employment.

7 Twenty-Six Things to Remember About Discrimination

This book is not a typical discussion of race and gender discrimination at work. Many of the claims are controversial, both for liberals and for conservatives. Few readers will agree with everything I have said. Some readers will agree with nothing.

The discussion so far has been complex. Because multiple unorthodox claims are made in each chapter, it is easy to lose sight of the larger argument being made. Therefore, in the interest of making my main points clear, I present here the twenty-six primary claims of the book. They come with no evidence and no defense. Those readers who want to assess whether these claims are reasonable are advised to go back to the chapters from which these main points were drawn. Some readers will go back to those chapters and come out unconvinced. However, there is a lot of data in those earlier chapters, and those data spell out a consistent story.

Here, then, are my basic twenty-six arguments:

A. Gender and racial inequality still exist in U.S.-society. Progress is being made in reducing discrimination, but inequality continues to persist. Note that male-female differences in employment opportunities have declined substantially, but that racial differences in employment are as high as they were before the Civil Rights Era.

B. Employers play a particularly important role in determining levels of gender and racial equality because it is they who choose whom to hire, whom to promote, and whom to pay well. Women and minorities do not choose what jobs they work in. Responsibility for hiring in most capitalist nations remains with management.

C. Prejudice and attitudes do not explain discrimination at work because in the corporate world-people are-not always able-to act on their personal preferences. If corporate economic constraints rule out racism, even a white supremacist will grit his teeth and hire and promote blacks. If corporate economic constraints do not rule out racism, even a minute amount of racial prejudice is sufficient to severely limit minority opportunity.

D. Shortage of labor can make discriminatory employers open up opportunities to minorities. Black-white gaps in employment were eased, though not eliminated, during periods of economic expansion.

E. Discrimination costs firms money, since the disadvantaged tend to work for lower wages than do white males. As such, discrimination is most likely to occur in firms that can afford to pay such a wage premium.

F. Capital-intense firms can finance discrimination more easily than can labor-intense firms, because personnel costs are a smaller part of the budget of the capital-intense firm.

G. This explains why women do white-collar work-while men do blue-collar work, and why women do light manufacturing while men do heavy manufacturing.

H. Cultural explanations of occupational sex-typing do not work very well. Most "universal principles of sex roles" have vast numbers of exceptions. Many men do jobs with female attributes; many women do jobs with male attributes.

I. Physical strength explanations of occupational sex-typing do not work well, either. Most male jobs involve very little physical strength.

J. Women are less likely than men to hold high-status jobs or have jobs with decision-making authority.

K.   This is not because of high female turnover or weak female commitment to the labor force. Women's quit rates are not consistently higher than men's.

L.   In some cases historically and in the third world, women are confined to low-status positions as a strategy for increasing turnover in the labor force. This process is known as *synthetic turnover.*

M.   In other cases, women's entry into high-status male jobs is restricted by the visibility problems facing any minority trying to break into the ranks of a job held by a majority. Workers who stand out rise quickly if they are successful all the time, but their conspicuousness insures dramatic punishment for failure.

N.   A more important factor confining women to subordinate jobs is employee discrimination. Males in occupations with substantial labor power often restrict entry into their occupations as a strategy for reducing the labor supply for their jobs-, and thus raising wages by artificial scarcity. These restrictions raise the labor costs for the employers of these workers-by removing companies' ability to hire cheap labor.

O.   Only the strongest workers, notably craft workers and professionals, have been able to restrict women from entering their occupations.

P.   Managers and top executives are the other example of strong workers who have restricted entrance into their professions at the expense of both women and their employers. Women are obtaining entry into managerial ranks, but some of these old processes still exist.

Q.   The primary cause of the gender pay differential is overcrowding, the concentration of women's employment prospects among a limited number of jobs, and occupations relative to the greater prospects enjoyed by men.

R.   Interrupted work careers play a part in the gap as well, primarily by giving women relatively low seniority in bureaucratic internal labor markets.

S.   The undervaluation of women's work by employers makes a third contribution. Workers of both sexes in occupations that are heavily female or have female characteristics are likely to be paid less.

T. Women also suffer from the dynamics of production constraint theory. Male supervisors assign women-to jobs with intrinsic low productivity-Forcing-women to work in labor-intensive settings and undervalued occupations insures a low market return to their labor.-They suffer as well from male supervisors taking false credit for their work.

U. Low rates of black employment cannot be explained by poor African-American educational qualifications. Median levels of black educational attainment are nearly identical to those for whites. Test score differences are declining drastically.

V. Low levels of black economic attainment can not be explained by IQ differentials. IQ correlates with childhood academic performance but declines in importance in adulthood. Equations predicting adult earnings or employment for adult blacks or whites from IQ generally fit the data poorly.

W. Low rates of black employment cannot be explained by black disinterest in looking for jobs. Studies of poverty populations in the U.S. find very low rates of shiftlessness or avoidance of work.

X. Low rates of black employment are hard to explain by spatial mismatch. Black and white commuting radii are fairly similar, and most blacks can reach plenty of jobs.

Y. Employer discrimination is the primary obstacle to increasing black employment. Audit studies in which black and white actors with identical credentials apply for the same job show employers take the white candidate more seriously and are more likely to offer the white a position.

Z. Employer discrimination is particularly marked in our nation's suburbs. Black job candidates have a lower probability of being hired in a firm in a white suburb than they are in the inner city. The color line in some cities is extremely marked, with conspicuous borders on major streets or county lines. There is as a result a virtual apartheid of employment opportunities.

Some readers may feel that twenty-six arguments are too many. I have trouble remembering more than ten arguments at a time. On a bad day,

I can remember even less. For those people who do not want to remember twenty-six separate claims, I conclude the book with a short, sweet minimal list of four.

1. RACE AND GENDER INEQUALITY IS CAUSED BY EMPLOYERS.

2. DISCRIMINATION COSTS THEM MONEY—MONEY THAT THEY SOMETIMES HAVE.

3. SOMETIMES LABOR SCARCITY OR THE NEED TO ECONOMIZE ON WAGES INDUCES THEM TO OPEN UP HIRING TO EVERYONE WHO IS QUALIFIED. IN THIS CASE, THE FREE MARKET WILL ELIMINATE DISCRIMINATION OF ITS OWN ACCORD.

4. WHEN THE MARKET DOES NOT ELIMINATE DISCRIMINATION, THE ONLY REMEDY THAT REMAINS IS LAW.

Appendix A:
Glossary

Ascriptive Status. Any feature with which one is born.

Boundary Heightening. The exaggeration of majority group member's distinctive majority traits as a strategy for challenging potentially hostile minority members.

Buffering from Competition. The degree to which a firm's survival does not depend on obtaining the lowest possible costs.

Buffering from Labor Costs. The degree to which a firm's survival does not depend on obtaining the lowest possible labor costs.

Capital. Non-human factors of production. Generally, money, technology, and raw materials.

Capital Intensive. Using more capital than labor.

Capitalism. 1) A system of production with private control of the means of production. 2) In Hartmann's theory, the impetus of firm owners to maximize profits.

Comparable Worth Theory. The claim that women are underpaid because male employers systematically undervalue their contribution to production.

Competitive Free Market. *See* Perfect Competition.

Craft Worker. A highly skilled blue-collar worker, such as a tool and die maker, a stained-glass repair person, or a specialized industrial electrician.

Culture of Poverty Argument. The argument that past oppression has left blacks (or other poor people) with a culture of poverty, a belief that they can no longer succeed, making them exert less objective effort to succeed at school or work.

Decision Theory. A theory of organizational irrationality.

Demand for Labor. The number of workers an employer is willing to hire.

Demand-Side Explanations of Sex-typing. Explanations of sex-typing that invoke the behavior or preferences of employers.

Differential Visibility Theory. The explanation of the confinement of an ascriptive group to low-status jobs in terms of the greater visibility of minorities.

Discrimination. The provision of unequal benefits to people of different ascriptive statuses despite identical qualifications and merit.

Employee Discrimination Models. The explanation of the confinement of an ascriptive group to low-status jobs in terms of the self interested, exclusionary activity of workers.

Empirical. Factual. Of or referring to real evidence as opposed to empty theory.

Employment. The condition of having a job. NOT the opposite of unemployment, because it is possible to be neither employed nor unemployed (withdrawn from the labor market).

Human Capital. Skills

Human Capital Theory. Any explanation of labor-market outcomes, including occupational sex-typing or gendered wage differentials, which invoke differential possession of skills.

Index of Occupational Dissimilarity. *See* Occupational Dissimilarity, Index of.

Inequality. The unequal allocation of benefits.

Internal Labor Market Theory. The argument that wages are determined by bureaucratic logic rather than market or human capital factors.

Labor. Human factors that go into production. Generally paired with capital, the non-human factors.

Labor Cost Buffering. *See* Buffering from Labor Costs.

Labor Intensive. Using more labor than capital.

Liquidity of Capital and Labor. The ability of firms to move either capital or labor to where it would be most profitable at a moment's notice. There are no obstacles to getting out of investments or to shedding workers.

Marginal Revenue Product. Strictly, the value of the output produced by the most recent worker the employer has hired. More generally, the value of output created by workers.

Occupational Dissimilarity, Index of. An indicator of occupational sex-typing, or the degree to which men and women are segregated into different jobs. Ranges from 0 (All jobs are gender-mixed) to 1 (All jobs are all-male or all-female with no mixing).

Occupational Typing. The degree to which occupations are associated with distinctive ascriptive groups.

Occupational Sex-typing. 1) The degree to which jobs are designated as male or female. 2) The process by which this comes about.

Organizational Slack. The level of surplus resources or "fat" in an organization.

Overcrowding Hypothesis. The claim that women's low pay is caused by occupational sex-typing crowding women into a limited number of occupations reducing their bargaining power.

Patriarchy. The tendency of men to exploit women for their own non-economic advantage. Such advantages might include making women do all the domestic work, increasing male sexual access to women, or increasing male access to high-status positions within society.

Perfect Competition. A theoretical condition in which firms trade goods with no one firm having any lasting advantages or disadvantages. Usually associated in traditional economics with perfect rationality.

Physical Strength Theories of Sex-typing. The claim that women do not get jobs involving physical strength.

Prejudice. An attitude of hostility held by members of one ascriptive group toward members of another group.

Primary Utility. A top priority goal for a company.

Production Constraint Theory. The argument that women are underpaid relative to men because men objectively lower female productivity.

Secondary Utility. A lower priority goal for a company.Sex-Role Theories of Sex-typing. Explanations of sex-typing arguing that women do jobs similar to feminine tasks they do at home and men do jobs similar to masculine tasks they do at home.

Sex-typing. *See* Occupational Sex-typing.

Shiftlessness. Being unwilling to get a job out of pure laziness or disinterest in exerting oneself.

Slack. *See* organizational slack.

Spatial Mismatch. The degree to which jobs are located far from centers of black residence.

Spatial Mismatch Theory. An explanation of black unemployment in terms of the increasing movement of jobs away from centers of black residence.

Status Segregation. The confinement of people to low-status jobs by virtue of their ascriptive status.

Supply of Labor. The number of workers willing to apply for a given job.

Supply Side Explanations of Sex-typing. Explanations of sex-typing that invoke the behavior or preferences of women themselves.

Synthetic Turnover. The use of gender to artificially increase turnover among workers.

Synthetic Turnover Theory. The explanation of women's confinement to low-status jobs in terms of employers' use of gender to artificially increase turnover.

Tautology. A trivial theory because it explains a phenomenon with itself.

Traditional Explanation of Sex-typing. Habit or tradition supports the explanation that a job is male or female because it has always been that way.

Trend. A change in some phenomenon over time.

Turnover. The degree to which employees are likely to leave a job. Although this can be caused by firing, generally turnover refers to voluntary quits.

Unemployment. The condition of not having a job but still searching for a job. Not to be confused with withdrawal from the labor market.

Utility. Something positive an actor tries to obtain. Money, pleasure, leisure, status, and sex are examples of utilities.

Withdrawal From the Labor Market. The condition of not having a job and not searching for a job. Not to be confused with unemployment.

Appendix B:
A Socratic Guide to Race and
Gender Discrimination at Work

The arguments in this book are complex and non-standard. As a result, it is not uncommon for subtleties to become lost in the haze. I provide an overview of the book here in question form. Any one who can answer all of these questions may not necessarily be a smarter person. However, they can replicate the book's arguments in the book's voice. I leave it to the reader to decide whether that voice is convincing or unconvincing.

1. What are the obstacles to a neutral, fair, and scientific discussion of race and gender issues at work?
2. What are the advantages of using statistics in the study of discrimination?
3. Does the presence of inequality demonstrate the presence of discrimination? Why or why not?
4. What is the difference between prejudice and discrimination?
5. What else besides the amount prejudice determines the amount of discrimination in a society?
6. Why do trends in racial inequality matter intellectually?
7. What has been the trend in racial differences in employment in the United States?
8. What has been the trend in racial differences in unemployment in the United States?
9. When does a decline in racial differences in unemployment NOT signify meaningful improvement in racial economic equality?
10. What has been the trend in racial differences in earnings in the United States?
11. How much of the racial income gap is caused by hours worked, education or region?
12. What does it mean to say that part of the income gap is caused by 1) hours worked, 2) education, or 3) region?

13. After adjusting for hours, education, and region, has the black-white income gap increased or decreased over time?
14. What has been the trend in racial differences in educational attainment?
15. What has been the trend in racial differences in test scores?
16. What does the test score data suggest about claims of black educational disadvantage based on either unequal school funding or family problems?
17. Why have black-white differences in years of schooling completed decreased over time?
18. If black-white differences in education have diminished, but black-white differences in employment persist, what does that imply for discrimination?
19. What are the trends in gender differences in earnings in the United States?
20. What are the trends in occupational dissimilarity between men and women in the United States?
21. What is occupational sex-typing and why does it matter?
22. Are there jobs that are at least 90 percent male or 90 percent female in the United States? If so, what are they? If not, why not?
23. What, if any, occupations have become more integrated by gender recently?
24. What is the percent of female doctors? Lawyers? Managers? What is the percent of females who directly supervise a staff?
25. According to the North Carolina Employment and Health Survey of 1989, how do male and female managers differ in their access to power?
26. What is the percent of female CEOs in the Fortune 1000? Of members of Fortune 1000 board of directors?
27. Do male and female members of Fortune 1000 board of directors differ in their functions?
28. If women managers are less likely to hold top jobs than are male managers, is this necessarily the result of discrimination? Why or why not?
29. According to Reskin and Ross, are gender differences in access to power the result of differences in seniority?
30. According to Kay and Hagan, are there gender differences in the likelihood of attorneys making partner? Are these because of seniority?
31. According to Nesbitt, are there gender differences in the success of Episcopal and Unitarian clergy? Are these because of seniority?
32. What is the difference between status segregation and occupational typing?

33. Are male-female differences in the United States most characterized by status segregation or occupational typing?
34. Are black-white differences in the United States most characterized by status segregation or occupational typing?
35. What is the Becker model of discrimination?
36. What three conditions have to hold for perfect competition to exist?
37. Under conditions of perfect competition, what happens to any firm that is less than fully cost efficient?
38. According to Becker, what happens to the wages of a firm that discriminates?
39. According to Becker, once discrimination causes a wage differential between firms, what will happen next?
40. According to Becker, does discrimination gain or lose money for corporations?
41. According to Becker, does the free market tolerate or eliminate discrimination?
42. What are Becker's two answers to why racial differences in wages and employment exist today?
43. What critiques could be made of Becker's two answers?
44. What is the Hartmann model of discrimination? In what way is it similar to or different from the Becker model?
45. According to Hartmann, which is more important in providing obstacles to women's advancement, capitalism or patriarchy? Why?
46. What is Decision Theory?
47. Why in real life don't organizations always act rationally?
48. What is "organizational slack" and how does this relate to organizational rationality?
49. Why is discrimination a secondary utility?
50. What is buffering from competition?
51. How does buffering from competition relate to discrimination?
52. Is it true that large monopolistic firms are more likely to discriminate than small competitive ones?
53. What makes large firms more likely to discriminate than small ones? What causes small firms to be more likely to discriminate than large ones? What happens when you put this all together?
54. How did the tighter economic conditions of the 1980s and 1990s affect discrimination in the United States overall?
55. Why did these tighter economic conditions affect male-female differences differently than they affected black-white differences?
56. Which is easier—to use blacks to undercut expensive white labor or women to undercut expensive male labor? Why?
57. What are some real-world examples of the substitution of women for men in an occupation to obtain lower wage rates?

58. What are supply-side explanations of occupational sex-typing? Give some concrete examples.
59. What are demand-side explanations of occupational sex-typing? Give some concrete examples.
60. Are there any logical problems with supply-side theories?
61. What is the point of the sex-worker example in Chapter 3?
62. In the nineteenth century, sexual ideologies were very traditional. Did this limit the ability of firms to find women willing to take paid employment? Support your answer with actual historical examples.
63. Does the fact that nineteenth-century women tended to work at relatively menial and low-paid jobs support supply- or demand-side interpretations of women's work? Why?
64. When in the twentieth century did female labor force participation increase?
65. What three supply-side explanations of labor force participation did Oppenheimer examine? What evidence supports or contradicts each of these?
66. According to Oppenheimer, why did female labor force participation increase in the 1950s?
67. Under what conditions are supply-side considerations most likely to have an effect?
68. How do scholars use "tradition" to explain occupational sex-typing?
69. Are explanations that invoke "tradition" tautological or not? Why?
70. What is a "sex-role" explanation of occupational sex-typing? Give some concrete examples.
71. What kinds of jobs fit sex-role explanations? What kinds of jobs don't? Are there very many exceptions to the sex-role rules?
72. Does the work experience of Mexican women on the United States-Mexico border support or contradict sex-role explanations of sex-typing? Why so?
73. What are the two major problems with physical-strength interpretations of occupational sex-typing?
74. How much strength do male jobs typically require? Give examples.
75. What might be a good counter to the argument that women should not work jobs such as police officer or fire fighter because women are more likely to claim physical strength tests required for those jobs? (Assume for this question that women really are more likely to flunk these tests than are men.)
76. What is labor cost buffering and how does it relate to occupational sex-type?
77. Define labor intensive and capital intensive. Which type of workplace is more likely to hire women and why?
78. How can labor cost buffering theory explain why women work in white-collar jobs and men work in blue-collar job?
79. What are the problems with alternative theories of why women work in white-collar jobs and men work in blue-collar jobs?

80. How can labor cost buffering theory explain why women work in light industry and men work in heavy industry?

81. Why are men more likely to work in firms that sell "gold mine" products?

82. Why do French restaurants have male waiters but truck stops have female waitresses?

83. How does labor cost buffering explain the predominance of men in engineering?

84. What are the primary findings of the Bridges study? What theory does it support?

85. What are the primary findings of the Cohn study of nineteenth-century office employment? What theory does it support and why?

86. Can labor cost buffering theory explain the findings of the Poster study of women in Indian multinationals?

87. List four different plausible explanations of women's confinement to low-status jobs.

88. What is the human capital explanation of the confinement of women to low-status jobs?

89. What is the difference between firm-general and firm-specific skills? Provide examples of each.

90. According to human capital theorists, which type of job is more likely to be staffed by women, jobs with firm-general or jobs with firm-specific skills? Why?

91. According to human capital theory, why do women have shorter careers than men?

92. If employers divided the labor force into workers likely to have children and workers not likely to have children, would their split be male-female? If not, what would it be?

93. What does the empirical evidence show about the extent to whether women have higher turnover than men?

94. What does the Viscusi study show about male and female turnover?

95. Is it really true that employers can not tolerate turnover and will do everything to minimize it? Explain your answer.

96. What is the empirical evidence on the extent to which female access to top jobs is determined by their education or experience?

97. Define synthetic turnover.

98. What is the synthetic turnover explanation of women's concentration in low-status jobs?

99. Synthetic turnover is generally only required with certain forms of payment systems. What payment systems are these, and why do they create the need for synthetic turnover?

100. Why are Japanese firms particularly prone to use synthetic turnover?

101. What does the story about British telegraphs in the nineteenth century illustrate about women's access to high status jobs?

102. What is a marriage bar? Is it anything like a salad bar?
103. Trace the history of the use of marriage bars throughout the world. Give as many examples of their use as possible.
104. Why has the use of marriage bars dropped off in many countries?
105. Were marriage bars ever used in the United States? Why was the United States less likely to use marriage bars than were other nations?
106. Why are marriage bars more common in South Korea than in Taiwan?
107. Explain differential visibility models of women's confinement to low-status jobs.
108. Is enhanced visibility a professional asset or a liability? Explain your answer?
109. According to Kanter, why are women more visible than men?
110. What is boundary heightening? How does it affect women's careers?
111. Why is network isolation dangerous in a corporate setting?
112. Why is having a reputation for being likely to succeed a cause of actual success?
113. How does the past success or failure of previous "role models" of a minority group affect the career prospects of present members of that group?
114. According to Kanter, how do women and ethnic minorities overcome the obstacles of minority status?
115. What empirical support is there for Kanter's theory of differential visibility?
116. What is the employee discrimination theory of women's confinement to low status jobs?
117. Which are more important in motivating employee resistance to women and minorities, economic or non-economic factors? Why?
118. Why don't employee resistance models apply in many cases?
119. What are the three situations in which employee resistance models can be very important?
120. What differentiates professionals, managers, and craft workers from other workers in regard to employee discrimination theory?
121. Give historical examples of male workers attempting to exclude women from blue-collar professions.
122. What historically have been the obstacles to women practicing medicine in the United States? Give concrete examples.
123. What factors besides legal ones lowered male resistance to female doctors in recent years?
124. What are the four primary explanations of women's low pay?
125. Explain the overcrowding hypothesis.
126. How does overcrowding relate to supply and demand?
127. How does female withdrawal from the labor market complicate the overcrowding hypothesis?

128. Why does it sometimes make sense to disbelieve people's claim that they are uninterested in obtaining paid employment?

129. Not all men are sexist. Does this support or not support the overcrowding hypothesis?

130. How do the predictions of overcrowding theory differ from those of a "gender hate" theory? Which is best supported by evidence?

131. What facts support the overcrowding hypothesis?

132. What is the human capital explanation of low female pay?

133. How plausible are human capital claims that skills degenerate rapidly when people leave the labor force? Give examples to back up your position.

134. Does the existence of burnout support or not support human capital theory?

135. What is the difference between a human capital and an internal labor market theory?

136. What did Medoff and Abraham find about the productivity of more-experienced as opposed to less-experienced executives? How does one explain this?

137. Discuss the findings of the Kilbourne et. al test of human capital theory. How do these findings relate to parallel analyses?

138. What does East German data suggest about the validity of human capital explanations of low female pay?

139. What is the comparable worth explanation of low female wages?

140. What does comparable worth theory predict about the wage consequences of working in an occupation staffed heavily by women? Is this prediction validated by evidence?

141. Are there any logical problems with comparable worth theory? If so, what are they? If not, why not?

142. People often differ in their gender attitudes. Is this a problem for comparable worth theory?

143. Can employers lower wages by holding certain types of work in contempt? Is this a problem for comparable worth theory?

144. According to Paula England, what types of gender-related job attributes are associated with low pay? How does this support or not support comparable worth theory?

145. Explain the production constraint explanation of low female pay. Is this a feminist or a non-feminist theory?

146. Does low productivity only come from low effort or low skill? Explain your answer.

147. If low female productivity were to exist, would it necessarily imply that women are lazy, unskilled, or at fault in the work world? Why or why not?

148. What are the three primary mechanisms by which men objectively lower women's productivity?
149. Why does female concentration in labor intensive jobs lower their pay?
150. What is the role of consumers in producing low female pay?
151. How do comparable worth theory and productivity constraint theory differ in their allocation of responsibility for low female pay between employers and consumers?
152. How is it possible for men to steal credit for women's productivity? Give concrete examples?
153. What kinds of jobs best allow someone to claim false credit for other people's productivity?
154. How does occupational sex-typing lower women's wages? List as many mechanisms as possible.
155. What are the most politicized and unflattering explanations of low black employment?
156. What is Spatial Mismatch theory? How is this an unpoliticized explanation of low black employment?
157. What are the main points illustrated by the Chapter 6 maps of Detroit and Atlanta?
158. To what extent can the findings in the Chapter 6 maps be explained as discrimination by white consumers?
159. To what extent can the findings in the Chapter 6 maps be explained by blacks being unable to reach jobs in white neighborhoods?
160. To what extent can the findings in the Chapter 6 maps be explained by educational qualifications?
161. Is there any evidence for the claim that blacks are less willing to travel to get to a job than are whites?
162. What are the primary findings of the Tienda and Stier study of shiftlessness in Chicago?
163. What kind of people might say they are uninterested in working but have legitimate reasons for doing so?
164. To what extent can low black employment be explained by shiftlessness?
165. What did Bound and Freeman find on the relationship between black education and black economic well being?
166. What are the problems with Herrnstein and Murray's argument that black poverty can be explained by IQs that are lower than those of whites?
167. What does the Wisconsin High School Senior study show about the relationship between IQ and adult economic attainment?
168. Do the findings of the Wisconsin High School Senior study on IQ and adult economic attainment make sense? Why or why not?

169. In general, to what extent do IQ differences help to explain racial differences in employment?
170. Which race is nearer the most jobs—blacks or whites? Why?
171. What does Table 6.2 show about the relation of spatial mismatch to racial gaps in employment?
172. What are the strengths and weaknesses of spatial mismatch theories of black unemployment?
173. What evidence exists for the presence of overt employer discrimination against black job candidates?
174. What is an audit study and how does it work? What are the main findings of audit studies of the employee interview process?
175. What are the main findings of surveys of employer racial attitudes?
176. What are the most important arguments in Cohn's *Race and Gender Discrimination at Work?*

Appendix C:
Problems for Deeper Thought

The Socratic questions in the previous section assume that everything in the book is perfectly true, and ask a set of right answer/wrong answer questions about the book. The more thoughtful, or intelligent, reader may not be overwhelmingly convinced of the fundamental correctness of everything in this volume. Here are some contemplative questions for more serious analysis.

1. What is the weakest claim in this book? What argument either has the most tenuous logic, or the smallest amount of factual support?
2. What is the most surprising claim in the book? What, if any, argument seems to run the most against what you would have considered "standard wisdom" concerning race and gender? Do you believe this claim?
3. By the logic of this book, will race and gender discrimination increase or decrease in the next thirty years? Will the same things occur for both race and gender? Do you believe these predictions?
4. Why are elementary school teachers female when secondary school teachers are more likely to be male?
5. Why is librarian a female job?
6. Why is gardener a male job when many women garden at home?
7. Why is nurse a female job when it is highly skilled?
8. Is it ever economically rational to discriminate? Why or why not?
9. Under what conditions could race and gender equality have come about without government intervention in the form of equal opportunity laws? Try to keep your answer as plausible as possible. After doing this, how plausible is your "most-plausible" answer?
10. If the models of this book are correct, what changes in ethnic and gender inequality might one expect in a modernizing country such as Mexico or India?
11. Imagine that in two different modernizing countries, gender inequality in one went up and in the other it went down. How might one use the material in this book to explain this?

12. How many different sources of labor cost buffering can you imagine? Be creative.

13. Is human capital theory completely worthless or does it have some redeeming virtues?

14. Does the content of people's racial or gender feelings ever matter or are all economic outcomes shaped by narrow economic forces? When do people's prejudices and role ideologies make a difference and when are they irrelevant?

15. Are there any other ways in which men interfere with women's productivity at work besides the ways mentioned in this book? Or alternatively, is male interference with female productivity a myth?

16. Why have women risen to the top in politics far faster than they have in corporate America?

17. If someone asked you for a concrete, social policy that would remedy racial disparities in employment in the United States, what would you recommend?

18. If someone asked you to comment on the effectiveness of the standard solutions liberals and conservatives recommend on how to eliminate black poverty in the United States, what comments might you make?

19. Do any of the models in this book apply to family owned and operated businesses? Explain your answer in detail. (You may have to answer this question differently for different models.)

20. Imagine you had a million dollars to do one study that would scientifically resolve any debate in the study of race and gender inequality at work. What study might you do? Specifically identify which two theories or explanations you would like to be able to adjudicate between, what data you would collect, what pattern of data would support Theory A and what pattern of data would support Theory B.

*For Extra Credit: Actually do the study.

References

Abbott, Edith. 1910. *Women in Industry: Study in American Economic History.* New York: Appleton.

Anderson, B.W. 1974. "Empirical Generalizations on Labor Turnover." Pp. 33–59 in *Studies in Labor and Manpower,* edited by Richard Pegnetter. Iowa City: Iowa: University of Iowa Press.

Arrow, Kenneth. 1973. *Information and Economic Behavior.* Stockholm: Federation of Swedish Industries.

Ashenfelter, Orley. 1971. "Discrimination and Trade Unions." Pp. 83–118 in *Discrimination in Labor Markets,* edited by Orley Ashenfelter and Albert Rees. Princeton: Princeton University Press.

Banfield, Edward. 1958. *Moral Basis of a Backward Society.* Glencoe: Free Press.

Baron, Ava. 1991. *Work Engendered: Towards a New History of American Labor.* Ithaca: Cornell University Press.

Becker, Gary. 1957. *Economics of Discrimination.* Chicago: University of Chicago Press.

_____. 1971. *Human Capital: A Theoretical and Empirical Analysis with Special Reference to Education.* 2d ed. New York: Columbia University Press.

Berg, Ivar. 1970. *Education and Jobs: Great Training Robbery.* New York: Praeger.

Bernstein, Jared. 1995. *Where's the Payoff: The Gap Between Black Academic Progress and Economic Gains.* Washington, D.C.: Economic Policy Institute.

Bergmann, Barbara. 1986. *Economic Emergence of Women.* New York: Basic Books.

Bernhardt, Annette, Martina Morris, and Mark Handcock. 1995. "Women's Gains or Men's Losses? Closer Look at the Shrinking Gender Gap in Earnings." *American Journal of Sociology* 101: 302–328.

Bilmoria, Diana, and Sandy Kristin Piderit. 1994. "Board Committee Membership: Effects of Sex Based Bias." *Academy of Management Journal* 37: 1453–1477.

Blau, Francine, and Marianne Ferber. 1986. *Economics of Women, Men and Work.* Englewood Cliffs, N.J.: Prentice-Hall.

Bonner, Thomas Neville. 1992. *To the Ends of the Earth: Women's Search for Education in Medicine.* Cambridge, Mass.: Harvard University Press.

Bound, John, and Richard Freeman. 1992. "What Went Wrong: Erosion of Relative Earnings and Employment Among Young Black Men in the 1980 s." *Quarterly Journal of Economics* 62: 201–232.

Bridges, William. 1980. "Industry Marginality and Female Employment: A New Appraisal." *American Sociological Review* 45: 58–75.

———. 1982. "Sexual Segregation of Occupations: Theories of Labor Stratification in Industry." *American Journal of Sociology* 95: 616–659.

Brinton, Mary, Yean-Ju Lee, and William Parish. 1995. "Married Women's Employment in Rapidly Industrializing Societies: Examples from East Asia." *American Journal of Sociology 100*: 1099–1031.

Burstein, Paul. 1985. *Discrimination, Jobs and Politics.* Chicago: University of Chicago Press.

Caplow, Theodore. 1954. *Sociology of Work.* Minneapolis: University of Minnesota Press.

Carroll, Jackson, Barbara Hargrove, and Adair Lummis. 1983. *Women of the Cloth: New Opportunity for the Churches.* San Francisco: Harper and Row.

Chaves, Mark. 1997. *Ordaining Women: Culture and Conflict in Religions Organizations.* Cambridge, Mass.: Harvard University Press.

Cobble, Sue. 1991. *Dishing It Out: Waitresses and Their Unions in the Twentieth Century.* Champaign-Urbana, Illinois: University of Illinois Press.

Cockburn, Cynthia. 1988. *Machinery of Dominance: Women, Men and Technical Know-How.* Boston: Northeastern University Press.

Cohen, Lisa, Joseph Broschak, and Heather Haveman. 1998. "And Then There Were More?: Effect of Organizational Sex Composition on the Hiring and Promotion of Managers." *American Sociological Review* 63: 711–728.

Cohn, Samuel. 1985. *Process of Occupational Sex- Typing: Feminization of Clerical Labor in Great Britain.* Philadelphia: Temple University Press.

———. 1990. "Market-Like Forces and Social Stratification: How NeoclassicalTheories of Wages Can Survive Recent Sociological Critiques." *Industrial and Labor Relations Review* 68:714–730.

Cohn, Samuel, and Mark Fossett. 1996. "What Spatial Mismatch?: Proximity of Blacks to Employment in Boston and Houston." *Social Forces* 75: 557–573.

Cooke, Thomas. 1993. "Proximity to Job Opportunities and African American Male Unemployment: Test of the Spatial Mismatch Hypothesis in Indianapolis." *Professional Geographer* 45: 407–415.

Corcoran, Mary, and Greg Duncan. 1979. "Work History, Labor Force Attachment and Earnings Differences Between the Races and Sexes." *Journal of Human Resources* 14: 3–20.

Corcoran, Mary, Greg Duncan, and Michael Ponza. 1984. "Work Experience, Job Segregation and Wages." Pp. 171–191 in *Sex Segregation in the Workplace: Trends, Explanations, Remedies,* edited by Barbara Reskin. Washington, D. C.: National Academy of Sciences.

Cotter, David, JoAnn DeFiore, Joan Hermsen, Brenda Marsteller Kowalewski, and Reeve Vanneman. 1995. "Occupational Gender Segregation and the Earnings Gap: Changes in the 1980 s." *Social Science Research* 24: 439–454.

———. 1997. "All Women Benefit: The Macro-Level Effect of Occupational Integration on Gender Earnings Inequality." *American Sociological Review* 62: 714–734.

———. 1998. "Demand For Female Labor." *American Journal of Sociology* 103: 1673–1712.

Cotton, Jeremiah. 1989. "Opening the Gap: Decline in Black Economic Indicators in the 1980 s." *Social Science Quarterly* 70: 803–810.

Cyert, Richard, and James March. 1963. *Behavioral Theory of the Firm.* Englewood Cliffs, N.J.: Prentice-Hall.

Davidoff, Leonore, and Catherine Hall. 1987. *Family Fortunes: Men and Women of the English Middle Class 1750–1850.* Chicago: University of Chicago Press.

Davies, Margery. 1982. *Woman's Place Is at the Typewriter: Office Work and Office Workers 1870–1930.* Philadelphia: Temple University Press.

Deutsch, Claudia. 1996. "Women Lawyers Strive for Chance to Make It Rain." *New York Times,* 21 May.

Dreeben, Robert, and Adam Gamoran. 1986. "Race, Instruction and Learning." *American Sociological Review* 51: 660–669.

D'Souza, Dinesh. 1995. *End of Racism: Prospects for a Multiracial Society.* Glencoe, Illinois: Free Press.

Dublin, Thomas. 1979. *Women at Work: Transformation of Work and Community in Lowell, Massachusetts 1826–60.* New York: Columbia University Press.

Edgeworth, F. Y. 1922. "Equal Pay to Men and Women." *Economics Journal* 32: 431–457.

Edwards, Richard. 1979. *Contested Terrain: Transformation of the Workplace in the Twentieth Century.* New York: Basic Books.

Ellwood, David. 1986. "Spatial Mismatch Hypothesis: Are There Teenage Jobs Missing in the Ghetto?" Pp. 147–90 in *Black Youth Unemployment Crisis,* edited by Richard Freeman and Harry Holzer. Chicago: University of Chicago Press.

Engels, Friedrich. 1964. *Origins of the Family, Private Property and the State.* New York: International Publishers.

England, Paula. 1982. "Failure of Human Capital Theory to Explain Occupational Segregation." *Journal of Human Resources* 17: 338–350.

———. 1984. "Wage Appreciation and Depreciation: A Test of Neoclassical Economic Explanations of Occupational Sex Segregation." *Social Forces* 62: 726–749.

———. 1992. *Comparable Worth: Theories and Evidence.* New York: A. De Gruyter.

Epstein, Cynthia Fuchs. 1970. *Woman's Place: Options and Limits in Professional Careers.* Berkeley: University of California Press.

———. 1981. *Women in Law.* New York: Basic Books.

Farley, John. 1987. "Disproportionate Black and Hispanic Unemployment in U.S. Metropolitan Areas: Roles of Racial Inequality, Segregation and Discrimination in Male Joblessness." *American Journal of Economics and Sociology* 46: 129–150.

Farley, Reynolds. 1985. *Blacks and Whites: Narrowing the Gap?* Cambridge, Mass.: Harvard University Press.

———. 1996. *New American Reality: Who We Are, How We Got Here, Where We Are Going.* New York: Russell Sage Foundation.

Form, William and Delbert Miller. 1964. *Industrial Sociology: Sociology of Work Organizations.* New York: Harper and Row.

Fremon, Charlotte. 1970. *Occupational Patterns in Urban Employment Change 1965–67.* Washington, D.C.: Urban Institute.

Gabin, Nancy. 1990. *Feminism in the Labor Movement: Women and the United Auto Workers 1935–75.* Ithaca: Cornell University Press.

Garfinkel, Irwin, and Sara McLanahan. 1986. *Single Mothers and Their Children: A New American Dilemma.* Washington, D.C.: Urban Institute.

Goldin, Claudia. 1990. *Understanding the Gender Gap: Economic History of American Women.* New York: Oxford University Press.

Gordon, David. 1996. *Fat and Mean: Corporate Squeeze of Working Americans and the Myth of Managerial Downsizing.* New York: Martin Kessler.

Gordon, Peter, Ajay Kuman, and Harry Richardson. 1988. "Spatial Mismatch Hypothesis: Some New Evidence." *Urban Studies* 26: 315–326.

Gould, Stephen Jay. 1994. "Curveball: Review of Herrnstein and Murray's The Bell Curve ." *New Yorker* (November 28): 139–149.

Greytak, David. 1974. "Journey to Work: Racial Differences and City Size." *Traffic Quarterly* 28: 241–256.

Gross, Edward. 1968. "Plus Ça Change: Sexual Segregations of Occupations Over Time." *Social Problems* 16: 198–208.

Hacker, Andrew. 1995. *Two Nations: Black and White, Seperate, Hostile, Unequal.* New York: Ballentine

Halaby, Charles. 1979. "Job-Specific Sex Differences in Organizational Reward Attainment: Wage Discrimination Versus Rank Segregation." *Social Forces* 58: 108–127."

Harrison, Bennett. 1974. "Discrimination and Space: Suburbanization and Black Employment in Cities." Pp. 21–53 in George Von Furstenburg et al. eds., Patterns of Racial Discrimination, Volume I, Housing. Lexington: Lexington.

Hartmann, Heidi. 1976. "Capitalism, Patriarchy and Job Segregation by Sex." Pp. 137–170 in *Women in the Workplace,* edited by Martha Blaxall and Barbara Reagan. Chicago: University of Chicago Press.

Herrnstein, Richard, and Charles Murray. 1994. *Bell Curve: Intelligence and Class Structure in American Life.* New York: Free Press.

Hicks, John. 1964. *Theory of Wages.* New York: Saint Martin's Press.

Hill, Herbert. 1994. "Race and Ethnicity. Organized Labor: Historical Sources of Resistance to Affirmative Action." *Journal of Intergroup Relations* 12:5–49.

Holcombe, Lee. 1973. *Victorian Ladies at Work.* Hamden, Conn.: Archon.

Holzer, Harry. 1991. "Spatial Mismatch Hypothesis: What Has the Evidence Shown?" *Urban Studies* 28: 105–122.

_____. 1996. *What Do Employers Want? Job Prospects for Less Educated Workers.* New York: Russell Sage Foundation.

Holzer, Harry, and Keith Ihlandfeldt. 1996. "Spatial Factors and Employment of Blacks at Firm Level." *New England Economic Review:* 65–86.

Ihlanfeldt, Keith, and Marilyn Young. 1996. "Spatial Distribution of Black Employment Between the Central City and the Suburbs." *Economic Inquiry* 34: 693–707.

International Labor Office. 1962. "Discrimination in Employment or Occupations on the Basis of Marital Status." *International Labor Review* 85: 368–389.

Ireson, Carol. 1978. "Girls' Socialization for Work." Pp. 176–200 in *Women Working: Theories and Facts in Perspective,* edited by Ann Stromberg and Shirley Harkness. Palo Alto, Calif.: Mayfield.

Jacobs, Jerry. 1989. "Long Term Trends in Occupational Segregation by Sex." *American Journal of Sociology* 95: 160–173.

Jencks, Christopher, Susan Bartlett, Mary Corcoran, James Crouse, David Eaglesfield, Gregory Jackson, Kent McClelland, Peter Mueser, Michael Olneck, Joseph Schwartz, Sherry Ward, and Jill Williams. 1979. *Who Gets Ahead; Determinants of Economic Success in America.* New York: Basic Books.

Jensen, Arthur. 1971. "How Much Can We Boost IQ and Scholastic Achievement?" *Harvard Educational Review* 39: 1–123.

Kain, John. 1968. "Housing Segregation, Negro Employment and Metropolitan Decentralization." *Quarterly Journal of Economics* 82: 175–197.

_____. 1992. "Spatial Mismatch Hypothesis: Three Decades Later." *Housing Policy Debate* 3: 371–460.

Kalleberg, Arne, Michael Wallace, and Robert Althauser. 1981. "Economic Segregation, Worker Power and Income Inequality." *American Journal of Sociology* 87: 651–683.

Kanter, Rosabeth Moss. 1977. *Men and Women of the Corporation.* New York: Basic Books.

Kasarda, John. 1990. "Urban Industrial Transition and the Underclass." *Annals of the American Academy of Political and Social Science* 501: 26–47.

Kay, Fiona, and John Hagan. 1998. "Raising the Bar: the Gender Stratification of Law School Capital." *American Sociological Review* 63: 728–742

Kessler-Harris, Alice. 1975. "Stratifying by Sex: Understanding the History of Working Women." Pp. 217–42 in *Labor Market Segmentation,* edited by Richard Edwards, et. al. Lexington, Mass., Heath.

_____. 1982. *Out To Work: History of Wage Earning Women in the United States.* New York; Oxford University Press.

Killingsworth, Mark. 1983. *Labor Supply.* Cambridge: Cambridge University Press.

_____. 1990. *Economics of Comparable Worth.* Kalamazoo, Mich.: W.E. Upjohn Institute for Employment Research.

Kilbourne, Barbara Stanek, Paula England, George Farkas, Kurt Beron, and Dorothea Weir. 1994. "Returns to Skill, Compensating Differentials and Gender Bias: Effects of Occupational Characteristics on the Wages of White Women and Men." *American Journal of Sociology* 100: 689–720.

King, Mary. 1992. "Occupational Segregation by Race and Sex." *Monthly Labor Review* 115: 30–36.

Kirschenman, Jolene, and Katherine Neckerman. 1991. "We'd Love to Hire Them But … : The Meaning of Race for Employers." Pp. 203–34 in *Urban Underclass,* edited by Christopher Jenks and Paul Petersen. Washington, D.C. : Brookings Institute.

Konrad, Alison, and Jeffery Pfeffer. 1991. "Understanding the Hiring of Women and Minorities in Educational Institutions." *Sociology of Education* 64: 141–157.

Kozol, Jonathan. 1967. *Death at an Early Age: The Destruction of the Hearts and Minds of Negro Children in the Boston Public Schools.* New York: Houghton Mifflin.

Leonard, Jonathan. 1986. "Space, Time and Unemployment: Los Angeles 1980." Unpublished manuscript.

Lester, Richard. 1951. *Labor and Industrial Relations: A General Analysis.* New York: Macmillan.

Lewis, Oscar. 1963. *Children of Sanchez: Autobiography of a Mexican Family.* New York: Vintage Books.

Marder, Janet. 1996. "Are Women Changing the Rabbinate? A Reform Perspective." Pp. 271–290 in *Religious Institutions and Women's Leadership: New Roles Inside the Mainstream,* edited by Catherine Wessinger. Columbia, S.C.: University of South Carolina Press.

Marshall, Ray. 1965. *Negro and Organized Labor.* New York: John Wiley.

Massey, Douglas, and Nancy Denton. 1993. *American Apartheid: Segregation and the Making of the Underclass.* Cambridge, Mass.: Harvard University Press.

Medoff, James, and Katherine Abraham. 1981. "Are Those Who Are Paid More Really More Productive? The Case of Experience." *Journal of Human Resources* 16: 186–216.

Mishel, Philip and Ruy Teixera. 1994. *Myth of Coming Labor Shortage: Jobs, Skills, and Incoming of America's Workforce 2000.* Washington D.C.: Economic Okey Institute.

Moss, Philip, and Chris Tilly. 1991. *Why Black Men Are Doing Worse in the Labor Market: Review of Supply Side and Demand Side Explanations.* Report prepared for the Social Science Research Council. New York: Social Science Research Council.

Moss, Philip and Chris Tilly. 1995. "Raised Hurdles for Black Men: Evidence from Interviews with Employers." New York: Russell Sage Foundation Web page.

Moynihan, Daniel. 1965. *Negro Family: Case for National Action.* Washington D.C.: U.S. Department of Labor.

Murray, Charles. 1984. *Losing Ground: American Social Policy 1950–1980.* New York: Basic Books.

Nam, Charles, and Mary Powers. 1983. *Socioeconomic Approach to Status Measurement.* Houston: Cap and Gown Press.

National Whitley Council. 1945–6. *Report on Marriage Bars in the Civil Service.* United Kingdom: House of Commons Sessional Papers 10: 871–894.

Nesbitt, Paula. 1997. "Clergy Feminization: Controlled Labor or Transformative Change?" *Journal for the Scientific Study of Religion* 36: 585–599.

Oppenheimer, Valerie Kincaide. 1970. *Female Labor Force in the United States: Demographic and Economic Factors Governing Its Growth and Changing Composition.* Berkeley: University of California Press.

Osterman, Paul. 1984. *Internal Labor Markets.* Cambridge, Mass.: MIT Press.

Petersen, Trond and Laurie Morgan. 1995. "Separate and Unequal: Occupation-Establishment Sex Segregation and the Gender Wage Gap." *American Journal of Sociology*: 329–365.

Pfeffer, Jeffery, and Alison Davis-Blake. 1987. "Effect of the Proportion Women on Salaries: Case of College Administrators." *Administrative Sciences Quarterly* 32: 1–24.

Piore, Michael, and Peter Doeringer. 1971. *Internal Labor Markets and Manpower Analysis.* Lexington, Mass.: Lexington Books.

Polachek, Solomon, 1981. "Occupational Self-Selection: A Human Capital Approach to Sex Differences in Occupational Structure." *Review of Economics and Statistics* 58: 60–69.

Pollard, Sydney. 1965. *Genesis of Modern Management: Study of the Industrial Revolution in Great Britain.* Cambridge, Mass.: Harvard University Press.

Poster, Winifed. 1998. "Globalization, Gender and the Workforce: Women and Men in a Multinational Corporation in India." *Journal of Developing Societies* 14:40–65.

Preston, Samuel. 1976. *Mortality Patterns in National Populations.* New York: Academic Press.

Price, James. 1977. *Study of Turnover.* Ames, Iowa: Iowa State University.

Prichard, Rebecca. 1996. "Grandes Dames, Femmes Fortes and Matrones: Reformed Women Ministering." Pp. 39–57 in *Religious Institutions and Women's Leadership: New Roles Inside the Mainstream,* edited by Catherine Wessinger. Columbia, S.C.: University of South Carolina Press.

Raphael, Stephen. 1998. "Inter and Intra-Ethnic Comparisons of the Central City Suburban Youth Employment Differential: Evidence from the Oakland Metropolitan Area." *Industrial and Labor Relations Review* 51: 503–524.

Reskin, Barbara, and Irene Padavic. 1994. *Women and Men At Work.* Thousand Oaks, Calif.: Pine Forge Press.

Reskin, Barbara, and Patricia Roos. 1990. *Job Queues and Gender Queues: Explaining Women's Inroads into Male Occupations.* Philadelphia: Temple University Press.

Reskin, Barbara, and Catherine Ross. 1992. "Jobs, Authority and Earnings Among Managers: Continuing Significance of Sex." *Work and Occupations* 19: 342–365.

Ridgeway, Cecilia. 1997. "Interaction and the Conservation of Gender Inequality: Considering Employment." *American Sociological Review* 62: 218–235.

Rose, Sonya. 1992. *Limited Livelihoods: Gender and Class in Nineteenth Century England.* Berkeley: University of California Press.

Rumberger, Russell. 1982. *Structure of Work and Underutilization of College Educated Workers.* Stanford: Stanford University Press.

Ryan, William. 1976. *Blaming the Victim.* New York: Vintage Books.

Scharf, Lois. 1980. *To Work and to Wed: Family Employment, Feminism, and the Great Oppression.* Westport, Conn.: Greenwood.

Seccombe, Wally. 1974. " Housewife and Her Labor Under Capitalism" *New Left Review* 83: 187–226.

Sewell, William, and Robert Hauser. 1975. *Education, Occupations and Earnings: Achievement in the Early Career.* New York: Academic Press.

Shallcross, Ruth. 1940. *Shall Married Women Work?* Public Affairs Pamphlet #49. No publisher.

Simon, Herbert. 1957. *Administrative Behavior.* New York: Macmillan.

Slichter, Sumner. 1947. *Challenge of Industrial Relations: Trade Unions, Management and the Public Interest.* Ithaca: Cornell University Press.

Smith, Catherine Begnoche. 1979. "Influence of Internal Opportunity Structure and Sex of Worker on Turnover Patterns." *Administrative Sciences Quarterly* 24: 362–381.

Smith, Vicki. 1990. *Managing in the Corporate Interest: Control and Resistance in an American Bank.* Berkeley: University of California Press.

Sørensen, Annemette, and Heike Trappe. 1995. "Persistence of Gender Inequality in Earnings in the German Democratic Republic." *American Sociological Review* 60: 398–406.

Sorensen, Elaine. 1989. "Wage Effects of Occupational Sex Composition: Review and New Findings." Pp. 57–79 in *Comparable Worth: Analyses and Evidence*, edited by M. Anne Hall and Mark Killingsworth. Ithaca: Institute of Labor Relations: Cornell University.

Stevenson, Mary. 1984. *Determinants of Low Wages for Women Workers*. New York: Praeger.

Strober, Myra, and David Tyack. 1981. *Women and Men in the Schools: History of the Sexual Structuring of Educational Employment*. Washington, D.C.: National Institute of Education.

Struyk, R. J., M. A. Turner, and M. Fix. 1991. *Opportunities Denied: Opportunities Diminished: Discrimination in Hiring*. Washington, D.C.: Urban Institute.

Thurow, Lester. 1975. *Generating Inequality*. New York: Basic Books.

Tienda, Marta, and Haya Stier. 1991. "Joblessness and Shiftlessness: Labor Force Activity in Chicago's Inner City." Pp. 135–154 in *Urban Underclass*, edited by Christopher Jencks and Paul Peterson. Washington, D.C.: Brookings Institution.

Tomaskovic-Devey, Donald. 1993. *Gender and Racial Inequality at Work*. Ithaca: Institute of Labor Relations, Cornell University.

Treiman, Donald, and Heidi Hartmann, eds. 1981. *Women, Work and Wages: Equal Pay for Jobs of Equal Value*. Washington, D.C.: National Academy of Sciences.

Truell, Peter. 1996. "Success and Sharp Elbows." *New York Times,* 2 July.

Viscusi, Kip. 1980. "Sex Differences in Worker Quitting." *Review of Economics and Statistics* 62: 388–398.

Wallace, Michael, and Arne Kalleberg. 1981. "Economic Organization of Firms and Labor Market Consequences: Towards a Specification of Dual Economy Theory." Pp. 77–118 in *Sociological Perspectives on Labor Markets,* edited by Ivar Berg. New York: Academic Press.

Walsh, Mary Roth. 1977. *Doctors Wanted: No Women Need Apply—Sexual Barriers in the Medical Profession, 1835–1975*. New Haven: Yale University Press.

Wellington, Alison. 1994. "Accounting for the Male/Female Wage Gap Among Whites: 1976 and 1985." *American Sociological Review* 59: 839–848.

Western, Bruce, and Katherine Beckett. 1999. "How Unregulated is the U.S. Labor Market? Penal System as a Labor Market Institution." *American Journal of Sociology* 104: 1030–1060.

Williams, Christine. 1989. *Gender Differences at Work: Women and Men in Nontraditional Occupations*. Berkeley: University of California Press.

Wooten, Barbara. 1997. "Gender Differences in Occupational Employment." *Monthly Labor Review* (April): 15–24.

Zikmund, Barbara Brown, Adair Lummis, and Patricia Chang. 1998. Clergy Women: An Uphill Calling.St. Louis: Westminster/John Knox Press.

Zweigenhaft, Richard, and William Domhoff. 1998. *Diversity in the Power Elite: Have Women and Minorities Reached the Top?* New Haven: Yale University Press.

Index